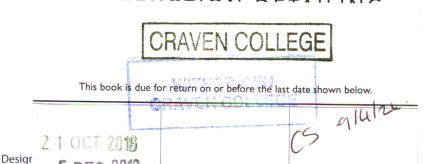
ensure that the designer's intent is clear and to enable the highest quality construction. *Construction Detailing for Landscape and Garden Design* contains the elements most often used when detailing surfaces, with key information on standards, guidance and construction that the practitioner must be aware of. Accompanying the text are 2D and 3D images with suggestions of measurements, design considerations and materials.

Key topics covered in this book are:

- vehicular paving
- pedestrian paving and patios
- steps and ramps
- margins, edges and kerbs
- drainage channels

To be used in conjunction with the book is an innovative online library of freely downloadable CAD (SketchUp format) details, which link directly to those in the book. These details are available for the reader to edit, adapt and use in their own designs – and make the task of detailing for projects that little bit easier.

PAUL HENSEY is a practising garden and landscape designer. He has been a registered member of the Society of Garden Designers since 2007 and was made a Fellow in early 2016. Originally trained as an industrial designer, Paul has used CAD systems for over 20 years. Early in his career he was the head of design for an international construction products manufacturer, giving him an invaluable insight into construction detailing and an appetite for understanding manufacturing techniques and the use of novel materials in gardens and landscapes. Paul has been the technical journalist for the *Garden Design Journal* since 2009 and writes their monthly feature on best practice and construction. A lecturer at the University of Portsmouth, Paul also teaches at several other colleges on garden design and CAD. Paul has won numerous RHS medals and is acknowledged for his contemporary and innovative gardens.

CONSTRUCTION DETAILING FOR LANDSCAPE AND GARDEN DESIGN

SURFACE, STEPS AND MARGINS

PAUL HENSEY

Routledge
Taylor & Francis Group

LONDON AND NEW YORK

First published 2016

by Routledge

2 Park Square, Milton Park, Abingdon, Oxon OX14 4RN

and by Routledge

711 Third Avenue, New York, NY 10017

Routledge is an imprint of the Taylor & Francis Group, an informa business

British Library Cataloguing-in-Publication Data
A catalogue record for this book is available from the British Library

Library of Congress Cataloging in Publication Data
Hensey, Paul, author.
Construction detailing for landscape and garden design : surface, steps and margins / Paul Hensey.
pages cm
Includes bibliographical references and index.
ISBN 978-0-415-74628-1 (pbk. : alk. paper) -- ISBN 978-1-315-68196-2 (ebook) 1. Landscape construction. 2. Landscape design. 3. Gardens--Design. I. Title.
TH380.H38 2016
712--dc23
2015035193

ISBN: 978-0-415-74628-1 (pbk)
ISBN: 978-1-315-68196-2 (ebk)

Typeset in Avenir by
Servis Filmsetting Ltd, Stockport, Cheshire

MIX
Paper from responsible sources
FSC® C013056
www.fsc.org

Printed and bound in Great Britain by
TJ International Ltd, Padstow, Cornwall

To Jane,

I know what it is to live entirely for and with what I love best on earth.

Charlotte Brontë, *Jane Eyre*

Contents

Figures

Tables

Acknowledgements

This book would not have been possible without the continual support and advice from countless designers, contractors and manufacturers who have given both their time and advice, trusting that I will put it to good use.

The technical challenges of producing the illustrations and related download materials could not have been possible without the support and tolerance of many CAD forums, but in particular www.SketchUcation.com and Matt Donley, at www.mastersketchup.com.

The illustrations have only been possible through the generosity of the devoted SketchUp community and those who create and release plugins and extensions, often free of charge for us with lesser coding abilities to use creatively. A list of all of the plugins used is given in Appendix E.

In compiling this book and the associated CAD files, I naïvely tried to reinvent several wheels, along with making every mistake known to publishing. This volume would undoubtedly have been a collection of unusable notes and mislabelled diagrams, without the perseverance and determination of my copy-editor, Susan Dunsmore. Her professionalism in dealing with a determined amateur has made me look better than I deserve.

Finally, thanks to Keith Edmond, friend and CAD devotee, who offered daily suggestions and advice, keeping me up to date and focused when I was floundering.

Note on the text

The companion website for this book can be found at www.routledge.com/cw/hensey.

The 3D CAD downloads that accompany this book are available for SketchUp only.

The purchase of this book entitles the reader access to view and download the 3D CAD files that support the illustrations. Access to the files is perpetual and not time-limited.

The 3D SketchUp files can be edited and used for both private and commercial work, but not resold or distributed, either free of charge or for payment. The publisher reserves the right to limit, restrict or prohibit access to the 3D download files without notice or apology.

The words that appear in the Glossary are given in bold on their first occurrence in the chapter.

Introduction

Like many designers, it was an early ambition of mine to ensure that my work flow was as efficient as possible. That during quieter periods, between projects in my early career, I would create document and specification templates, gain an understanding of materials and perhaps most important of all, create a library of standardised construction details. Perhaps it is a good thing that those drawings never did materialise. With the development of CAD (computer aided design) tools and specifically 3D CAD, its adoption and subsequent replacement of the drawing board, those details would now be in a somewhat redundant format.

Therein lies the motivation for this book. Construction detailing is now much more accessible that it has ever been. Books have been written on the subject, suppliers usefully provide sections, drawings and assemblies of their components and expert advice is never far away. Despite the prevalence of information, the original problem remains. Not necessarily what the construction detail is (with a little research, advice can usually be found for most circumstances and problems), but is the data available, in a useful and more importantly, usable format? The information currently offered and supplied remains low tech and locked in the two-dimensional world, as simple illustrations (PDFs, JPEGs). It is virtually uneditable and requires some considerable investment of time to redraw or adapt to fit a project's specific requirements. The usefulness and life of the static PDF, and two-dimensional technical download are limited. Enlightened companies, manufacturers and suppliers are making their products available as 3D objects and assembled structures, for designers to download into their construction software and place easily in the designed landscapes. What is missing is the mundane, the detailing of surfaces and channels, joints and attachments in a way that allows a designer freedom to edit and reconfigure to suit a specific application. This book aims to address that problem. The images presented here are by necessity 2D and static, they do, however, represent another tier of information. All of the illustrations presented have been created as 3D CAD models and are available to download (see below), making this more of a catalogue than a book. They have been created within SketchUp and organised with both a simple layer structure and using 'scenes' to create specific screen views and orientations. Details of the CAD files are available on the download site at: www.routledge.com/cw/hensey

The 3D models are not simply 'mass' models. They are constructed from the components that they represent. Textures from actual unit materials have been applied, and despite the limitations of print restricting this book's illustrations to monotone, all models are in colour.

In addition to the 3D models, each detail has a sectional view. These are available both as a separate view within SketchUp and as a 2D drawing within Layout (SketchUp Pro's drawing package). These are linked and any changes to the SketchUp model are reflected in the Layout drawing. While the SketchUp 2D section is 'naked', dimensionally accurate but without any notes, the Layout drawing is fully annotated, along with dimensions and text.

Some illustrations in this book are shown only as simple elevations, for instance, paving patterns. These are actually assembled from individual 3D model components and show in plan, for clarity. They can be reconfigured to suit, although a large selection of patterns has been created.

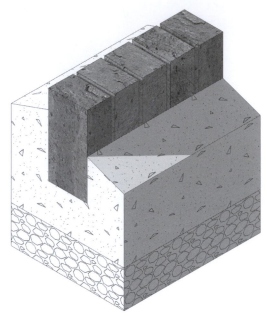

Figure 0.1 Bricks

Figure 0.2 Bricks, section

HOW TO USE THIS BOOK

All of the components and materials in this book have been created as 3D CAD models, using the SketchUp software. The illustrations in this book have been derived from these models.

While manufacturers have willingly supplied some information, to aid in the creation of 3D models, they have not supplied fully dimensioned drawings, as this would be handing over their intellectual property. As such, the models created are as accurate as possible within the limitations of the information supplied. They are fair representations but not of sufficient quality or detail for manufacturing purposes. While every care has been made to ensure the accuracy of the information presented, products and specifications frequently change, and errors, omissions and mistakes are possible. Updates and corrections will be made as quickly as possible; these will be included in any subsequent printed editions but the material available from the website will always be the most up to date. The website requires a registration process and notification of any updates will be issued when they are made.

All CAD software has limitations. The representation of curves and curved surfaces is one such compromise. Curved components (e.g. **kerbs**) may appear faceted due to the method employed by SketchUp to represent blends and organic forms. The precise placement of adjoining units may not be possible due to this approximation. In reality, such precision is simply not achievable and inconsistent gaps and joints due to human workmanship and the dimensional tolerances are the norm. Such inaccuracies should be anticipated and accounted for, allowing the contractor to make any necessary adjustments on site, while maintaining the intent of the designer.

Access to the 3D CAD models (available for SketchUp only)

Every illustration, that has an accompanying download, has a figure number. This is the number for the download file and should be used to find the SketchUp model. Instructions on how to search, access and use the files are given on the book's website at www.routledge.com/cw/hensey

Figure 0.3 Bricks, exploded view

Requirements

The download files were created in SketchUp version 2014 and 2015 (Pro) . They can be opened in these and later releases of the software, in either SketchUp Make (free) or Pro. The Layout files (dimensioned drawings) can only be opened in SketchUp Pro. SketchUp files can be opened in either Mac or PC versions of the software.

The 3D CAD models are intended to be used as supplementary details within a larger project. Some of the textures and methods used are quite memory-intensive and care should be taken to avoid too many detailed elements within a single SketchUp project, as they may consume memory and cause the model to run slowly. Advice is given on the website on the use of these models and the best way to effectively include and manage them within a design project.

The *SketchUp Workflow for Architecture* by Michael Brightman (2013) gives a detailed overview of how to integrate SketchUp into a design workflow that involves construction detailing.

MATERIALS

All constructed features are achieved through the assembly of smaller, individual components: sub-assemblies. The size to which individual units are manufactured varies between countries, regions and even factories. With metrication, manufacturing has become standardised, for instance, while the British Standard range of kerbs has dimensions often directly converted from imperial to metric (e.g. kerb stones are typically 915mm long, the metric equivalent of 1 yard), there are now equivalent products in metric modules; 1000mm, 1500mm, etc. Care should be taken in the selection of components to ensure that the dimensional sizes of unlike materials work together. **Paving**, for instance, looks better if the joints of brick trims and inset patterns are aligned to the joints of the paving units themselves. The standard sizing of materials creates a useful reference and gauge to help the designer in organising a space. It saves time, labour and materials if the sizes of features and structures are derived from a module of the principal materials used. Cuts can be difficult to manage and place. Where cuts are inevitable, their location and alignment should be detailed. A **contractor's** opinion on what is aesthetically acceptable may not be the same as the designer's. Small pieces of cut paving, placed in the wrong location, such as on a road surface, can also create an unacceptable risk; avoided through forethought and appreciation of the materials being used.

Materials are manufactured in batches. The process may be continuous, but the batch is said to end when the production equipment is switched off (at the end of a shift, for example), when there is a stoppage to allow maintenance work, or replenishment of raw materials is required. The combination of new raw materials, different operators and changes in the atmosphere, can all contribute to a variation in the supplied product. This variation is called the **tolerance** and every manufactured component has a range of variation within which it is considered to be acceptable and fit for purpose. This is usually found in the small print of the product's **specification**. This permitted variation is usually expressed as +/- mm (e.g. +/-5mm).

A 400mm square paving slab with +/−5mm may be delivered at a maximum size of 405mm or minimum size of 395mm, and it would be within tolerance and considered fit for purpose.

Every batch will be identified on the order/delivery documentation. When materials are ordered, it is preferable if they are supplied from the same batch to reduce variation in both physical and aesthetic attributes. Products from the same batch are more likely to have the same dimensional characteristics and tolerance range. Where construction is on such a large scale that use of components from a single batch is not possible, or where on-site storage is problematic and necessitates using materials as they are delivered, a system of randomised selection is used. This technique is used by bricklayers, roofers and those laying extensive areas of paving. Multiple packs or pallets of the paving/roofing materials are opened simultaneously and the pieces drawn randomly from all packs as work progresses. This prevents tolerance variations from affecting any one area, for instance, having to create wider or narrower joints to fit in with previously laid units. Importantly, it also randomises the colours so that any variations are evenly distributed and appear intentional rather than introducing unsightly and unappealing bands of colour variations, typical if only one pallet were used at once. While such techniques are the responsibility of the contractor, the designer should be aware of tolerances and variations, designing details that minimise waste and effort.

STANDARDS AND REGULATIONS

These construction details should not be used as a substitute or as a replacement for any written specifications. They are intended to supplement Landscape and Garden Construction specifications and provide clarity for a contractor. Written specifications and clauses are beyond the scope of this book. Products, standards and specifications change, and the designer should ensure that they are using the correct and most up-to-date references available. The breadth of products and construction techniques available is considerable. These construction details are intended as generic and common examples. Full written specifications are best obtained from the material supplier and manufacturers and included in a unified specification document, such as those provided by the National Building Specification (NBS) (UK), or Heather's Model Specification for Landscape and Garden Design Construction (UK), see Appendix B.

Guidance on the design, construction and installation of features and structures is included in a wide range of publications, regulation documents and Standards. Such documents are constantly being updated, revised or harmonised with other organisations with similar interests. The references given are correct at the time of going to press but designers should satisfy themselves that they are using the most up-to-date and relevant guidance, code or standard.

The regulations for private spaces are different and less onerous than those surfaces and structures that are intended for use by the public or large groups of people. It is expected, however, that a designer will apply any guidance in a reasonable and considered way; the guidance for the ratio of ramps and steps and their protection, for instance, is the result of considerable research and should be used as the basis for any design involving changes of level.

References
Brightman, M. (2013) *SketchUp Workflow for Architecture*. Chichester: John Wiley & Co. Ltd.
National Building Specification (NBS) (UK). Available at: www.thenbs.com
Heather's Model Specification for Landscape and Garden Design Construction (UK). Available at: http://sgd.org.uk/industry-heathers-model-specifications-2014.aspx

CHAPTER 1

Vehicular paving

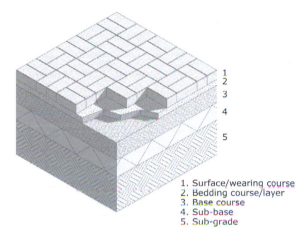

1. Surface/wearing course
2. Bedding course/layer
3. Base course
4. Sub-base
5. Sub-grade

Figure 1.1 General build-up of a road or parking surface

INTRODUCTION

Well-designed pavements can give direction, can look attractive, as well as reduce hazards and improve safety. Poorly constructed pavements, pedestrian or vehicular, can at best look unappealing and at worst result in a surface that is unsafe and potentially hazardous.

The design of pavements and surfaces for vehicular use requires a specialist knowledge that considers the service, context and design criteria, the intended maximum intensity of use, the local geology, the climate and the budget.

The location of the pavement will to some degree influence the choice of materials, aesthetic detailing and the finishes specified. The pre-existing structure/profile of the **sub-grades** will influence the bearing capacity of the structural layers of the pavement.

The selection of pavement material is determined by the functional requirements of the site, the aesthetics of the final wearing surface and the performance criteria to meet the intended intensity of use.

In the UK, the Highways Agency offers guidance on the construction of vehicular and pedestrian paving and this should be consulted in conjunction with a site-specific geo-survey identifying the nature of the soil and sub-grades.

The use of **permeable** or **impermeable** materials may be determined by the intensity of use of the final surface as well as by the condition of the substrate and, additionally, by legislation.

The suitability of the sub-grade is critical to a successful and sustainable structure; it is essential that the load-bearing capacity of the sub-grade be established, as this will determine the subsequent composition and thicknesses of all supported materials. This is assessed through subsoil samples. A common measure used is the **California Bearing Ratio (CBR)**; results less than 5 per cent will require deeper excavations and additional, or thicker layers of materials (known as capping layers). These are necessary to achieve a firm working platform without excessive deformation, and which will allow the overlaid materials to be fully compacted. Where low CBR sub-grades are encountered, ground stabilisation may be more cost-effective. A CBR of 5 per cent or more indicates that capping layers may not be required. Prior to project commencement, all sites should be independently inspected and assessed by a qualified engineer. A full engineering specification will be needed for most vehicular pavements, although some standard solutions will often be suitable in most circumstances and can be used at the project's appraisal or development stage. Where traffic loading is in excess of those commonly anticipated for public highways, specialised design advice should be sought. Field guidance for estimating sub-grade strength is shown in Table 1.1.

Table 1.1 Field guidance for estimating sub-grade strengths

Consistency	Indicator		Strength		
	Tactile	Visual	Mechanical	CBR	CU
			SPT*	%	kN/sqm
Very soft	Squeezes through fingers	Man walking sinks >75mm	4–82	<1	<25
Soft	Easily moulded with hand pressure	Man walking sinks 50–70mm	2–4	Approx 1	Approx 25
Medium	Moulded with moderate hand pressure	Man walking sinks 25mm	4–8	1–2	25–40
Firm	Moulded with strong hand pressure	Utility truck ruts 10–25mm	8–15	2–4	40–75
Stiff	Cannot be moulded by hand	Loaded construction vehicle ruts 25mm	15–30	4–6	75–150

Source: Rennison and Allen, Department of Mechanical Engineering, Sheffield University, via Fiberweb Geosynthetics Ltd, www.terram.com, March 2009.

* Standard Penetration Test

The visible surface of a road or driveway is known as the wear layer. This is supported by a series of individual layers, ranging from a single, thick course of cast concrete to the more stratified constructions used to stabilise block paving. Usually the smaller the module of the material used on the uppermost surface, the more stratified the construction is in section. The materials used in road construction have unique characteristics and it is necessary to understand their behaviour and properties in order to create the best construction.

All pavements and road installations must comply to the requirements set out in BS 7533, Part 3.

SUB-GRADE

Sub-grade is the term used to describe the bare earth, after it has been prepared (i.e. stripped of vegetation and excavated to the required level). Top soil contains a high ratio of organic matter and this must be removed to reveal the more stable and inert subsoil. The subsoil is then excavated to the formation level, i.e. the level at which the construction will start. Correct preparation is essential; undulations may compromise the final construction and should be rectified at this stage, giving a solid platform on which to build. The sub-grade level should correspond to the final wearing layer, giving a uniformly strong structure and planar drainage. Inaccurate or uneven excavations that use the subsequent **sub-base** and bedding courses to correct undulations or create the required falls follow poor practice and will cause uneven load distribution.

GEOTEXTILES

Geotextiles are non-woven construction membranes; different from the landscape fabrics (used as weed suppressants or as a non-load-bearing separation barrier between soils and mulches) used in general landscape works. A well-constructed road or driveway will be impenetrable to most weeds, however, certain species such as *Equisetum arvense* (horsetail) and *Fallopian japonica* (Japanese knotweed) may force their way through; they also have root systems that can extend well below the usual excavation depth for a road. Their removal, if present, may require specialist contractors. An initial site investigation, prior to the removal of the top soil, should be conducted to determine if such pernicious vegetation is present or in close proximity. Most vegetation in road surfaces is a result of seeds caught in gaps and taking advantage of any micro-conditions, flourishing in an abundance of moisture and nutrients carried in run-off; geotextiles cannot prevent this type of growth.

In road and vehicular pavement construction, a geotextile or fabric membrane creates a separation barrier, preventing one layer of material from amalgamating into another, while allowing water to percolate through. The separation between layers can be at either the sub-base/sub-grade interface or between the sub-base and the laying course. An argument for it being between the sub-base and sub-grade is that it prevents the migration of clean material into the ground. Geotextiles also work well over made-up sub-grades where consolidation may be uneven, and as a barrier on top of wet/heavy clays to prevent material migration.

Small domestic construction projects, such as a domestic driveway, do not always require a membrane, if the sub-layers are prepared and compacted correctly.

SUB-BASE

This is usually the first constructed layer of a load-bearing structure. Laid onto the excavated/prepared subsoil, it is essential to support and dissipate the load of the overlaid road/carriageway surface. Collapsed driveways and road surfaces are invariably attributed to the poor or incorrect specification and construction of the sub-base.

There are three types of sub-base:

- *unbound*: used for residential projects (drives);
- *commonly crushed rock or crushed concrete*: the ratio of dust, fines and particular aggregates is controlled to ensure a firm and void-free layer when compacted;
- **cement bound** (*CBM*): used almost exclusively on public roads or highways where the sub-grade is unreliable or the surface is designed for heavy loads.

Unbound sub-base materials are composed of the following materials:

- DTp1
- ballast
- planings
- crusher-run stone

- **quarry scalpings**
- hardcore

DTp1 (Department of Transport specifications UK)

DTp1 is also known as MoT1 (UK), 804 Type A (Ireland), 40mm down/to dust. A sub-base material, of premium aggregate, Type 1 is the most appropriate, although not essential for pedestrian trafficked areas.

Ballast

Ballast is typically an uncontrolled mix of gravel and fines originating from quarry or dredging works. It is suitable for use under pedestrianised surfaces and low-load trafficked areas (e.g. domestic driveways). It is unsuitable for high-load use or frequently used trafficked surfaces. As the source may be unknown, ballast may be composed of eroded particles (e.g. from a river bed) which have smoothed edges and therefore it is unsuitable as a load-bearing structure.

Planings

Planings are material derived from the resurfacing operations in highway maintenance. Old road surfaces are 'planed' down to a stable, solid layer and the crushed surface materials are collectively described as 'planings'. The quality of the material depends entirely on the roads that have been repaired and as such can vary enormously. At its worst, a batch consisting of mostly asphalt will degrade and create considerable problems. Planings are a risk and best avoided.

Crusher run

Crusher run refers to stone that has been crushed. This material is usually sieved and specified according to the maximum particle size, e.g. 60mm to dust. The material is an uncontrolled mix of everything from dust up to the specified aggregate size. Crushed stone has sharp edges and so binds well. For domestic drives 50mm crusher run is acceptable, the larger the construction, the larger the specified particle should be (e.g. 50mm, 75mm, 100mm).

Quarry scalpings

Scalpings consists of crushed and recycled stone material, derived from the everyday operations of a quarry. The material produced will depend on the products manufactured/operations at the quarry. The variety of material is considerable and only local knowledge will identify if the scalpings/waste are suitable as a load-bearing fill.

Hardcore

Hardcore is a universal term for sub-base materials. It is so generic that it is virtually meaningless and is an unsuitable description or term to use in specifications or on drawings.

Old bricks, broken paving and the like are unsuitable as a sub-base, but may be described as hardcore. The pieces are too large and irregular and will inevitably create voids. Such materials needs to be crushed to a more uniform size (e.g. 100mm or 75mm) and blended with fines and dusts to create a consistent material that will consolidate well, without voids.

Depth of construction for permeable driveways

From the finished surface of a proposed drive or pavement there is normally 200mm to 250mm of layered material forming the construction. Geotextiles are recommended to prevent migration and cross-contamination between layers; particularly important for permeable paving solutions.

Where services and utilities lie beneath the intended paved area, some form of intervention is required. Services and ducts may require redirection around the paved area or relocating to a more suitable depth. This work may have to be undertaken by either the utility provider or a specialist contractor. The presence of services and ducts should be established before design

work is started and certainly as a matter of course before excavations are made.

BASE OR BEDDING LAYERS

These are stiff, tough layers, also know as binder layers. They generally fall into two categories: flexible and rigid.

'Flexible' courses are better described as being semi-rigid; usually constructed from bitumen bound materials, they are capable of minor flexion. Rigid courses are usually constructed from concrete and remain inflexible.

The base course forms an intermediate layer between the loose sub-grade/base beneath and the surfacing layers above. The requirements of the surface-wearing layer dictate whether the base layer needs to retain a degree of flexion or be completely rigid. In general, a flexible surface layer will require a flexible (or semi-rigid) base layer and a rigid surface will similarly require a rigid base (e.g. a flexible wearing surface, such as **tarmac**, will require a semi-rigid base layer). A road surface designed for heavy loads would benefit from a rigid base structure.

Bedding layer or laying course

This is the layer that supports the uppermost surface layer or laid materials. It needs to be flexible enough to accommodate variations in the thicknesses of any top course materials, maintaining an even finished paving/surface layer.

The choice of surface material will determine the composition and thickness of this layer. A rigid surface usually requires a rigid (bound) bedding, whereas an unbound bedding is suitable for a wearing surface laid with a flexible or unit material.

- *Bound bedding*: Surfaces with **bound** bedding are impermeable and therefore the fall of the pavement and peripheral drainage form an essential part of the design criteria. Often cement-based, bitumen bound bedding is used but this is not typical in the UK, although common in the USA.

- *Unbound bedding*: An **unbound** bed should be free draining and not retain water. It is typically a fine granular material, such as sand. Suitable sands are either coarse grit, bedding or concreting sand: Class M or Zone 2. Building sand is less angular, containing a high ratio of clay and is not suitable. Crushed rock or stone dust can be suitable but must be of the correct grade.
- *Cement/mortar bedding*: Unit materials laid onto a rigid concrete base are usually set in a wet layer mortar or fine concrete layer, of which there are several grades or onto a semi-dry mix (40–70mm, 1:4 cement: concreting sand, grade M) layer, over which is poured a 1:1 **slurry** prior to laying the paving units, to improve adhesion. Joints are left open and finished with a semi-dry mortar or stiff mortar, once set.

Rigid surfaces may be set onto a variety of concrete beds, consisting of fine aggregate, coarse aggregate, cement and water. Fine concrete incorporates 6mm aggregate, medium concrete incorporates 10–20mm gravel and coarse concrete contains 20–40mm particles.

The nature of the application will determine the type and structure of the concrete to be used. Concrete and mortars have two defining characteristics: cement content and slump, which is the measure of the material wetness; there is an optimal value either side of which will be detrimental to the final strength of the concrete mix. Ideally the water/cement (w/c) ratio is approximately 1:2 (e.g. 1kg water:2kg cement).

There are several common varieties of mortars and concretes used in bedding mixes:

- *Slurry mix*: A fine concrete, used as a wet grout for pavers and setts. Poured onto the finished surface, it fills all the voids between units, excess slurry is brushed off.
- *Wet mix*: Prepared using the optimal water/cement ratio (1:2), this is the commonest type of mix for bedding.
- *Moist mix*: This is a stiff mix with only sufficient water to allow the cement to cure; when squeezed, there should be no residual moisture. It can be useful where a more fluid bed would disrupt previously laid units.
- *Semi-dry mix*: No water is added to this mix, relying on the water content of the sand to activate the cement. A benefit is that such mixes remain workable for extended periods of time and previously laid units are not disrupted. There is typically no adhesion between the mix and the laid units.
- *Dry mix*: This is usually used exclusively for jointing and is brushed into the final laid surface. The cement/sand mixture causes no/minimal staining on laid units. The consistency of the cured mix is dependent on the water content of the surrounding materials as well as the weather. Inconsistent curing can result in the mix washing out or crumbling, where insufficient moisture was present.

Synthetic mortars can have the benefit of not staining natural materials. Epoxy resin (in powder form also known as polymeric mortar) or polybutadiene bases are supplied pre-mixed with sand. They are more expensive than their cement equivalents though they are stronger, with a variety of grades for different applications and are supplied ready to use.

WEARING OR PAVING SURFACE

There are several qualities that will direct the designer to specify one material over another:

- What does it look like?
- Is the pattern achievable from the material? Is it acceptable? Is it attractive?
- The surface finish should be relatively smooth and hard wearing, i.e. does not abrade.
- Small unit materials are far better than large unit paving which is prone to cracking. The small units will dissipate the load more effectively.

There are two classifications of surface materials: **rigid paving** and **flexible paving**.

Rigid paving

Rigid paving is usually more expensive than flexible alternatives. Post-construction alterations and excavations, such as laying/replacing service pipes can be difficult. Rigid structures are suitable for steep slopes/surfaces, areas of high intensity and impact and where the surface needs to be impenetrable to surface chemicals (e.g. petrol forecourts). All road materials are subject to movement due to ground compaction as well as expansion and contraction cycles from seasonal environmental changes. Rigid paving cannot be laid as a continuous surface and movement joints are required.

For concrete surfaces, such joints are necessary to avoid cracks as well as to compensate for longitudinal expansion. Dummy, or fake, joints, are used to control any crack formation or propagation. Slab lengths should not exceed ×25 their thickness, with a maximum length of 5–6m. In situ concrete can be post-treated to enhance the surface qualities, such as brushing to improve traction.

Flexible paving

Flexible paving is by far the most common form of road construction. It is quick to lay, usable almost immediately after laying, and is relatively cheap.

Gravel is a good flexible material, it must be angular, as pea gravel/river bed gravel will not support any load. Even angular gravel will migrate and edge restraints are required. Intermediate features may be included to minimise material migration.

Self-binding gravels can be **porous** but with a clay content they become impermeable, such as **hoggin**. The surface clay will eventually wash away, after which the hoggin will be less messy.

Macadam is an historic development from loose gravel, whereby graded gravels, in a determined ratio, were compacted to form an impermeable surface. **Tarmacadam** introduces a bitumen binder to the graded gravel. More recently, clear binders such as Clearmac® and Sureset have been developed, that allow the character of the gravel to help form the road surface aesthetic.

The composition of asphalt is determined by the type of bitumastic binder used. Soft bonding agents are suitable for low intensity use, while harder grades suit surfaces with a higher frequency of use/wear. The granular size of the macadam varies: driveways and surfaces used infrequently or to low intensity: 6mm; public roads and highways 10–14mm.

Unit paving has the most scope for aesthetic variations. The brick, pavers, cobbles and combinations are capable of being used to create a wide variety of effects and patterns. It is good practice that, in order to reduce the effect of any surface irregularities, patterns are laid across rather than along a surface.

Unit materials, natural or man-made, may carry a wear value. This may assist in selecting a suitable surface for the intended application. Highway Design Document 36/06 outlines the minimum **PSV** values for particular sites and traffic frequencies. Note HD36/06 states: 'Where designers are knowledgeable or have other experience of particular site conditions, an alternative PSV value can be specified.'

> PSV = polished stone value, i.e. how much an aggregate polishes after repeated wear
> **PPV** = polished paver value, i.e. the value applied to the surface as a whole

Materials not intended for public or road use may not carry a PPV/PSV value.

OTHER FEATURES

Edge restraints

All pavements created from unit materials require an edge restraint. This prevents the lateral migration of the structural layers as well as providing a means for drainage.

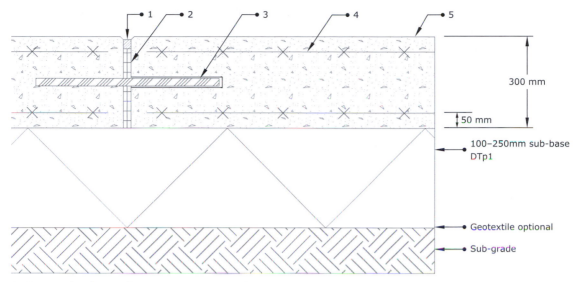

1. Waterproof sealant used to cap joint min. 25mm depth
2. Compressible fillerboard (e.g. Flexcell) 25mm drilled to accommodate dowels
3. Stainless steel (grade 250) jointing dowel: 600mm × 25mm diam., set level and parallel, one side sleeved, at 300mm centres
4. Reinforcing mesh(e.g. A142): set 50mm from all external surfaces
5. Concrete (C32/40)*

   Joints should be located at a maximum of ×30 the slab thickness (e.g. 250mm thickness = 6.25m)
   Frequently joints are set closer to reflect the aesthetics of other site features.

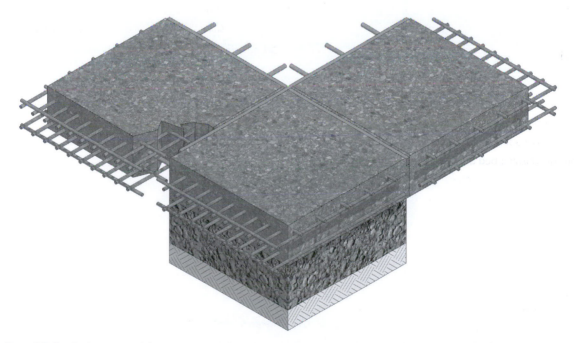

Figure 1.2 Cast in situ concrete joints

Source: * *Manual of Contract Documents for Highway Works*, vol. 1, *Specification for Highway Works*. www.standardsforhighways.co.uk/mchw

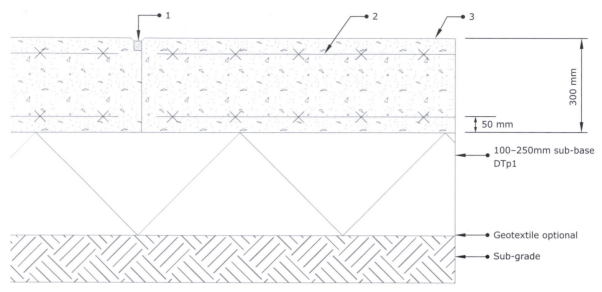

1. Waterproof sealant used to cap joint min. 25mm depth
2. Reinforcing mesh (e.g. A142): set 50mm from all external surfaces
3. Concrete (C32/40)*

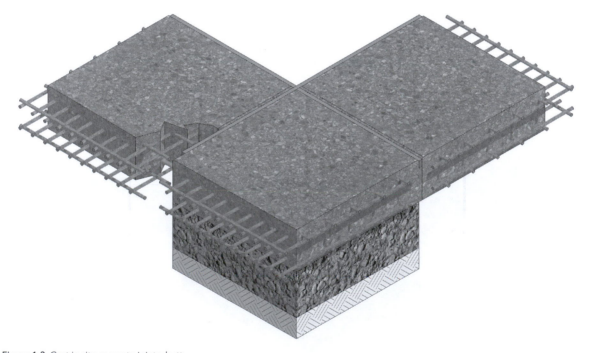

Figure 1.3 Cast in situ concrete joints: butt

Source: * *Manual of Contract Documents for Highway Works*, vol. 1, *Specification for Highway Works*. www.standardsforhighways.co.uk/mchw

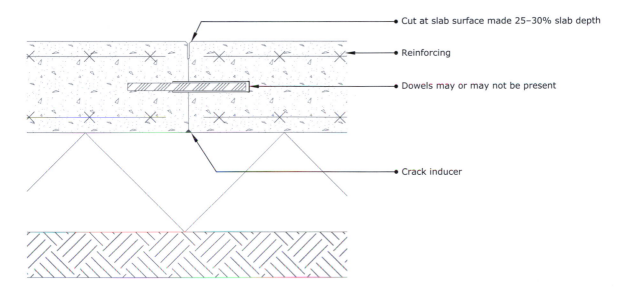

- Cut at slab surface made 25–30% slab depth
- Reinforcing
- Dowels may or may not be present
- Crack inducer

To prevent cracks from appearing in cast concrete slabs, it is necessary to subdivide a space (particularly if the area has several changes of direction) into minor rectangles. While the entire slab might be created in one pouring, the smaller sections will be made by inducing cracks after the concrete has set. The induced crack pattern should be designed prior to slab construction. Reinforcing should be constructed (if required) so that it is contained within the crack lines.

Joints should be located at changes in direction and every 2.5–3.5m.
The cut lines are subsequently sealed.

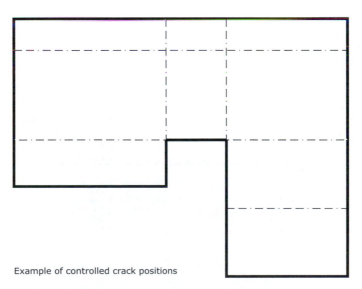

Example of controlled crack positions

Figure 1.4 Concrete slabs cast in situ, controlling cracks
Source: www.concretenetwork.com

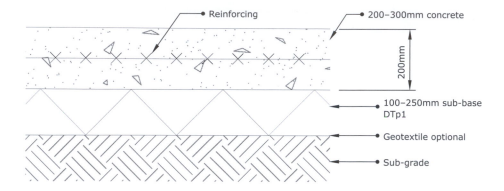

The strength class of the concrete will depend on the application and loads imposed on the wearing surface. For light vehicular applications, such as driveways, strength class C25 is adequate. Roads and high load-bearing surfaces are subject to Highway Agency regulations and expert advice should be obtained (in the UK, Guidance on the Specifications for Highway Works, Road Pavements: Concrete Materials; Series NG1000).

In addition to the wearing material, the surface finish must be specified. This might be a brushed or scattered aggregate to give traction. This is a skilled procedure that requires the creation of a uniform finish applied at the optimum time between compaction and curing.

Reinforcing mesh (sometimes referred to as 'fabric')

Mesh type	size (mm)/ Wire diam.	Where used
A142	200x200 (6)	Light use slabs, parking
A193	200x200 (7)	General use, can be used to replace A142 and A252
A252	200x200 (8)	Heavy duty use, roads and slabs +200mm

The thickness of the sub-base will be determined by the depth of the top soil and the type of sub-base present. The sub-base should be constructed on consolidated sub-grade material and never over top soil. If the local top soil extends to 300mm, for instance, the sub-base should be made at least as deep. Heavy clay soils that are liable to heave and subsidence will also require a deeper sub-base to compensate. Manufacturers' advice should be sought for specific applications.

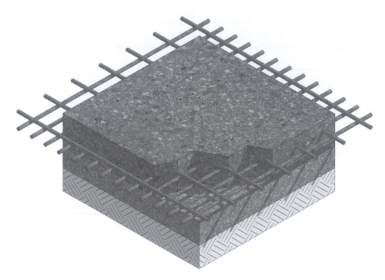

Figure 1.5 Reinforced concrete as a parking or road surface: impermeable

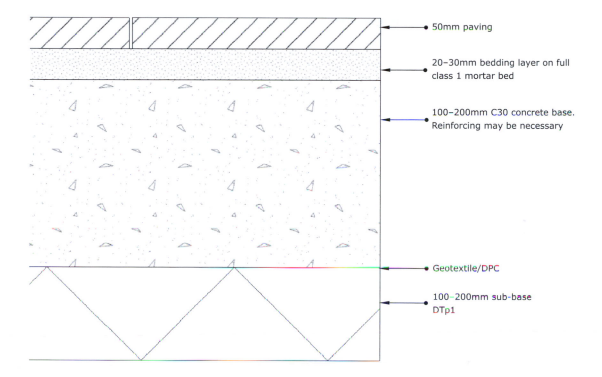

- 50mm paving
- 20–30mm bedding layer on full class 1 mortar bed
- 100–200mm C30 concrete base. Reinforcing may be necessary
- Geotextile/DPC
- 100–200mm sub-base DTp1

Where there is only occasional, light traffic – driveways, for instance – the construction of the supporting layers can be simplified, compared to that for road or highway applications.

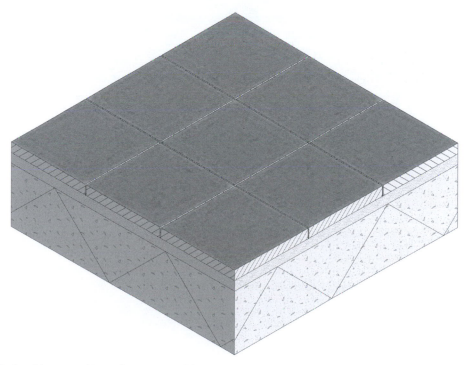

Figure 1.6 Paving slabs as a parking surface: impermeable

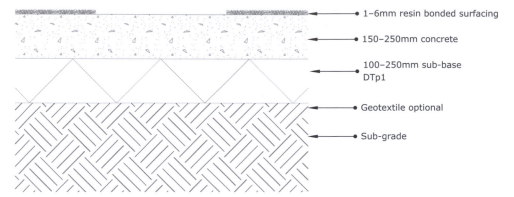

- 1–6mm resin bonded surfacing
- 150–250mm concrete
- 100–250mm sub-base DTp1
- Geotextile optional
- Sub-grade

There is a wide range of aggregate blends that are used in resin bound surface applications. The thickness of the surfacing layer will be determined by the size of the aggregates used. An antislip aggregate can be applied to the final wearing surface as it cures.

The concrete sub-surface should be shot-blasted to remove laitance. Resin bonded aggregates can be applied to asphalt concrete (macadam). The bitumen binder should be 40/60 pen. **Pen** is the term used to measure the softness of a bitumen surface.

Manufacturers' guidance and recommendations for surface preparation and application should be followed.

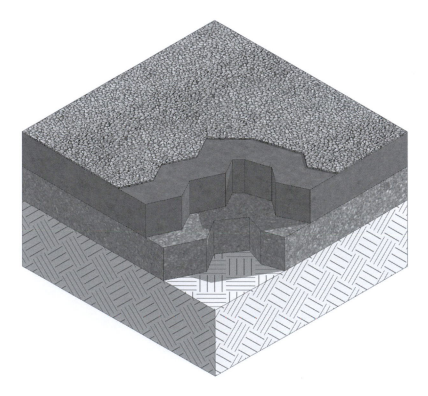

Figure 1.7 Resin bonded aggregate as a parking or road surface: impermeable

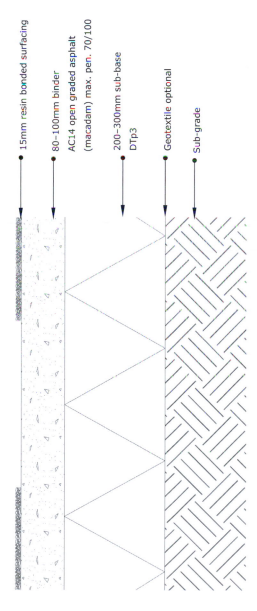

15mm resin bonded surfacing

80–100mm binder
AC14 open graded asphalt
(macadam) max. pen. 70/100

200–300mm sub-base
DTp3

Geotextile optional

Sub-grade

There is a wide range of aggregate blends that are used in resin bound surface applications. The thickness of the surfacing layer will be determined by the size of the aggregates used. An antislip aggregate can be applied to the final wearing surface as it cures.

Application	Wearing layer (min. mm)	Binder layer (mm)	pen	Granular sub-base DTp3
Driveways	15	80	100/150	200
Carparks/ light access	18	100	70/100	300
General access	18	70	70/100	300

Figure 1.8 Resin bonded aggregate as a parking or road surface: permeable

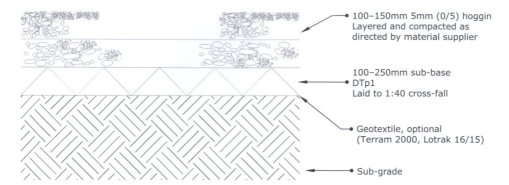

100–150mm 5mm (0/5) hoggin
Layered and compacted as
directed by material supplier

100–250mm sub-base
DTp1
Laid to 1:40 cross-fall

Geotextile, optional
(Terram 2000, Lotrak 16/15)

Sub-grade

Hoggin, a blend of clay and fine particles, is an inexpensive method of surface construction. Historically, the material would have been dug on site (sometimes this method is referred to as an 'as dug' road or path), pre-blended material is readily available, nationwide. The hoggin has to be compacted in thin layers, and the preferred technique will be advised by the material supplier. The composition of the sub-grade may result in surface undulations and indents over time. These are easily repaired and levelled with the addition of material to correct the problem. Compacted hoggin can be virtually impermeable and a fall or camber 1:50 (2%) is recommended.

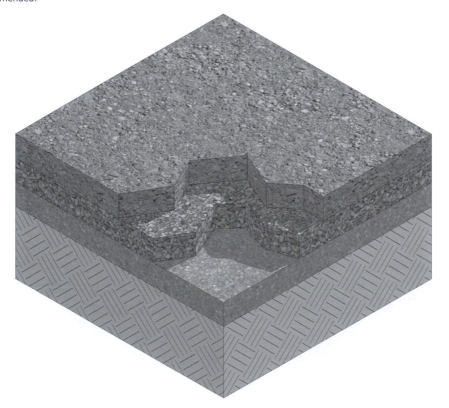

Figure 1.9 Hoggin: impermeable

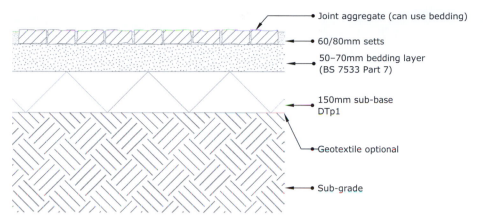

- Joint aggregate (can use bedding)
- 60/80mm setts
- 50–70mm bedding layer (BS 7533 Part 7)
- 150mm sub-base DTp1
- Geotextile optional
- Sub-grade

Setts, 60–80mm, are recommended as they dissipate imposed forces easily. Setts of this size are recommended for decorative/fan laying patterns. Larger setts (100mm) may be used with difficulty as it will be difficult to lay to the required pattern without cutting.

A topping aggregate may be required to fill or repair setts. Use a hard carboniferous limestone dust (BS 7533 part 7).

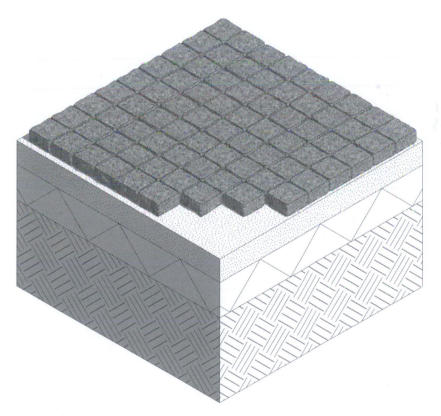

Figure 1.10 Setts as a road surface: impermeable

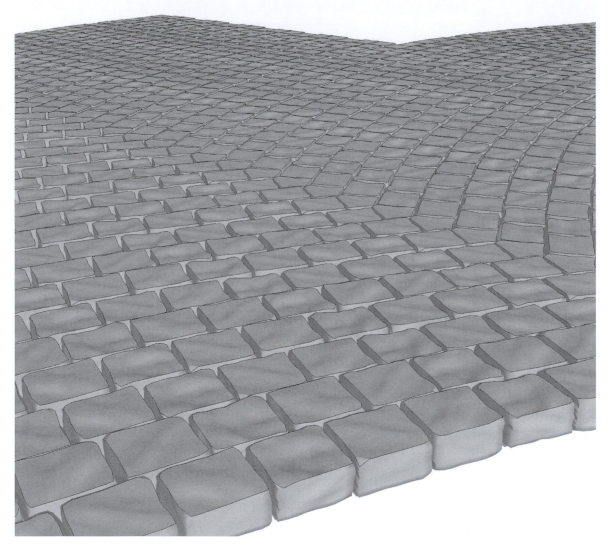

Arcs are the most effective pattern for setts used as paving for roads. Like an arch, the curve/s of the pattern distributes the lateral loads, maintaining the integrity of the surface. The curve of the setts will be determined by the width of the road. There are several sizes of sett available, 60–80mm is an effective size for average road traffic applications. Larger setts will create wider joints and the arc forms will not be as stable. Cropped, rather than sawn edge, setts should be used as they achieve a high degree of interlock.

Figure 1.11 Completed sett pattern

Source: The Porphyry Manual (1998).

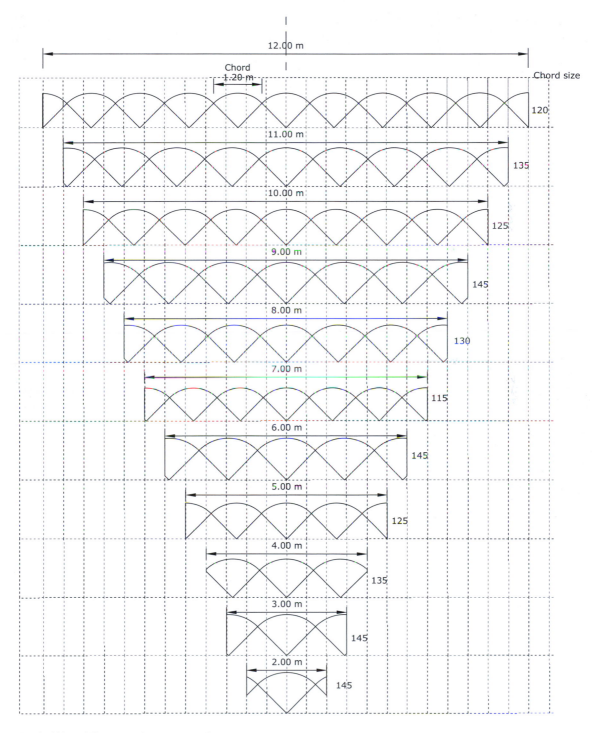

Road width and the appropriate segment size to use.

Select the closest pattern for the required road width.

The pattern should be set out from the road centre. There will be variation in the road width and the necessary adjustments to the pattern can be made at the road/kerb interface.

Figure 1.11 (Continued)

(Continued)

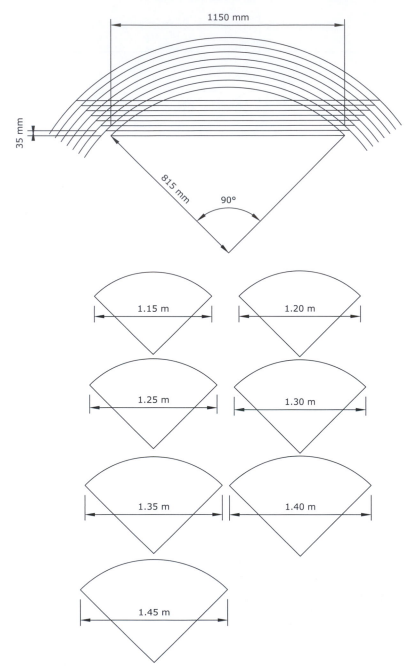

Creating the required chord and segment
(a chord is a line, at 90 deg to the radius, that connects two points on the diameter)

Figure 1.11 (Continued)

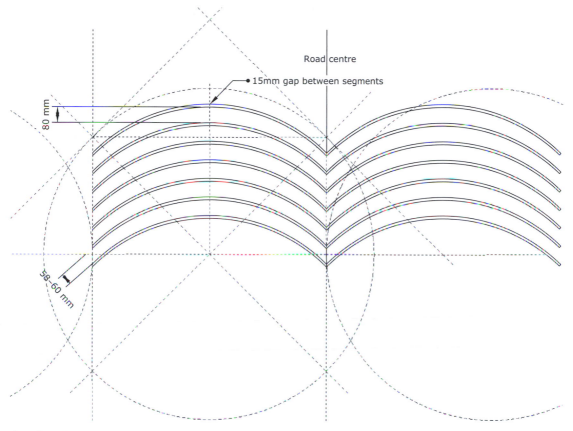

Road centre

15mm gap between segments

80 mm

58–60 mm

The selected segment is repeated in columns, with 80mm gaps at the segment centre. This will result in 60mm gaps at the edge and intersection of the arc with the adjoining geometry. The 80mm setts are laid from the centre of the arc out and the smaller setts, down to 60mm, at the edges of the arc radii. The intersection of two arcs may require the shaping of a specific sett unit to fill the gap effectively.

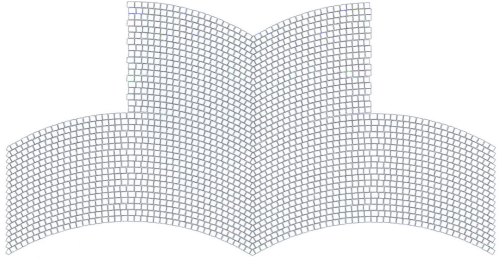

Completed sett pattern.

Figure 1.11 (Continued)

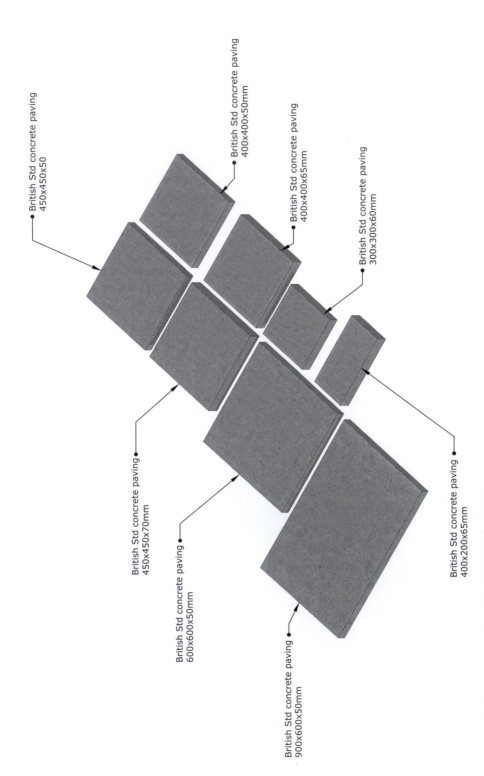

British Std concrete paving
450x450x50

British Std concrete paving
400x400x50mm

British Std concrete paving
400x400x65mm

British Std concrete paving
300x300x60mm

British Std concrete paving
450x450x70mm

British Std concrete paving
600x600x50mm

British Std concrete paving
900x600x50mm

British Std concrete paving
400x200x65mm

Figure 1.12 Common paving sizes in the British Standard metric range

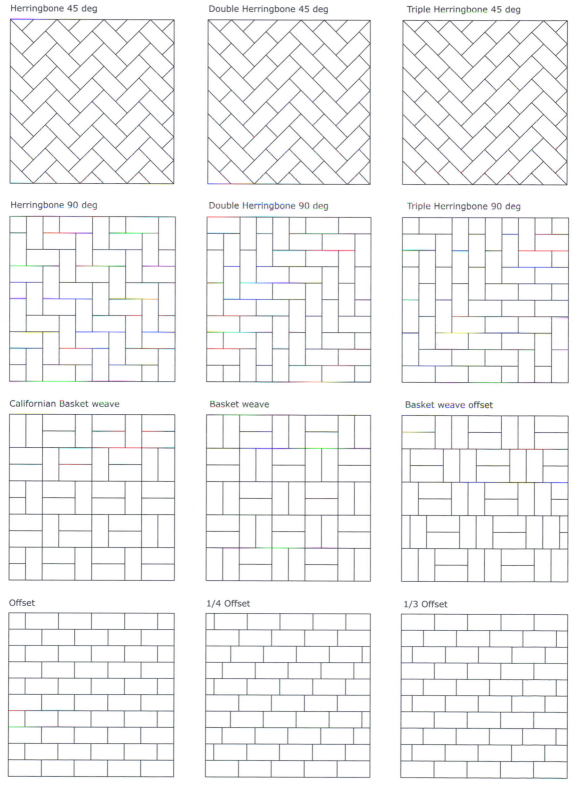

Herringbone 45 deg

Double Herringbone 45 deg

Triple Herringbone 45 deg

Herringbone 90 deg

Double Herringbone 90 deg

Triple Herringbone 90 deg

Californian Basket weave

Basket weave

Basket weave offset

Offset

1/4 Offset

1/3 Offset

Figure 1.13 Block paving patterns

(Continued)

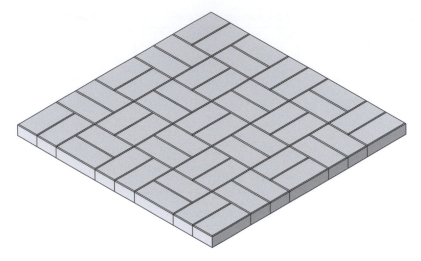

Block paving patterns

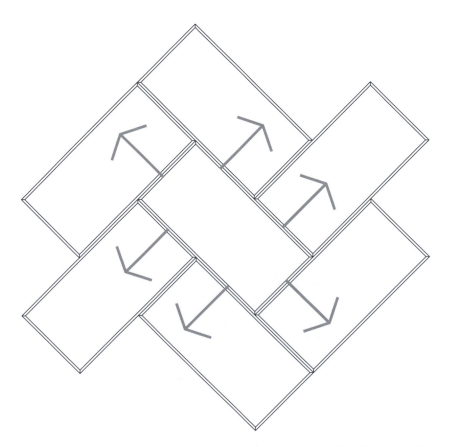

Block paving for roads can be laid to a range of patterns. The strongest bond is where a block is in contact with as many of its neighbours as possible (max. x6) as this most effectively distributes loads and lateral forces.

Figure 1.13 (Continued)

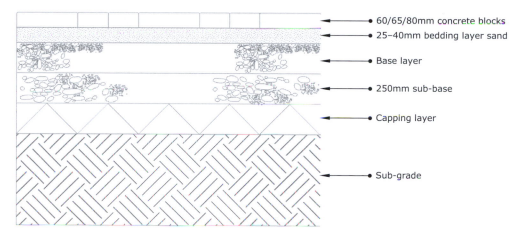

- 60/65/80mm concrete blocks
- 25–40mm bedding layer sand
- Base layer
- 250mm sub-base
- Capping layer
- Sub-grade

Capping layer
A capping layer is not always required and usually only where any sub-grade has a CBR of 5% or less. This should be constructed from granular or cement bound material, approved by the Local Highways Authority.
CBR <2% requires 600mm capping layer.
CBR 2–5% requires 350mm capping layer.

Sub-base
The thickness of the sub-base will be determined by the volume of traffic anticipated and if a capping layer is present. No capping layer requires 250mm.
A capping layer, if present, reduces the sub-base requirement to 150mm for space serving up to 4 dwellings, 200mm for 5–20 dwellings and 225mm for over 20 dwellings/large sites.

Base layer
Where required, this should be of either cement bound material (CBM) or dense bituminous macadam (DBM).
The thickness of the base layer will be determined by the volume of traffic anticipated:
infrequent use/access roads require no base layer

standard use roads 130–180mm

heavy use/load 200–250mm.

Where the wearing surface is exposed to exceptional circumstances, such as frost heave, heavy goods turning, speeds in excess of 50kph, additional depth is required and will be advised by the Local Highways Authority.

See BS 7533:1992 Guide to structural design of pavements constructed with clay or concrete block pavers.

Figure 1.14 Concrete block paving as a road surface: impermeable

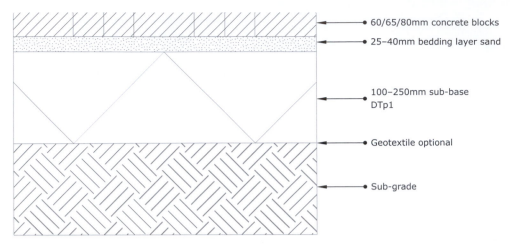

- 60/65/80mm concrete blocks
- 25–40mm bedding layer sand
- 100–250mm sub-base DTp1
- Geotextile optional
- Sub-grade

Where there is only occasional, light traffic – driveways, for instance – the construction of the supporting layers can be simplified, compared to that for road or highway applications.

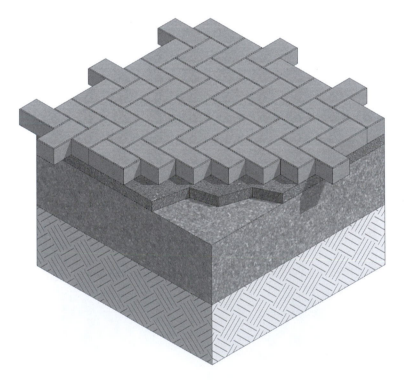

Figure 1.15 Concrete block paving as a parking or road surface: impermeable

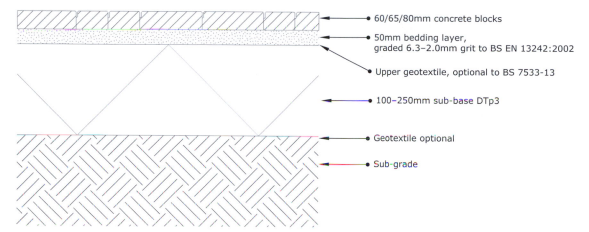

- 60/65/80mm concrete blocks
- 50mm bedding layer, graded 6.3–2.0mm grit to BS EN 13242:2002
- Upper geotextile, optional to BS 7533-13
- 100–250mm sub-base DTp3
- Geotextile optional
- Sub-grade

While there are many **bond** patterns possible, the most effective is herringbone. The joint width should be min. 6mm, filled with graded 6.3–2.0mm grit to BS EN 13242:2002. All joints should be firmly filled. Care should be taken not to spill soil over or contaminate the grit during construction as this may compromise the infiltration mechanism.

Permeable paving relies on the correct grade of aggregates. Material should be categorised as LA30, F120 and MDE20 (Table A.3 BS EN 7533-13:2009). The grit should be insoluble in hydrochloric acid and be a naturally occurring aggregate. Where there is only occasional, light traffic, such as driveways, the construction of the supporting layers can be simplified, compared to that for road or highway applications.

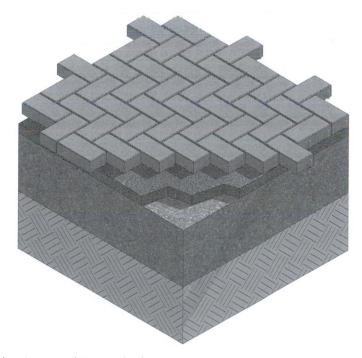

Figure 1.16 Concrete block paving as a parking or road surface: permeable

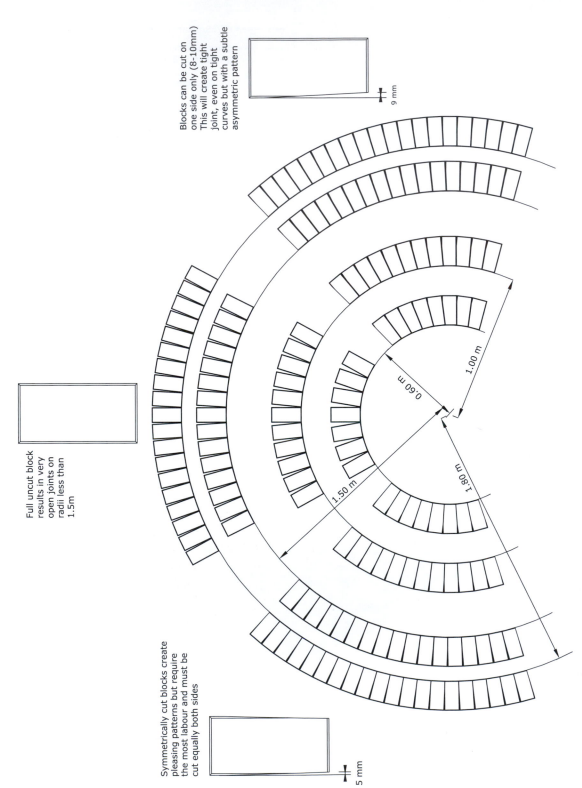

Blocks can be cut on one side only (8-10mm) This will create tight joint, even on tight curves but with a subtle asymmetric pattern

9 mm

Full uncut block results in very open joints on radii less than 1.5m

Symmetrically cut blocks create pleasing patterns but require the most labour and must be cut equally both sides

5 mm

1.00 m

0.60 m

1.80 m

1.50 m

Figure 1.17 Laying standard paving blocks to curves

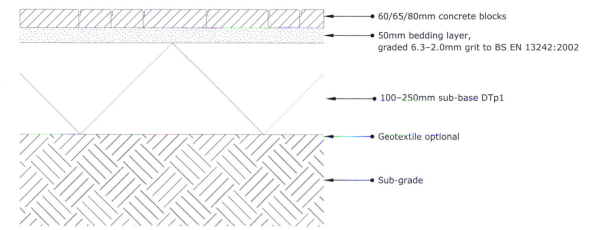

- 60/65/80mm concrete blocks
- 50mm bedding layer, graded 6.3–2.0mm grit to BS EN 13242:2002
- 100–250mm sub-base DTp1
- Geotextile optional
- Sub-grade

Decorative concrete block paving is available in a wide range of shapes and styles. Most is designed for impermeable applications. Pattern repeats/bond permutations are usually limited, making such blocks unsuitable for road and highway construction although ideal for driveways and small access roads.

The irregular edge detail of most decorative blocks will require the specification of specialised edge or kerb pieces.

Where there is only occasional, light traffic – driveways, for instance – the construction of the supporting layers can be simplified, compared to that for road or highway applications.

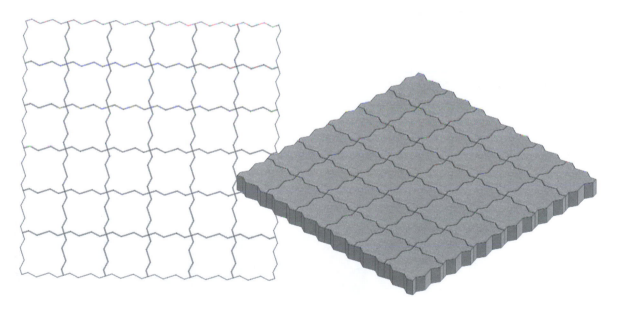

Figure 1.18 Decorative concrete block paving as a parking or road surface: impermeable

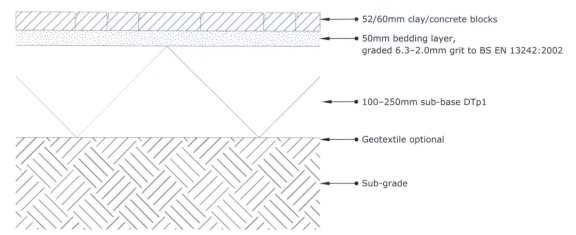

- 52/60mm clay/concrete blocks
- 50mm bedding layer, graded 6.3–2.0mm grit to BS EN 13242:2002
- 100–250mm sub-base DTp1
- Geotextile optional
- Sub-grade

Elongated pavers give a distinct aesthetic, whether manufactured from concrete or clay. They can be used for light use roads, driveways or pedestrian footpaths. A herringbone bond is recommended for trafficked areas, whereas a footpath can be laid to a staggered bond laid either across or along the main path axis. The tumbled/hand-finished characteristics of these blocks mean that they do not form tight joints, making them somewhat permeable although not to the extent of paving specifically designed for that purpose.

Illustrated: Retro (concrete)
(190x50x60mm); Tobermore

Illustrated: Clay Paver
(215x70x52mm); Vande Moortel

Figure 1.19 Elongated paving blocks

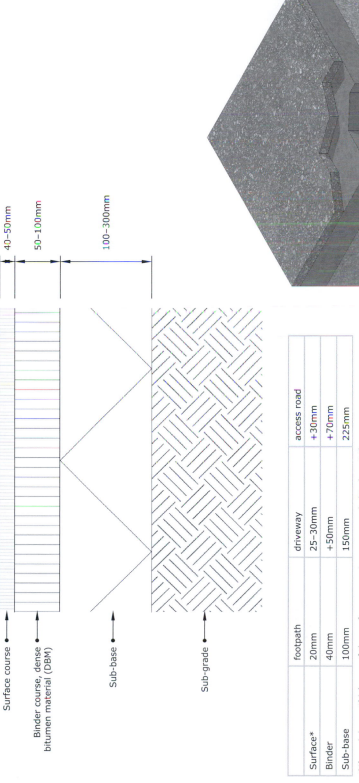

40–50mm

50–100mm

100–300mm

Surface course

Binder course, dense bitumen material (DBM)

Sub-base

Sub-grade

	footpath	driveway	access road
Surface*	20mm	25–30mm	+30mm
Binder	40mm	+50mm	+70mm
Sub-base	100mm	150mm	225mm

*the minimum thickness of the surface course is recommended to be x4 the largest aggregate size used or x2.5 the largest size of aggregate in the binder course (e.g. 20mm aggregate=50mm asphalt)

Bitumen is graded on stiffness (penetration ('pen') in tenths of a mm of a 100g needle dropped onto a bitumen sample for 5 seconds at 25°C and softening point. Lower value (pen) bitumens are stiffer (i.e. 40/60 pen is stiffer than 160/220 pen).
Commonly used bitumen grades in the UK are:
40/60 pen (is used for heavily trafficked roads)
70/100 pen
100/150 pen (is the preferred grade for most applications in the UK)
160/220 pen (is easier to apply and often used for hand-laid work)

Figure 1.20 Asphalt over a flexible base

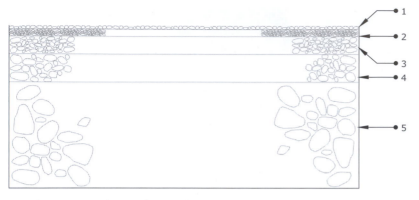

1. Surface course, asphalt or macadam (6 or 10mm aggregate) 20–40mm thick
2. Binder course, 40–70mm dense bitumen macadam (DBM 20mm)
3. Base, 100–150mm, Type 1 (DTp1/803) or Type 3 (DTp3 used for permeable surface courses)
4. Sub-base, 100–250mm consolidated hardcore with optional geotextile
5. Sub-grade

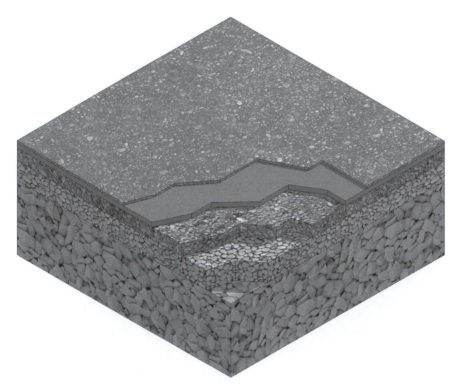

Figure 1.21 Bitumen macadam course

Sub-drains

Drains are usually located at the periphery of a pavement and below the aggregate sub-base. This is an essential component in vehicular pavements built over heavy or colloidal (clay) soils, to prevent heave.

SUDS (sustainable urban drainage systems)

SUDS are a series of water management practices and structures designed to drain surface water in a sustainable manner. Legislation was introduced in the UK to ensure that construction now takes account of water management and there is a direct impact on the type of surfaces/sub-surfaces that can be laid, for instance, for driveways: 'Often source control components are within the curtilage of properties and maintained by the property owner or manager and can include green roofs, permeable surfaces, rainwater harvesting, soak-aways, permeable surface & water butts' (www.susdrain.org).

While vehicular areas may use a permeable paving, this is a construction method more suited to light traffic and pedestrian areas, see Chapter 2, Pedestrian Paving, for more information.

There are many alternative designs for hard-standing and areas of combined pedestrian and light vehicular use, such as domestic driveways:

Loose gravel

Gravel, laid over a simple sub-base, is the most simple form of construction. Decorative gravel and aggregates can significantly improve the appearance of a large area. Edging, in the form of **setts** or simple precast concrete units, is required to prevent migration and material loss. The advantages of loose gravel are:

- simple to construct;
- cheap;
- readily available materials;
- works well in combination with planted areas;
- will not require planning permission.

The disadvantages of loose gravel are:

- potential for loss/migration of gravel and aggregates;
- not suitable for sloped surfaces, without the use of a cellular structure;
- not suitable for disabled and wheelchair users.

'Tram lines'

To minimise and reduce the impact of hard surfaces, a path or driveway can be created that has two paved tracks. These **tram lines** are constructed from simple lines of bricks, blocks, asphalt or concrete, laid over a suitable sub-base. The area between and around the track can be surfaced in gravel or can be planted. The actual paved areas are so small that standing water will not cause problems, although a slight camber can help reduce ice formation in winter. Each track should be 300–600mm wide. The spacing of the tracks will be determined by the width between the tyres of the vehicle the track is designed to support.

The advantages of tram lines are:

- simple to construct;
- cheap;
- work well in combination with planted areas;
- will not require planning permission.

The disadvantages of tram lines are:

- require regular maintenance;
- fix the location a car or vehicle can be parked in;
- may not be suitable for disabled and wheelchair users if the adjoining surfaces are loose.

Reinforced grass and gravel

There are a number of systems available that increase the strength of a grass surface, preventing compaction of the soil. Both plastic and concrete reinforcement systems are available that strengthen the ground and reduce erosion. Most of these 'cellar' systems can also

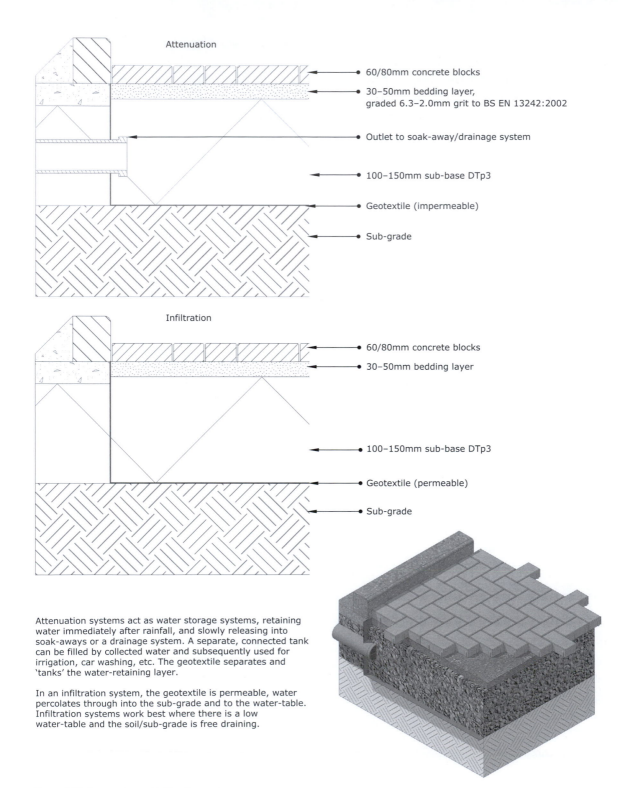

Attenuation

- 60/80mm concrete blocks
- 30–50mm bedding layer, graded 6.3–2.0mm grit to BS EN 13242:2002
- Outlet to soak-away/drainage system
- 100–150mm sub-base DTp3
- Geotextile (impermeable)
- Sub-grade

Infiltration

- 60/80mm concrete blocks
- 30–50mm bedding layer
- 100–150mm sub-base DTp3
- Geotextile (permeable)
- Sub-grade

Attenuation systems act as water storage systems, retaining water immediately after rainfall, and slowly releasing into soak-aways or a drainage system. A separate, connected tank can be filled by collected water and subsequently used for irrigation, car washing, etc. The geotextile separates and 'tanks' the water-retaining layer.

In an infiltration system, the geotextile is permeable, water percolates through into the sub-grade and to the water-table. Infiltration systems work best where there is a low water-table and the soil/sub-grade is free draining.

Figure 1.22 Attenuation and infiltration paving systems

be used with gravel. Some plastic systems have narrow edges, making them almost invisible but they are uncomfortable to walk on. The type of grass should be specified by the manufacturer of the system to ensure it is suitable for the intended location. Specific low-growing grass that does not need a lot of mowing can be used.

The advantages of **reinforced grass** are:

- simple to construct;
- minimal loss of vegetative area;
- attractive/invisible/discreet;
- works well in combination with planted areas;
- will not require planning permission.

The disadvantages of reinforced grass are:

- requires regular maintenance;
- may not be suitable for disabled and wheelchair users if the adjoining surfaces are loose;
- only temporary parking (not long-term) available;
- gravel may migrate somewhat.

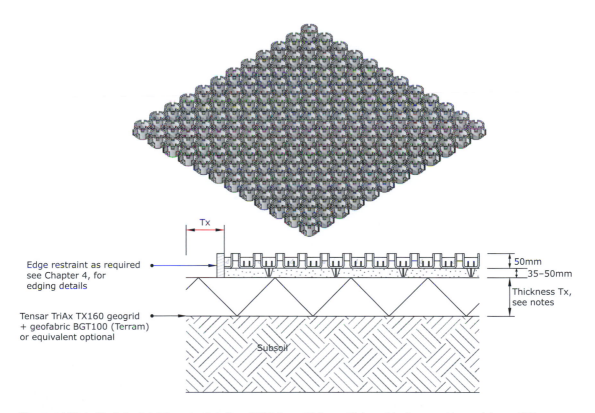

If a geogrid is omitted, the total Granular Sub-Base (GSB) layer thickness (Tx) must be increased by a minimum 50%.

DTp1 sub-base may be used provided that an adequate drainage system is installed. Alternatively, a permeable/ open-graded (reduced fines) sub-base layer (i.e. DTp3) may be specified.

If traffic axle loads will be greater than 60kN (6 Tonnes), the minimum sub-base thickness over a suitable geogrid shall be 150mm.

Where drains are omitted and a 'reduced fines' sub-base is specified for SUDS, this may be covered with a geotextile fabric (e.g. BGT100) to avoid contaminants leaching into the sub-base.

Specific advice on construction over weak ground should be sought.

Figure 1.23 Reinforced grass trackway (Bodpave85 shown)

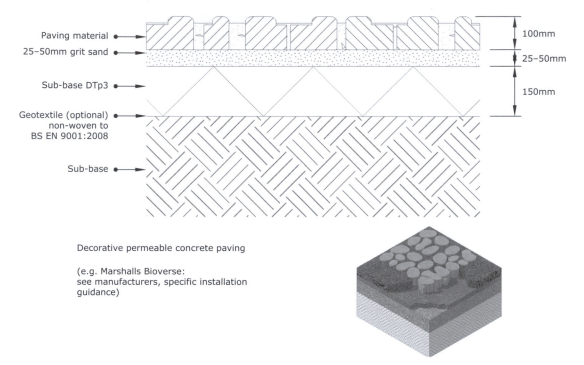

Paving material

25–50mm grit sand

Sub-base DTp3

Geotextile (optional)
non-woven to
BS EN 9001:2008

Sub-base

100mm

25–50mm

150mm

Decorative permeable concrete paving

(e.g. Marshalls Bioverse:
see manufacturers, specific installation
guidance)

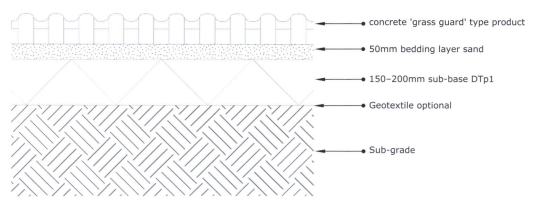

Figure 1.24 Decorative permeable concrete paving (Marshalls Bioverse shown)

concrete 'grass guard' type product

50mm bedding layer sand

150–200mm sub-base DTp1

Geotextile optional

Sub-grade

There are many versions of large format concrete matrix paving units that permit or encourage grass to grow through and within large cavities. They can be filled with soil and grass or wild flowers or gravel. Some systems are cast in situ over supplied moulds, although most are supplied as individual units. Where drainage is poor, surface water can be diverted to an attenuation tank.

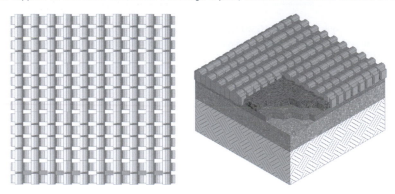

Figure 1.25 Concrete 'grassguard' as a parking surface: permeable

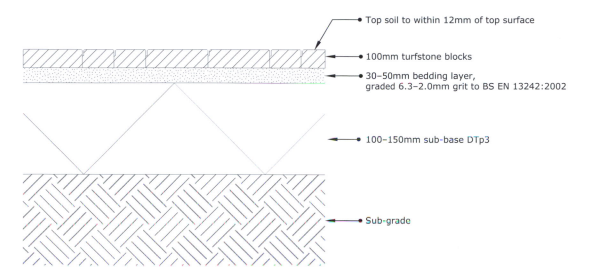

- Top soil to within 12mm of top surface
- 100mm turfstone blocks
- 30–50mm bedding layer, graded 6.3–2.0mm grit to BS EN 13242:2002
- 100–150mm sub-base DTp3
- Sub-grade

'Grass' paving solutions come in a range of materials and are application-specific. Heavy duty units, such as the Turfstone (Tobermore) are very thick (100mm) concrete and at 35kg/unit they require mechanical lifting facilities. The units achieve their full stability once the grass has formed a root network.

Illustrated: Turfstone; Tobermore

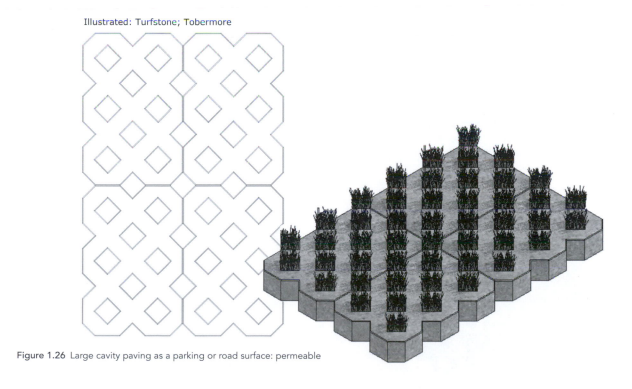

Figure 1.26 Large cavity paving as a parking or road surface: permeable

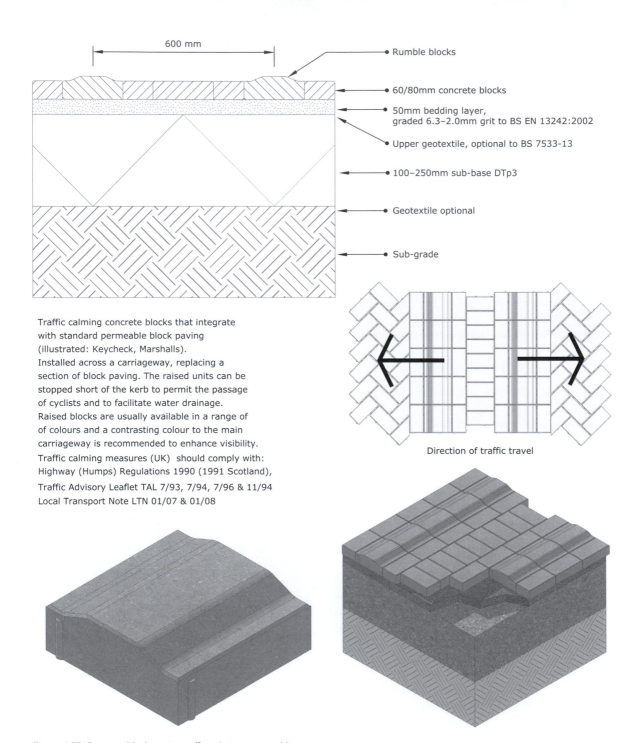

600 mm

Rumble blocks

60/80mm concrete blocks

50mm bedding layer,
graded 6.3–2.0mm grit to BS EN 13242:2002

Upper geotextile, optional to BS 7533-13

100–250mm sub-base DTp3

Geotextile optional

Sub-grade

Traffic calming concrete blocks that integrate
with standard permeable block paving
(illustrated: Keycheck, Marshalls).
Installed across a carriageway, replacing a
section of block paving. The raised units can be
stopped short of the kerb to permit the passage
of cyclists and to facilitate water drainage.
Raised blocks are usually available in a range of
of colours and a contrasting colour to the main
carriageway is recommended to enhance visibility.
Traffic calming measures (UK) should comply with:
Highway (Humps) Regulations 1990 (1991 Scotland),
Traffic Advisory Leaflet TAL 7/93, 7/94, 7/96 & 11/94
Local Transport Note LTN 01/07 & 01/08

Direction of traffic travel

Figure 1.27 Concrete block paving traffic calming: permeable

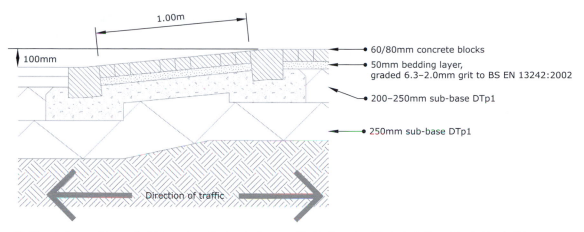

1.00m

100mm

● 60/80mm concrete blocks

● 50mm bedding layer,
graded 6.3–2.0mm grit to BS EN 13242:2002

● 200–250mm sub-base DTp1

● 250mm sub-base DTp1

Direction of traffic

Traffic calming road hump that integrates with standard permeable block paving (illustrated: Speedcheck, Marshalls).

Speed humps are usually (not always) constructed in 20mph zones. They cannot be used in isolation to slow traffic, but as part of a series of traffic calming measures. There are regulations that set the interval and vicinity to road entry points. The shape of speed humps is strictly regulated: 50–100mm in height, 2.75m long (min.) and to the full width of the carriageway (allowances can be made for drainage channels). The crown can be either rounded or flat (sometimes referred to as 'speed tables'). A height of 75–100mm is typical. Capital side gradients are typically 1:10, but reduced to 1:15 on bus routes.

The starter or crown blocks are usually available in a range of colours and a contrasting colour to the main carriageway is recommended to enhance visibility.

Traffic calming measures (UK) should comply with:
Highway (Humps) Regulations 1990 (1991 Scotland),
Traffic Advisory Leaflet TAL 7/93, 7/94, 7/96 & 11/94
Local Transport Note LTN 01/07 & 01/08

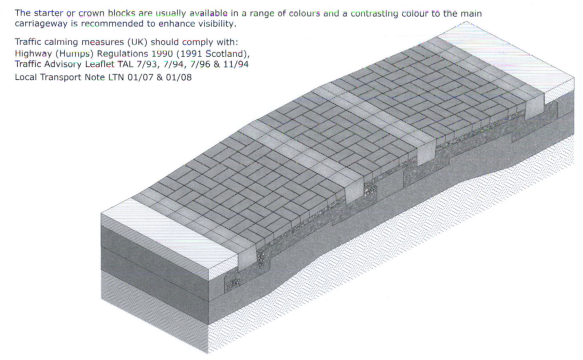

Figure 1.28 Concrete block paving traffic calming road hump: impermeable

GEN concrete might not be suitable for obtaining a satisfactory cast or finished surface nor be easily transported (e.g. pumped). The supplier should be consulted on the selection of a suitable mix. The mesh (**weld mesh**/fabric) must be set +50mm in from all external concrete faces. Two layers of mesh may be required for thicker (+200mm) slabs. The specification and installation of the reinforcing should be undertaken by a qualified installer/engineer.

CAR PARKING

General provision

Wherever conventional parking facilities and spaces are offered, provision should be made for disabled motorists. Car parks controlled by local authorities and those made available for public use should include disabled (Blue Badge) spaces, preferably covered and as close as possible to the facilities served by the car park. Setting down points are acceptable where designated bays cannot be close to the building or facilities.

Designated parking spaces should be on firm, level ground, with any variation between adjoining surfaces not exceeding 5mm difference.

The recommended distribution of parking spaces for disabled badge holders will vary between the authorities who have control of the site. The number of allocated spaces can also vary depending on the purpose of the associated building or facility, for instance, a leisure centre, railway station or place of work. In general, the requirement is for 4–6 per cent of the total capacity to be designated as disabled parking.

Bay design

The Department for Transport Leaflet Traffic Advisory Leaflet 5/95 and BS 8300 detail the design and provision of parking bays for conventional and disabled users.

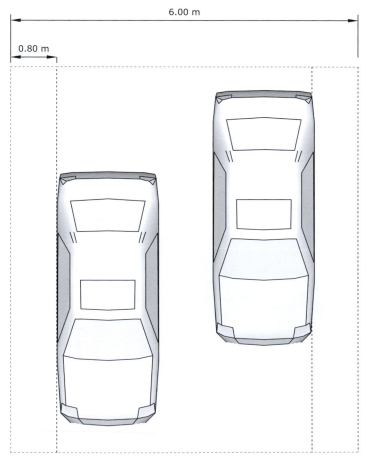

The suggested minimum width for a driveway, with two cars is 6m.
0.8m minimum should be allowed for opening doors.

Figure 1.29 Driveway widths

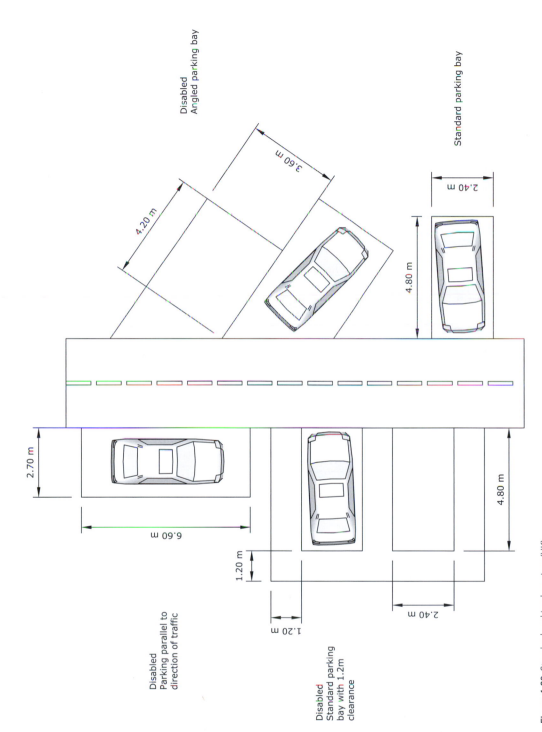

Disabled
Angled parking bay

3.60 m

4.20 m

Standard parking bay

2.40 m

4.80 m

2.70 m

6.60 m

1.20 m

4.80 m

1.20 m

2.40 m

Disabled
Parking parallel to
direction of traffic

Disabled
Standard parking
bay with 1.2m
clearance

Figure 1.30 Standard parking bay sizes (UK)

MATERIALS

Tables 1.2–1.10 show a range of measurements for the different materials used in vehicular paving.

Table 1.2 Concrete grades for vehicular use

Use	Designated mix	Standard prescribed mix (i.e. on site mix ratios)	Strength class	Consistence class (slump)
Heavy duty external paving with rubber-tyred vehicles*	PAV2	N/A		S2
Domestic driveways*	PAV1 Class II general purpose mortar	N/A		S2
	ST1	6 parts 10mm gravel 3 parts grit sand 1 part cement		
	ST4	4 parts 10mm gravel 2 parts grit sand 1 part cement		
HGV park			C40	
External hard-standing (reinforced)			C30	
External hard-standing (unreinforced)	PAV1			
Road sub-base	CBM3	16-1		
Kerbing	Gen0	ST1		

*Source = British Ready Mixed Concrete Association.

Table 1.3 Sub-base laying thickness

Uncompacted depth (mm)	Compacted depth (mm)
70	50
100	75
130	100
165	125
200	150
235	175
265	200
300	225

Source: McCormack (2011).

Table 1.4 Comparative capacities for waste removal/delivery

Delivery/removal method	m³	Weight capacity (kg)
Wheelbarrow	0.15 (80L–200L)	100
Skip (mini)	2	1500
Skip (midi)	3.2	3500
Skip (builders–8 yard)	6	8000
Truck (2 axle 10ft)		15,000–18,000
Truck (3 axle 14ft)		25,000

Source: Department of Transport, Truck specification gross weight vehicle limits.

Table 1.5 Gradients

Finished wearing surface	Min gradient/fall
Block paving	1:60
Smooth pavers/flags	1:60
Riven/rough pavers/flags	1:50
Setts/cobbles	1:50
Asphalt/bitumastic: hand-laid	1:50
Asphalt/bitumastic: machine-laid	1:75
Smooth concrete	1:75
Textured concrete	1:60
Resin bound/bonded	1:75

Table 1.6 Vehicular pavement materials

Type	Advantages	Disadvantages
Unit paving		
Block paving	Traction	Installation cost
	Good colour range	Differential settlement
	Various patterns achievable	Efflorescence
	Easily handled	
	Easily repaired	
	Permeable options	
Setts (natural)	Traction	Installation costs
	Natural	Differential settlement
	Easily repaired	Difficult to work
	Hard wearing	Suitable for low speed zones
	Durable	
	Long lasting	
Flags/pavers	Durable	Installation cost
	Hard-wearing	Mundane appearance
		Limited colours
		Traction
Limestone (natural stones?)	Easily worked	May weather/erode
	Variety of colours	
Sandstone	Easily worked	May weather/erode
	Variety of colours	
Slate	Durable	Poor traction when wet
	Variety of colours and textures	Installation costs
In situ paving		
Concrete	Easily installed	Jointing required
	Durable	Requires controlled preparation
	Long lasting	Prone to cracking
	Facilitates complex surfaces	Limited aesthetics

(Continued)

Table 1.6 (Continued)

Type	Advantages	Disadvantages
Tarmacadam	Durable	Edges must be kerbed/supported
	Easily installed	Deteriorates with petrochemicals
	Facilitates complex surfaces	Freeze/thaw damage
	Cheap	
	Can be permeable	
	Low maintenance costs	
Resin bonded	Range of colours/aggregates	Installation costs
	Can be permeable	Difficult to repair
	Facilitates complex surfaces	May be prone to petrochemical attack
	Traction can be enhanced	
Soft/loose paving		
Gravel	Economical	Regular maintenance
	Range of colours/textures	Edges must be kerbed
		Prone to vegetative growth

Table 1.7 Soil bearing loads

Subsoil	Type	Bearing kN/m²
Rock	Strong igneous	10,000
(unweathered)	Strong limestone &	4,000
	sandstone	
	Slate	3,000
	Shale, mudstone	2,000
Non-cohesive soils	Dense gravel	>600
	Medium gravel	200–600
	Loose gravel	<200
	Compact sand	300
	Loose sand	100–200
Cohesive soil	Hard clays	300–600
(susceptible to long-	Stiff clay	150–300
term settlement)	Firm clay	75–150
	Silt/soft clay	>75

Source: Baden-Powell *et al.* (2011).

Table 1.8 Slump classifications

Class	Slump range mm	Target slump
S1	10–40	20
S2	50–90	70
S3	100–150	130
S4	160–210	180
S5	210 +	220

Source: BS 8500.

Table 1.9 Reinforcing mesh

Mesh type (UK)	Size	Used
A142	200mm sq 6mm diam. rod	Light use slabs/parking/ patios/shed bases/ steps
A193	200mm sq 7mm diam. rod	Can be used to replace A142 & A252 if required
A252	200mm sq 8mm diam. rod	Heavy duty slabs. Roads and concrete depths +200mm

References

Standards and regulations

BS 7533-13:2009 Pavements constructed with clay, natural stone or concrete pavers

BS 8500 Concrete. Complementary British Standard to BS EN 206-1

BS 8500-1 Method of specification

BS 8500-2 Specification constituent materials and concrete

BS 8300 Design of buildings and their approaches to meet the needs of disabled people, Code of practice

BS EN 206-1 Concrete. Specification, performance, production & conformity

British Ready Mixed Concrete Association, Do's & Don'ts of Ready Mixed Concrete. Available at: www.road,ix.com/fs/doc/publications/brmca-do-and-donts,pdf

Books

Baden-Powell, C., Hetreed, J. and Ross, A. (2011) *Architect's Pocket Book*. London: Routledge.

McCormack, T. (2011) *Driveways, Paths and Patios*. Ramsbury: Crowood Press.

Tomlo, P. and Filippi, F. (1998) *The Porphyry Manual*. Available at: www.milestoneimports.com

Vernon, S., Tennant, R. and Garmory, N. (2013) *Landscape Architect's Pocket Book*. London: Routledge.

Guidance and advisory publications

www.dft.gov.uk/ha/standards/dmrb/ design manual for roads and bridges

www.dft.gov.uk/ha/standards/mchw/ Highway Agency standards

www.gov.uk/government/uploads/system/uploads/attachment_data/file/82421/suds-consult-annexa-national-standards-111221.pdf national standards for sustainable urban drainage systems

www.sustainableaggregates.com/library/docs/wrap/L0315_PRCPS3003_TRL.pdf development of new materials for secondary and recycled aggregates in highway infrastructure, unpublished report

Suppliers

www.ayton.co.uk Clearmac® hot and cold applied paving

www.breedon-special-aggregates.co.uk self-binding gravel

www.ced.ltd.uk natural stone & paving supplier

www.drainageonline.co.uk drainage materials

www.londonstone.co.uk natural stone and paving supplier

www.marshalls .co.uk paving materials

www.resinbondedsurfaces.co.uk resin bonded surfaces

www.stonefirms.com Portland (Dorset) limestone

www.stowellconcrete.co.uk concrete products

www.sureset.co.uk resin bound surfaces

www.thomasarmstrong.co.uk permeable paving solutions

www.tobermore.co.uk attenuation designs

www.tobermore.co.uk paving materials

Online resources

www.concrete.net.au/publications/pdf/SkidResistance.pdf Information about PPV and wearing rates of road surfaces

www.pavingexpert.com Probably the best practical guide to the construction of paths, drives and roads

www.paving.org.uk Interpave, precast concrete paving and kerb association, permeable paving guidance

www.staffordshire.gov.uk/Resources/Documents/a/AppendixE.pdf Source of general highways information

www.sureset.co.uk/files/2013/07/QRSA7161-Straight-Driveway-Specification-0611.pdf Construction details for permeable and bound aggregate surfaces

Trade bodies and associations

www.environment-agency.gov.uk/suds government advice on SUDS

www.interlay.org.uk independent association of block paving contractors

www.interpave.org.uk Interpave: paving for rain

www.paving.org trade association for block paving manufacturers

CHAPTER 2

Pedestrian paving

INTRODUCTION

Gardens and landscapes, whether small or extensive, private or public, require access. For the most part, access is by pedestrian traffic, wheelchair and mobility aids and pushchairs. The components that are used to create hard landscapes and, in particular, the pedestrian paved surfaces, can define the character, ambience and success of the space. They can be used to effortlessly direct, encourage or even discourage use, to manage water and create a sense of connection with the wider landscape or urban setting, whether to complement or contrast. The selection of paving that addresses both the aesthetic requirements and practical needs of a site is not an insignificant decision. Paving might frequently be one of the single largest budget items in a project. Small courtyards and patio areas use such a small amount of paved material that the price/msq can have relatively little impact on the overall budget and therefore the choice is expansive. In larger landscapes and public spaces, the material selection is significantly influenced by the budget and the choice available can be limited.

Natural products are processed to be more consistent and easier to lay, while exploiting the character and differences inherent between individual pieces. Man-made products are no longer restructured into grey concrete slabs, modern composites can be almost indistinguishable from the real thing, but are manufactured with a stability, strength and precision not always found in natural products. Advances in material technology and processing mean that the choices available are continually expanding. Natural is not always best. The choice of paving should be informed by performance criteria as much as aesthetics; this is a decision that is exposed and permanent.

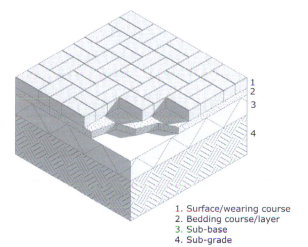

1. Surface/wearing course
2. Bedding course/layer
3. Sub-base
4. Sub-grade

Figure 2.1 Typical build-up of a paved pedestrian surface

Paving for pedestrian areas is subject to less loading and wear than vehicular paving and the choice of materials and finishes is much more extensive. It is preferable to use a limited palette of materials that complement each other or contrast to emphasise features and give guidance, for instance, at the edge of a path or drainage channels.

The size of the paving material will be somewhat dictated by the area to be covered. Small intimate areas and enclosed paths might use a range of small format units, whereas larger areas have more scope for selection. Paving for public spaces must comply with the applicable British or combined European standards. Whether private or public, the material selected must be fit for purpose and reliable.

Selecting paving

When selecting paving, the following considerations must be borne in mind:

- How many people, mobility aids, wheelchairs will travel over the surface and how frequently?
- Might there be occasional vehicular intrusion (e.g. fire brigade access)?
- What is the aspect or exposure of the areas to be paved?
- Choice of ancillary paving, such as stair treads.
- Determine the direction and falls of drainage and paved surfaces.

THE WEARING COURSE (PAVED SURFACE)

There is an almost unlimited choice of paving products available. Simplistically, they might be divided into: man-made, natural and flexible-type surfaces. There are permeable options available in all of these categories.

Man-made

Setts (cobbles), block paving and concrete/imitation stone are the commonest types. They range in thickness and are mostly a utility product. Perversely, some man-

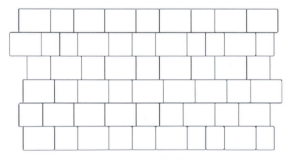

Small format paving, such as Tegula-style paving blocks, coursed with a random 3 size block pattern. All paving materials should be evaluated in situ, with samples, and ideally seen when both dry and wet

Tegula blocks
90 x 90 x 60mm, 90 x 120 x 60mm, 90 x 70 x 60mm

Figure 2.2 Tegula block paving

made products can be more expensive than the natural version they seek to imitate, travertine for instance. It is usually the case that the cheaper the product, the less cement and pigment are in the paving material and the poorer the quality. There are some very realistic man-made products, however, and it is worth considering their use, particularly where consistent colour and size are important. Highly textured surfaces are available and these can be effective for driveways, while also being guaranteed to withstand specific loads.

Wet cast concrete (open moulded)

These are usually products that copy or imitate a natural material. They are available in a relatively small range of standard-sized units (e.g. 600mm × 600mm, 300mm × 300mm). Good quality pieces can be almost indistinguishable from the stone that they replicate, frequently using actual natural components, **Yorkstone**, for instance, as the basis for the moulds used. The **riven** effect can be quite considerable and such paving will not be suitable for all areas (e.g. patios, where a level surface to support furniture is required). Wet cast/open moulded paving is lower in strength than **hydraulically bound** paving (see below) units and, unless indicated otherwise, is unsuitable for vehicular use. There is usually no mechanical pressure involved, instead the filled mould is left open to set. Due to the manufacturing process, there can be considerable variation between units in thickness and in planar dimensions and care must be taken when ordering that all pieces are supplied from the same **batch**. Colouring is achieved by the addition of dyes and pigments, usually to the uppermost surface only, While this can create a pleasing effect, the quality of the pigments and the application process can vary. The long-term weathering effects should be appreciated before such materials are specified.

Precast concrete (PCC)

Precast concrete is a highly versatile paving material. Mass production makes it consistent, very strong and cheaper than other paving materials. Frequently it is used for patios, public footpaths, as well as for drives, where a utilitarian and reliable pavement is required.

A basic range of paving was developed in the UK, which prescribed a uniform, hydraulically pressed product in a standardised range. It is still commonly referred to as 'British Standard' paving. In practice, only about half of the range is now commonly used. Sizes 900 × 600 × 50mm (D50), 750 × 600 × 50mm (C50) and 600 × 600 × 50mm (B50) are the commonest of these; 63mm and 70mm thickness sizes are available but may be subject to special order. The letter and numeric reference are detailed in the standard (BS 7533); each paving unit of a specific size and thickness combination has a unique reference and this is sometimes used by suppliers to identify the more popular units.

For small areas, smaller format paving is available,

laid similarly to block paving. PCCs are manufactured from hydraulically pressed concrete. Once only available in a drab grey, with a 'pimpled' surface, most suppliers now offer a much wider range of standard colours (buff, grey, charcoal or red, for instance), finishes and sizes.

Surface finishes range from brushed, exposed aggregate, geometric textures (as in tactile paving, see p. 72), as well as textures for specific purposes, such as increased traction or aggregates added for high wear use. Many products feature riven or natural stone effects. These are not usually as pronounced as those produced by open moulded methods. The texture range can also be limited, perhaps to four or five unique textures. Units

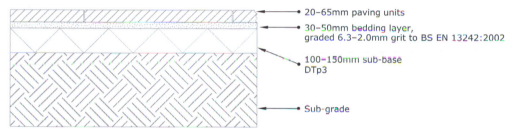

- 20–65mm paving units
- 30–50mm bedding layer, graded 6.3–2.0mm grit to BS EN 13242:2002
- 100–150mm sub-base DTp3
- Sub-grade

There is a wide range of paving materials: clay, concrete, porcelain, to name but a few, in a range of styles and formats. The specific laying recommendations will be given by the material supplier.

Driveways and pedestrian footpaths are category IV and require the simplest form of construction. As such, there is greater scope for aesthetic variation in material types and bond. The most mechanically efficient methods, as used in vehicular paving, do not necessarily suit pedestrianised areas and paths.

The thickness of the sub-base will be determined by the depth of the top soil and the type of sub-base present. The sub-base should be constructed on consolidated sub-grade material and never over top soil. If the local top soil extends to 300mm, for instance, the sub-base should be made at least as deep. Heavy clay soils that are liable to heave and subsidence will also require a deeper sub-base to compensate. Manufacturers' advice should be sought for specific applications.

Common (UK) sizes of paving units

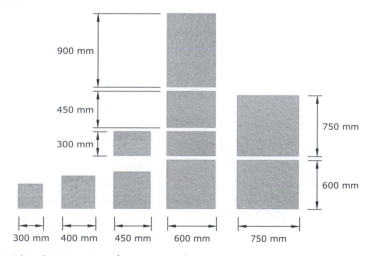

Figure 2.3 Standard paving materials and common sizes of paving materials

should be randomly picked as well as rotated to avoid lines and pattern clusters.

Concrete blocks, whether for wall construction, block paving, or kerb edging, are all PCC. Most have a colour from the addition of pigments and any wear or damage does not significantly alter the character of the material. Exposed aggregates, whether decorative or functional, comprise a thin layer, a few millimetres thick, at the wearing surface of the block or paver. Cut units will expose this striation and it can be unsightly. Some ranges have special pieces for finishing edges and corners where the aggregate is on more than one surface.

PCC paving is the predominant paving material in the UK. The website www.paving.org.uk offers guidance on specification, design and installation for all major UK manufacturers' products.

British Standard paving is dimensioned so that it readily combines with other materials to allow for edge details and pattern creation. For simple landscape work, drives and patios, some manufacturers offer software that will visualise their recommended patterns as well as provide a quantity of materials list.

Porcelain

Porcelain is a man-made product created from natural materials (feldspar, kaolin, quartz and clay). These materials are mixed with water and colour pigment, then pressed in moulds and baked in a kiln at temperatures up to 1240°C. Porcelain is worth considering where uniformity in colour and texture is desired. Modern porcelain paving is full-bodied, and the colour is carried through the entire thickness of the tile, making it virtually impervious to wear. It is supplied in a wide range of textures from smooth to riven and a very wide range of styles, colours and finishes. It can be almost indistinguishable from high quality **sawn** stone. Good quality porcelain paving is also fully vitrified; the tile is fired to temperatures high enough for the materials to form a single mass, making the tiles extremely hard with very low porosity (0.5 per cent). Due to its exceptionally low level of porosity, porcelain does not require sealing. Although tiles are uniform in size and thickness, **butt** jointing is not recommended. The hardness of the tiles

requires the use of a special porcelain blade to cut or drill the stone.

Porcelain is typically 20mm thick. Tiles are easier to handle than natural stone or their concrete counterparts and the strength of the material allows tiles up to 1200mm long. This reduced thickness can make step treads appear rather 'mean' and thin. Some suppliers offer special copings and tread tiles which have increased thickness. Some tiles have a patterned rear surface, ribs or a grid are common. This facilitates the application and retention of the adhesive. Porcelain is best laid on a full bed of tile adhesive, 5–8mm thick. Laid over a full adhesive bed, the tiles are best jointed with a specialist grout. The patterned rear surface can create an unsightly detail when it is used for copings, where the rib pattern is evident in the cut edge and on the overhang. Porcelain should be laid with a small joint of about 5mm. It lends itself to the use of pedestal systems, where low ribs create a uniform open joint.

Natural stone

There can be few materials that have the diversity of character, colour and texture as natural stone. A wide range of surface treatments can be used to extend and considerably improve its performance as well as the aesthetics. The range of stone available for paved surfaces is extensive. The character and aspect of the project may guide a designer in the selection of a suitable material. Riven and highly porous stone surfaces are likely to retain surface water and may not suit shaded or northern locations. While a stone can usually be supplied in a range of formats, sawn paving blocks, setts and gravel, for example, a project usually benefits from a combination of different stones and formats (granite setts and sandstone slabs, for instance).

Unlike other building materials, it is not always possible to distinguish one type of stone from another by visual inspection alone. Geological references are somewhat meaningless and obscure, whereas commercial categories can often be helpful but are not always clear or accurate. Different stone types are frequently marketed under a unified description, 'Indian'

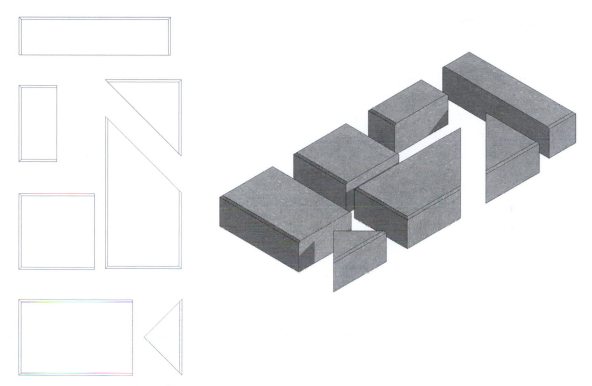

Figure 2.4 (a) Common brick cuts; (b) isometric section

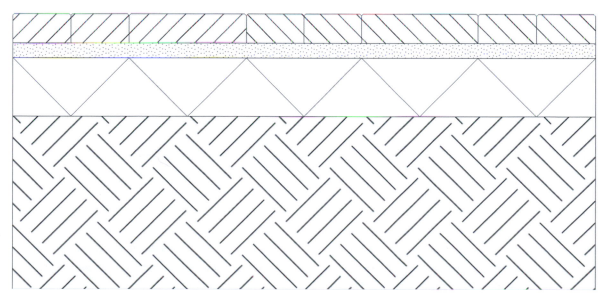

Figure 2.5 Concrete/clay block paving: impermeable

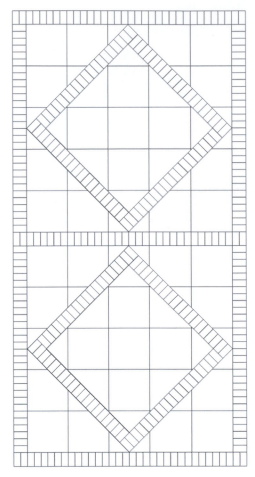

Figure 2.6 Brick and standard sized paving diamond plan

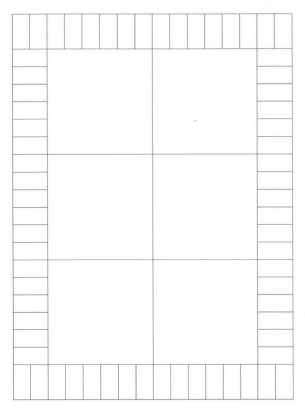

Figure 2.7 Paving with brick edge

stone, for example, might refer to both sandstone and limestone.

Each type of stone has characteristics and properties that influence where it might be used. Natural stone is invariably chosen for its aesthetic characteristics, colour, structure, texture and grain. Technical requirements are used to refine the selection; load, chemical and abrasion resistance, absorbency and thermal expansion. Frost resistance is of particular importance if the stone is to be laid in contact with the ground or in a location subject to shade and moisture. It is essential that a written specification for any specified stone is obtained from the supplier, as a minimum to include flexural strength and slip resistance. It is possible to be supplied with a batch of stone that is below the stated performance specification, and documentation that identifies

providence and quality will be helpful in rectifying any such problems.

Domestic paving, for pedestrian use, is typically 30–50mm, although imported stone can be as thin as 20mm. This should be used with caution; in particular, installation should be as recommended by the material supplier.

While manufactured/man-made paving is produced to predetermined sizes and shapes, it is possible for natural stone to be made to specific requirements. Here it is a distinct advantage to discuss the project directly with the quarry. This association with specific suppliers might come at a premium, but the quality of the advice and service and the knowledge that the material is both as local as possible as well as responsibly extracted more than compensates for price.

In addition to the aesthetic and mechanical qualities of stone, the sizes that can be supplied may influence a designer's decision. Not all stone types are supplied in the same format or thicknesses. This can be of particular importance when stone of different types is to be combined. Custom-cut supply is possible but may attract an extended delivery schedule and price.

UK indigenous stone

Yorkstone

New riven Yorkstone is a dense, hard-wearing sandstone, used as paving and cladding for centuries. It is naturally textured and ages to a dark patina. Reclaimed Yorkstone is prized for the weathered look and characteristic blemishes, veining and occasional marks and holes in the surface. Reclaimed materials are typically of considerable age and will have variations in thickness and size between slabs (from 40–140mm), and this will have an impact on the sub-base and bedding layers. Good quality stone can be reworked; riven edges can be sawn and highly contoured faces milled flat. This is useful where Yorkstone is being used for step treads and risers, where an even bedding and wearing surface are required. Edge chipping and minor damage are common, so this, combined with a variation in slab thickness, means that butt jointing is inappropriate. A joint of +15mm is usual for reclaimed stone paving. Yorkstone paving can vary in colour from dark blues through to light buffs, depending on the quarry of origin. Reclaimed material may be contaminated with oils or diesel oil, deposited when it was originally installed as a paving for a road or in an industrial site. Both the colour and degree of contamination are not always evident when reclaimed material is purchased and may only be revealed after the stone is milled or cleaned. Knowledge of providence is essential and a reputable source of reclaimed stone should be used.

Sandstone

Derived from compacted sand, there is a wide variety of sources making sandstone cost-effective.

Slate

Slate is formed from compacted clay; it is uniform in appearance with a limited palette of colours (dark blues, greens and purples), very low maintenance.

Limestone

Portland stone (Dorset) has been used for paving, steps and cladding for centuries. It is much denser and harder wearing than imported varieties and can be textured or polished.

Flexible paving

Flexible surfaces come in a wide variety of finishes and effects. **Hoggin** and asphalt are some of the least expensive methods to pave larger areas. If the space is poorly designed, they can appear somewhat monotone and devoid of the character found in more textured paving. Edge detailing and the design of the paved area can help reduce this effect. Gravels can offer a similar low price/msq. They are available in a huge variety of types and sizes. There is an aggregate to suit almost every type of design and application. Decorative aggregates should be specified as being sharp. The angular edges will form a stiff, self-binding surface that will not drift or migrate, unlike rounded river or pea gravels. Paved area gravels are usually 10–14mm, larger gravels may be uncomfortable to walk on in thin shoes and are more suited to decorative areas or as mulch. Gravels need to be laid to 75–100mm depth to achieve a consolidated surface. Self-binding gravels, such as **Breedon gravel**, are formed of a specific mix of particulates from about 12mm to dust (fines). They require specific layered installation and the supplier's instructions should be carefully followed. Relatively inexpensive, they will compact to a hard working surface suitable for vehicles as well as pedestrians. Of particular use is that any surface damage is easily and quickly repaired. They can become contaminated with soil, and suitable edging details should be used to prevent any migration of materials. Flexible surfaces can be laid over a range of laying courses but should never be placed directly onto soil or sub-grade. Without a permeable membrane or barrier, they will quickly be absorbed.

Gravels can be applied to a prepared surface, either bound (coated) in a resin or scattered over a surface coated with a proprietary adhesive or resin (referred to as a bonded surface). There is a wide selection of suitable aggregates that, with appropriate construction, can also be made permeable. The aggregates, bonding and binding agents will be specific to individual suppliers and must be mixed and applied as recommended.

STONE PROVIDENCE

Paving was historically the preserve of larger houses and estates and therefore was a status symbol. Concrete paving (from as early as the 1900s) provided a viable alternative to gravels, sands and setts, as used by the majority of the population for paved surfaces. Its use brought significant aesthetic and practical changes to garden design. As personal wealth and demand increased, the diversity of materials has expanded to the extent that the majority of stone used in the UK is imported, often from developing countries.

Indian sandstone, for instance, was found to be a viable and much cheaper alternative to indigenous stone. Its use was quickly followed by slate and granite from China and Brazil, limestone and slate from Spain and Portugal, and travertine from Turkey. Imported stone is generally thinner than that from native suppliers. A minimum of 50mm is required for surfaces where there may be occasional vehicle intrusion, even thicker if commercial or emergency vehicles access is required.

If the stone is not local, then it should be ethically sourced. Designers should be aware of the ethical trading policies of their suppliers (through the Ethical Trading Initiative, the ETI Code, Fair Trade stone or equivalent schemes). The environmental impact of quarrying and transportation over such distances may mean there is less than equivalence between such materials. Natural stone paving should, in the UK, meet BS 7533 class 2 (water absorption of less than 2.5 per cent, be CE marked and have a flexural strength of more than 12MP). Not all imported products will carry such certification, and documentation that addresses providence and fitness for purpose should be requested.

FINISHES

Natural stone is selected for its visual impact, and a surface treatment can either enhance or change a material's appearance for both visual and practical purposes. The type and quality of the material influence the price rather than the production method. Both Yorkstone and sandstone from India are hand-riven and are found at both ends of the price spectrum.

Natural stone is supplied as either riven or sawn. Stone can be sawn on four faces (the edges) while the upper and lower faces are left riven, or sawn to all six faces.

Polishing will enhance the grain and structure whereas flaming will dull a surface. The structure of a particular stone will lend itself to certain finishes and not others. Granite and slate, for instance, are not easily carved, chiselled or sandblasted, and sandstone does not readily or successfully flame.

Natural stone, once riven or ungauged, is usually hand-split on both sides, is uneven in thickness and with variation between slabs. It is a cost-effective medium, and lends a natural effect to the finished surface. Newly riven stone can be mechanically vibrated or tumbled. Edges and corners are subtly rounded, creating a vintage, weathered look. Not all stone can be treated like this.

Flaming is the application of intense heat to a smooth-cut stone face. The stone breaks into minute flakes and the surface is evenly textured. It is a versatile finish, particularly useful where improved traction is required.

Sandblasting and mechanical brushing can improve the natural characteristics of a surface. Traction can be improved and a more diffuse appearance created.

Gauged means lightly machined so that it will lie flat without rocking, the thickness can vary between slabs.

For sawn/calibrated stone, typically all the faces are smooth, the thickness is even across a slab, and all the slabs are identical. Calibrated paving is typical of public spaces and high traffic areas. Sawn paving lends a modern aesthetic, with usually tight geometric alignments and junctions. Sawn stone requires the most protection and ongoing maintenance.

There are various types of cut that can be achieved, with degrees of refinement:

- Both **chat-sawn** and **shot-sawn** are types of coarse finish created by using a slurry of abrasive material while cutting the stone.
- **Honed**: a smooth finish created by polishing, although not to a gloss finish.
- **Polishing** creates a buffed, glossy surface used particularly for cladding and decorative surfaces.

Within individual types of stone there can be additional grades, for example, travertine can be offered in Best, First, Economy and Commercial grades.

SEALING, PROTECTION AND MAINTENANCE

Once cut, stone will begin a process of oxidation and discoloration and the exposed surfaces develop a patina. The nature of this will depend on the type of stone and the environment in which the material is used (a city centre will cause faster and greater discoloration than a rural location). Sandstones will acquire a patina faster than most other stone types.

Most stone masonry is porous, whether with visible cavities as seen in travertines and concretes, or microporous, in such dense materials as granite and slate. On contact, stone will absorb liquids to a greater or lesser degree, depending on the type of stone. The ingress of liquids can cause a range of problems, from simple water-staining to more noticeable discoloration where liquids or juices or soils have been spilt or trodden into a surface. Stains in stone can run deep into the material body and be difficult or impossible to remove. The use of standard household cleaners, whether acids or bleaches, is not recommended.

In particular, algae can develop on the stone face in shaded and moist locations. In contrast, granite and slate, however, may not noticeably discolor, even over decades. In high traffic areas, cleaning is essential. Algae growth on unsealed stone may be removed with soapy water, whereas more stubborn problems such as chewing gum or graffiti may require specialist equipment to remove,

on flamed and deeply textured surfaces. The use of acid cleaners on any stone surface should be avoided if possible, in particular, on limestone. Even if the stone is not affected, the jointing materials and sub-base or supporting structure are likely to be. Chemical cleaners should be particular to the stone and type of stain. The building process can itself cause stains, calcium hydroxide in cement, lubricants and unbound aggregates can cause surface discoloration. Efflorescence is a naturally occurring process where a bloom of calcium carbonate or **lime** appears on the surface of a wall or paving. This can be avoided if the bedding concrete or cement is made with a low water content. The use of specialist cements (such as Trass, iron Portland or blast furnace cements) will also prevent efflorescence.

Stone can be sealed either in advance of installation or in situ. This can reduce the maintenance regime considerably and improve the long-term durability, surface characteristics and overall aesthetics of what is likely to be one of the most significant cost items in a scheme. There are three types of sealer:

1. *Topical coating/films (acrylics/polyurethanes)*: These are applied to the surface, blocking the stone's pores. These can be slippery when wet. They typically lend a glossy sheen to the surface, and moisture embedded or taken up from the stone surface in contact with the ground can be prevented from migrating to the uppermost surface of the paving.

2. *Penetrating sealers (silicone/siloxane/fluoropolymers)*: These are applied as a liquid to the uppermost, wearing surface and are partially absorbed into the stone. They can repel either oil (oleophobic) or water (hydrophobic). Household cleaners can be problematic and, similar to other polymer treatments, such as pointing compounds, may cause discoloration of the stone. Their limited ability to penetrate the body of the stone can result in erosion by mechanical abrasion (pedestrian traffic), and frequent reapplication (3–6 months) may be required. Specialist cleaning products may be required to maintain the sealed stone. Neither topical or penetrating sealers should be used on the underside of stone. This will

compromise the effectiveness of the adhesive bond between the stone and the sub-base.

3. Modified **silane impregnators** form a permanent molecular bond with the stone material. The pores are coated rather than blocked and the breathability of the material is maintained. The inherent surface qualities of the stone, whether natural or mechanically enhanced, are not changed or compromised. Due to the molecular bond, such impregnators are much more resistant to household cleaners and positively repel paints and graffiti. Life in service is considerable and reapplication is not usually necessary.

Not all coatings and impregnators are UV-resistant, which can result in surface deterioration.

The most effective method of sealant application is to pre-seal at source. Some topical and penetrating sealants may require more than a single coat. Application at site can be affected by local conditions and may be less than ideal. Stone should be completely dry prior to application and, if guarantees are offered, an approved contractor must be used.

variations of source and manufacture. It is both prudent and professional to look at an area of the product when laid, preferably with the client, and ensure that it is seen when dry as well as wet.

In addition to its appearance, any cut stone will have variation in the sizes it is supplied in. A dimensional range (**tolerance**) of +/−5mm is typical; this means that any single piece can be larger or smaller than the stated size and still be considered fit for purpose, e.g. 600mm-long paving can be supplied at 595 (min.) or 605 (max.). Tolerances should be taken into account when designing paving layouts so that there are no unexpected cuts.

Stone is supplied in a range of sizes, from miniature 'setts' to custom-cut slabs. Popular ranges derived from the paving sizes have been developed for the concrete paving market and this generally permits products from different suppliers to be used alongside one another. Different stones and suppliers may use specific sizes and tolerances and these should be considered before product ranges are selected or assumed to be compatible.

An additional 10 per cent material should be allowed for wastage, damage cuts and unsightly pieces.

BATCHES AND TOLERANCE

Natural stone is desirable foremost for its inherent variation. The aesthetic qualities that led to a material's selection may not, however, always give the required result. Exposed, quarried stone can reveal subtle, or occasionally less than subtle, patterning and this may not always be evident in the description or sample supplied. Materials extracted and processed at the same time, from the same source, are most likely to have the least degree of variation. Where an order is fulfilled by supply from several sources, the variation may be quite pronounced. This may be unavoidable, especially where large areas are to be paved. Randomly drawing on the stock from several open pallets will help in distributing any variation in the batch throughout the laid area and minimise the impact of local patterning and clusters of variation. Paving products, whether natural or man-made, are subject to

LAYING PATTERNS

When developing the design for a paved area, it is essential to draw the bond. Having a paving plan will greatly assist the contractor and will also remove any ambiguity, especially in areas where paved areas intersect, change direction or incorporate other materials. A golden rule is: ensure that your intent as a designer is clear and unambiguous.

Unlike areas with heavy traffic, for pedestrian and pedestrian/cycle combined paths, designers have a huge selection of materials available. Aesthetics and cost will play a large part in any selection criteria and choices should be made that complement the vernacular architecture as well as any adjacent surface materials. A limited or simple palette of materials will succeed better than a scheme that is busy or complex. Paving patterns succeed best where the junctions and interfaces with other areas are detailed to give a coherent and smooth transition. This may involve changes of direction, the integration of existing structures, and changes in levels.

The suitability of materials must be considered as part of the selection criteria. Extensively paved areas will require materials that are hard-wearing, robust and consistent. Smaller paths and areas may benefit from the use of more unique materials, styles and surfaces. Repair and maintenance should also be included in the selection of paving surfaces. A **monolithic** cast material will be considerably harder and more expensive to repair than a permeable block paved path. It is frequently by luck rather than design that any paved surface is free from the intrusion of access and inspection covers. The position of these is usually determined and set prior to the paving being considered and there is often little scope for relocating these, although there might be scope for rotating or adjusting the final level. As such, access and inspection covers must be successfully integrated into a paved surface. Covers should be selected that allow the paving to be inset, that is, included within the framework. Where possible, the covers should be aligned to follow the direction of a path or lie parallel to the path edge. Randomly skewed, plastic

or galvanised steel covers rarely look pleasing. With good planning, the excavated route of a path can also be used to distribute water and electrical services around a landscape. Junction points should have access chambers and covers to allow access for inspection, repair and even system expansion.

THE LAYING COURSE (BEDDING)

The **laying course** lies directly beneath and therefore supports the final paving material. It may be formed of **cast in situ (CIS)** concrete, a sub-base or even sub-grade. The type of **bedding** can vary and will be dictated somewhat by the extent of the paving type used and its application. **Permeable paving** will require a different laying course to paving stone pieces, the depth of which will be advised by the supplier of the permeable materials. The final paving layer may require some minor adjustments to ensure a level finish and the laying course must be capable of accommodating local adjustments.

There are two classes of material suitable for the laying course: unbound or loose and hydraulically bound (HB) or rigid.

Concrete or clay block paving: impermeable

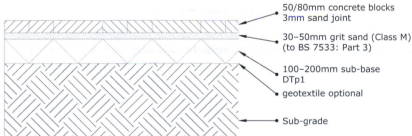

50/80mm concrete blocks
3mm sand joint

30–50mm grit sand (Class M)
(to BS 7533: Part 3)

100–200mm sub-base
DTp1
geotextile optional

Sub-grade

There is a wide range of block paving materials, clay as well as concrete and in a range of styles. The specific laying recommendations will be given by the material supplier. Clay joints, for instance, will be about 6mm to accommodate surface variations.

Driveways and pedestrian footpaths are category IV and require the simplest form of construction. As such, there is greater scope for aesthetic variation in material types and bond. The most mechanically efficient methods, as used in vehicular paving, do not necessarily suit pedestrianised areas and paths.

The thickness of the sub-base will be determined by the depth of the top soil and the type of sub-base present. The sub-base should be constructed on consolidated sub-grade material and never over top soil. If the local top soil extends to 300mm, for instance, the sub-base should be made at least as deep. Heavy clay soils that are liable to heave and subsidence will also require a deeper sub-base to compensate. Manufacturers' advice should be sought for specific applications.

Figure 2.8 Block paving with patterns

(Continued)

Examples of block paving laying patterns

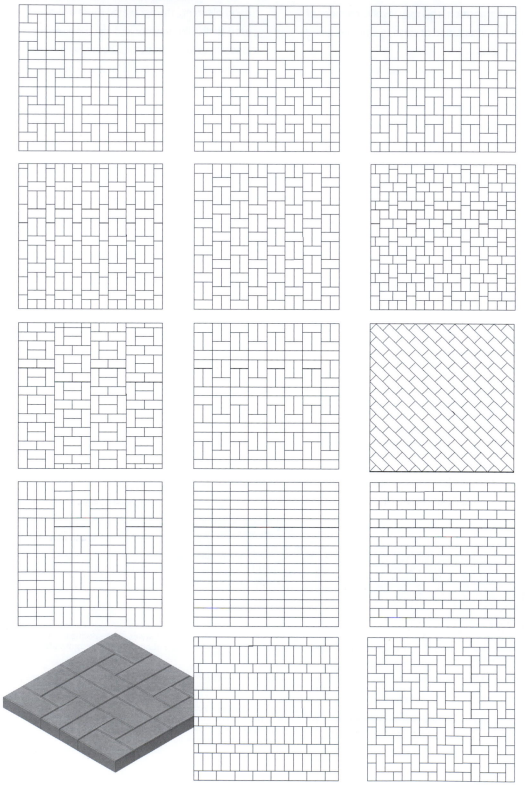

Figure 2.8 (Continued)

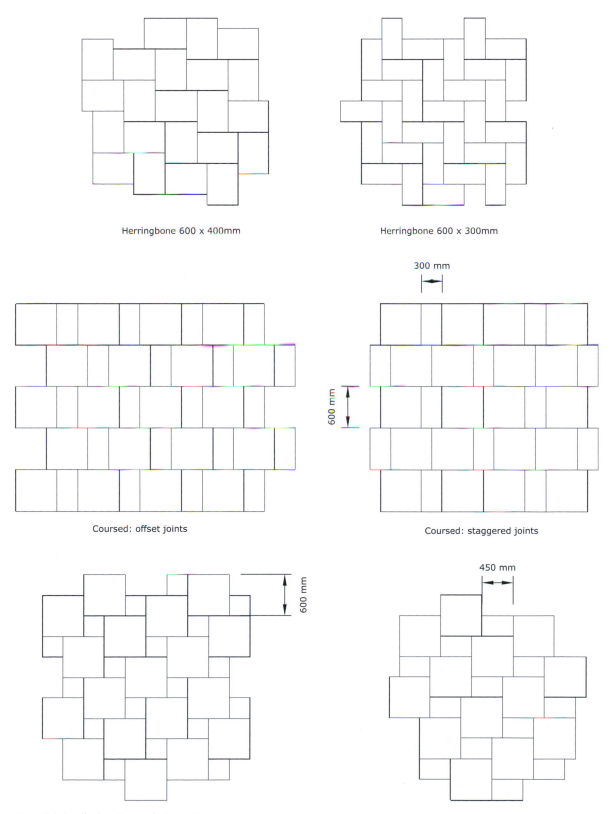

Herringbone 600 x 400mm

Herringbone 600 x 300mm

300 mm

Coursed: offset joints

600 mm

Coursed: staggered joints

600 mm

450 mm

Figure 2.9 Standard paving unit laying patterns

(Continued)

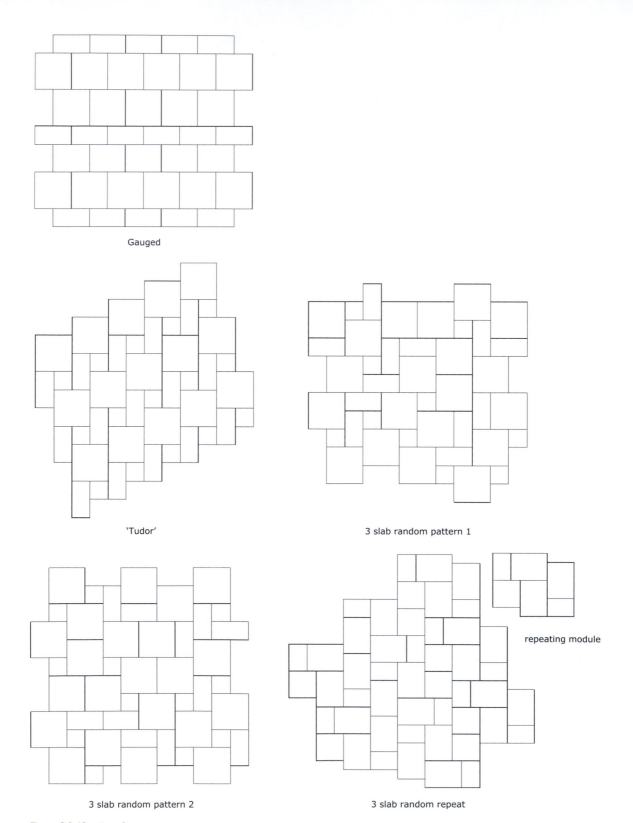

Gauged

'Tudor'

3 slab random pattern 1

3 slab random pattern 2

3 slab random repeat

repeating module

Figure 2.9 (Continued)

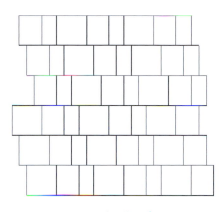

coursed pattern 1

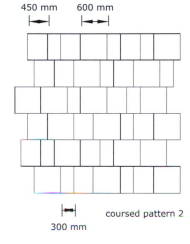

450 mm   600 mm

coursed pattern 2

300 mm

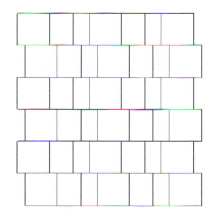

alternating coursed

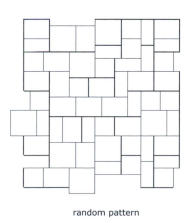

random pattern

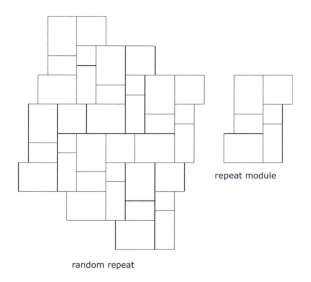

random repeat

repeat module

Figure 2.9 (Continued)

(Continued)

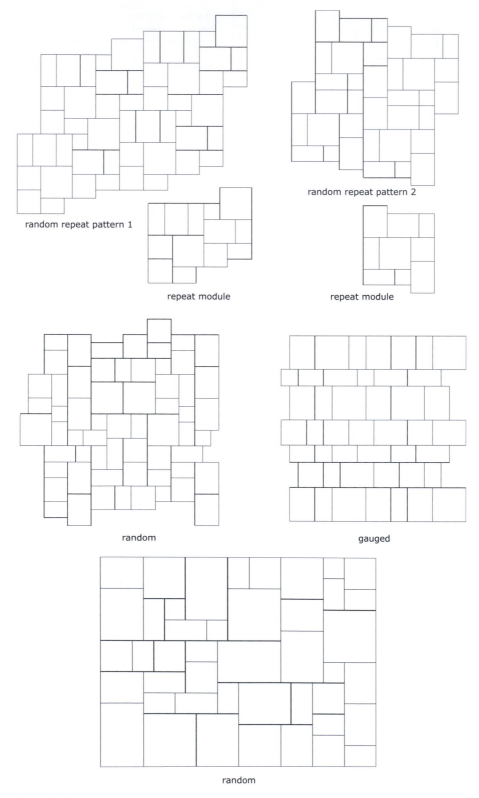

random repeat pattern 1

random repeat pattern 2

repeat module

repeat module

random

gauged

random

Figure 2.9 (Continued)

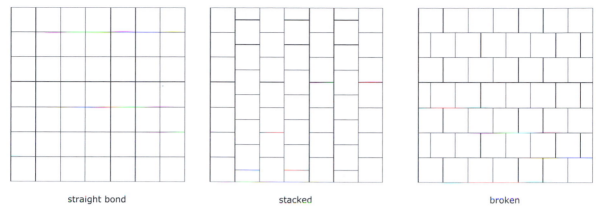

straight bond   stacked   broken

Figure 2.10 Common laying patterns for square paving materials

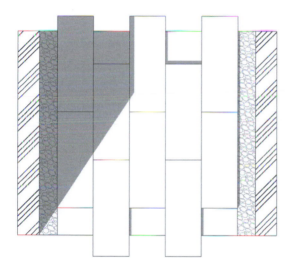
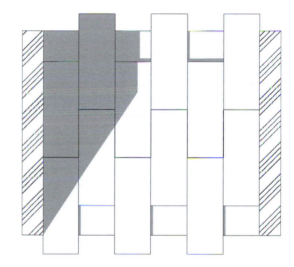

Figure 2.11 Paving tolerance. Paving tolerances need to be considered (see p. 152)

Unbound

This laying material is most commonly used on smaller paving materials. It has the advantage of being cheap and relatively easy to work with, with no curing or drying constraints. Its flexibility may result in undesired settlement and it requires complete consolidation to perform as intended. An essential component in the success of any paved area is the edging detail. This acts as a restraint, to contain the sub-base and the laying course. There are numerous designs for containment and one should be selected that is appropriate to the paving structure and complementary to the paving material and design (see Chapter 4, Margins, edges, kerbs and trims).

Unbound alternatives

There are acceptable alternatives to the use of grit sharp sand. It all must be 4mm to dust and of a sharp and angular quality to facilitate free draining.

- All-in **ballast** is an unregulated mix, created at the aggregate source. It requires inspection to determine if it is suitable.
- Crushed fines are derived from the quarrying and crushing of rock. Fines sourced from granite quarries are well suited to laying materials, whereas softer materials such as limestone are not. Whin and grit are specific fines produced exclusively from either whinstone or gritstone.

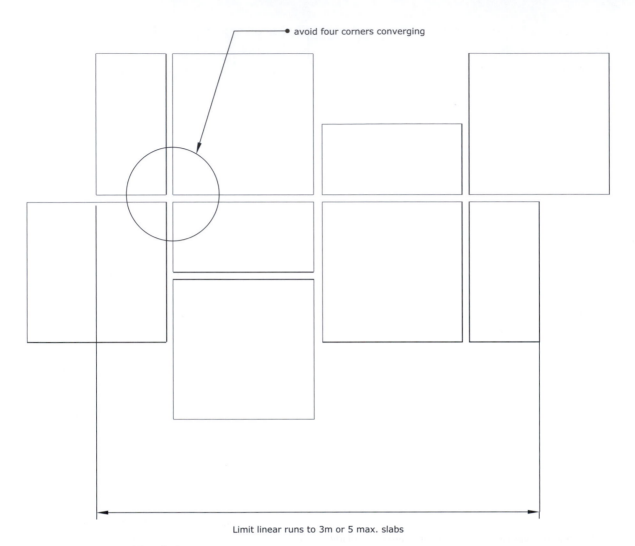

avoid four corners converging

Limit linear runs to 3m or 5 max. slabs

Figure 2.12 General guidelines for laying paving

Certified Class M sand Fine Aggregate to BS EN 12620:2002 is used for both bound and unbound. It is also known as coarse/grit/sharp/concreting sand. Table 2.1 compares bound and unbound in the laying course.

Building, soft or pointing sands are not a suitable laying course material. Being rounded in nature, there will be little interlock. Having a higher clay content, they are more hydroscopic and become waterlogged easily.

Bound

Typically large paving units of stone or concrete are laid on a full bed of mortar (sand and cement). Smaller

Table 2.1 Unbound vs bound laying course

Unbound sand	Bound (cement/lime added)
Unlimited working life	Robust, solid bed
Cheap	Resistant to movement
Readily available	Can accommodate incomplete consolidation
Clean, easy to work with	Creates a rigid pavement
Can move and settle	Expensive
Prone to undermining (water, insects)	

units (such as **paviors** and setts) are laid on coarse Class M grit sand but may be laid on a mortar bed if the circumstances dictate this is more appropriate. Pavements where there may be occasional vehicular traffic should be laid directly onto a minimum 100mm concrete bed. Slabs less than 50mm thick are not suitable for driveway use unless laid on a minimum 100mm concrete bed.

The method of **spot bedding** or dabbing (the practice of applying a dab or spot of mortar to each corner and perhaps also the centre) paving slabs, concrete or natural stone, is not recommended. The void created between the discs of solidified mortar permits colonisation by nesting insects as well as a reservoir for water run-off. This water may freeze and the slabs are susceptible to lifting.

The choice of cement, for both bedding and pointing, is critical to the successful installation of paving. While grey cement (**OPC**) is the most common, there are several manufacturers. While the characteristics of any supplier's cements will be consistent, there is a difference between those characteristics, and, in particular the colour, across suppliers. This will also, in part, be determined by the type of sand used. Grey cement, when used as a bedding, can cause staining on the paving's uppermost surface, as salts and oxides are drawn through the stone. The resultant stains are sometimes referred to as 'picture framing'. This problem can be more evident on white and light beige or buff-coloured paving as those stone types are particularly porous, for example, limestones and basalts.

White cement (WOPC) is also available, somewhat more expensive than ordinary grey cement, but it has distinct advantages. Mortar made with white cement does not usually transfer any stains to a paving's uppermost surface. A full bed of WOPC would be expensive, a simple technique is to apply a full slurry coat to the rear of a paving unit and allow it to set. This effectively seals the rear of the stone and prevents any leaching. Paving can then be set on a full bed that uses OPC (grey).

There are also proprietary sealants that can be used to achieve the same effect. **PVA** and SBR (styrene butadiene copolymer) are performance bonding agents that do the following:

- improve adhesion and bonding;
- are suitable for use in damp conditions;
- improve workability, strength and abrasion resistance;
- reduce mortar shrinkage and cracking and improve flexibility;
- improve chemical and water resistance;
- are non-corrosive to steel;
- allow reduction in the water content of a mortar.

Highly porous, unsealed stone can absorb the moisture from cements and mortars. Laid to an even and full bed, it will result in an even absorbency, and there should be no noticeable discoloration. Dabbing may be evident on the top stone surface due to such absorbency and may form noticeable areas of discoloration. The technique does not comply with the code of practice (BS 7533 Part 4), which requires 'uniform support'.

For bound materials, the binding agent is commonly cement or lime. It can be mixed with water to form a mortar or is frequently mixed dry. This keeps the bedding material flexible while laying, curing to form a rigid support for the pavement and so reduce the risk of post-construction settlement. Unlike unbound or loose materials, it will not be susceptible to any undermining by insects or water.

Lime mortar has been overtaken by the mass production of Portland cement-based mortars. They are, however, inherently more flexible than cement, making them very desirable as a laying course or bedding. Similar in structure to a Class V mortar, 1:3:10 cement:lime:sharp sand, working time will depend on the prevailing conditions. Lime mortar is especially useful in supporting Code 6 house construction, where cement-free specification is necessary.

SUB-BASE

See also Chapter 1, Vehicular paving, for a discussion of the sub-base. The sub-base needs to be appropriate to the type of paving installed and the strength of the ground on which it is constructed. The structural support for the **wearing course** or paved surface is similar to that used for vehicles but with variations in the required depths. There are two types of sub-base: flexible and rigid.

Flexible sub-bases are constructed of loose, granular materials and may be either permeable or non-porous. Rigid sub-bases are inflexible and typically made of CIS concrete. While there are porous forms of concrete, these are for special situations. The majority of rigid sub-bases are impermeable.

Permeable paving will require different materials from impermeable paving. The thickness of the sub-base will be determined by both the paving and wearing surface specified and the type of soil it is constructed on. Clay soils in particular can be problematic, as they are subject to expansion and contraction. This is even more pronounced where large trees are present.

Typical sub-base thicknesses are:

- impermeable soil: +400mm
- free draining soil: +150mm

Table 2.2 shows the sub-base thickness and capping required. The depth of the sub-base may be determined by the extent of the top soil present on site. It is pointless to specify a sub-base of 200mm if the top soil extends to 500mm. A sub-base needs to be constructed over non-friable or sub-grade material. It should never be built over top soil.

Table 2.2 Approximate CBR values for UK soil types

Type of soil	CBR (%)	
	Depth of water-table	
	Under 600mm	Over 600mm
Sand or gravel	60	20
Sand poorly graded	20	10
Sand well graded	40	15
Silt	2	1
Sandy clay	6–7	4–5
Silty clay	5	3
Heavy clay	2–3	1–2

It can be prudent to seek advice from a structural or soil engineer to advise on the appropriate depth and composition of the sub-base, especially where there are impermeable soils.

Care should be taken to avoid excessive and abrupt changes in sub-base thickness which might prove awkward to construct and be labour-intensive Dtp Type 1 is the most suitable sub-base material although not always necessary for pedestrian paved areas.

Types of sub base

1. *DTp1*: This is a granular material comprised of particles of stone 40mm to dust, providing a high degree of interlock. This is the highest grade of sub-base. Ideally suited to roads and areas subject to high loading. Must comply with the Department of Transport for Highway Works, clause 803.
2. *DTp2*: Contains a higher ratio of fines and therefore has reduced load-bearing properties. Suitable for some vehicular areas such as drives and mostly used for paved/pedestrian areas. Must comply with the Department of Transport for Highway Works, clause 804.
3. *DTp3*: Permeable, due to lack of fines and dust particulates. It is usually specified for use as a sub-base below gravel paving, grass paving systems, resin bound and permeable paving. Must comply with the Department of Transport for Highway Works, clause 805.

It is unacceptable to simply specify DTp1. Clarity is required in specifying the type of aggregate to be used, e.g. DTp1: crushed concrete. All sub-base materials should be compacted in layers not exceeding 100mm to ensure optimum performance. Once compacted, Type 1 and Type 2 are not permeable.

There are many types of aggregate available. Limestones are naturally alkaline and their use may alter the soil pH, locally. Road planings or scalpings are not recommended where there are planted areas in close proximity as they may contain hydrocarbons and other discharge from road use that is likely to be detrimental to plant health.

CIS (cast in situ) concrete may be required for areas that are either subject to occasional traffic incursions or where the paving material remains loose and subject to settlement (cobbles, setts) unless set over a rigid base. Large, monolithic areas of concrete will require the construction of movement joints, although the slab need not be as thick as those designed for vehicular traffic. A CIS concrete area is commonly called a 'raft'. For pedestrian and occasional light traffic, these are typically 100mm thick with reinforcing mesh, over a 100mm sub-base (depending on soil type and ground conditions). Reinforcing mesh is usually classified as:

- A412: suitable for patio slabs and low walls
- A393: this is more robust and used where more engineered structures are present.

CIS rafts should be no larger than 30–40m². This is to allow for expansion. Surfaces that are larger than this should be divided into a simple rectangular grid, of comparable areas. A simple expansion joint between two rafts is required, usually constructed from a 10mm-wide strip of fibrous, compressible flexible board. This is stopped 10–15mm from the concrete surface and sealed with a flexible expansion joint sealer. Where paving units are laid over a rigid sub-base and cover the expansion joints, care should be taken to consider the laying pattern. Movement in the sub-base will be reflected in the paved surface, pointed joints may collapse or the paving materials may fracture. Joints in paving materials should approximate those in the rigid sub-base so that any problems are mitigated as far as possible.

Where underground services and utilities are present and cannot be relocated or diverted, additional support and protection may have to be added to prevent damage.

SUB-GRADE

Chapter 1, Vehicular paving, also discussed the sub-grade. The strength and suitability of the soil to support the intended paved surface are determined by on-site analysis and tests, the most common of which is the **California Bearing Ratio (CBR)**. The higher the calculated percentage value, the more suitable the soil (Table 2.3). Pedestrian areas can tolerate a less structurally stable soil than areas to be used for higher load-bearing surfaces, such as roads and highways. The level of the water-table can also have a significant impact on the suitability of a soil. Drainage should be provided where the water-table is less than 600mm below the formation level.

Table 2.3 Sub-base thickness and capping requirements for CBR values

CBR value (soil at sub-grade level) (%)	Sub-grade strength	Sub-base thickness mm: pedestrian areas and driveways	Sub-base thickness mm: pedestrian areas with occasional traffic incursion	Notes
3 or less	Poor	+200mm	200–500	Capping is required
3–5	Normal	150–200	15–250	Typical CBR value Capping may be required
5–8	Good	100–150	100–150	Capping usually not necessary except on high volume/load surfaces
+8	Very good	100	100	Capping not usually required

Table 2.4 Paving joint widths

Material	Joint width
Natural stone: sawn edges	Min. 4mm, typical 7mm
Natural stone: riven edge	10–15mm
Natural stone: reclaimed	10–15mm but can require up to 20mm
Natural stone: cropped/riven setts	10–15mm but can require up to 20mm
Block paving: 6mm	10–15mm but can require up to 20mm
Porcelain paving	Min. 4mm

JOINTING

There are several methods of jointing paving materials:

- mortar pointing
- dry grout
- dry sand fill
- resin fill.

Paving should never be butt or close-jointed, this prevents paving from moving or expanding. Dry joints are typically 3–5mm wide (Table 2.4) and filled with sand or cement mix or dry sand (kiln-dried sand).

Uneven surfaces and gaps between paving slabs can cause problems for the **visually impaired** as well as weaken the paved structure and lead to localised failure. Joints in combined use area pavers should be no less than 2mm and no more than 5mm wide. Paving in pedestrian-only areas can have wider joints (6–10mm) filled with a compacted mortar. The permitted height variation over 1m is 3mm. Reclaimed stone may require joints up to 15mm, the variations in its surface height make it unsuitable for use in public or mixed use areas.

Flags laid onto a concrete or mortar bed will invariably have mortar joints; units laid onto sand are frequently tightly abutted or include a sand joint. Paving that follows a curve will benefit from using smaller units. The change in angle can be accommodated through the joints of the paving. There is a limit to how tight a radius can be achieved before the joints become excessive. Cuts on

tight radii can be either on one side of the paving unit or an equal cut, made symmetrically. Small areas or intricate detailing may justify the additional labour and time required. The designer should indicate the configuration of such cuts so that the appropriate techniques and sequence of laying can be accurately quoted.

Where there are changes of level that the paving must negotiate, small format paving requires fewer cuts. **Folded plane** or 'envelope' cuts in large slabs can detract from the overall appearance of a paved area whereas small units easily change direction and frequently eliminate the need for cutting altogether.

Stone has always been set and pointed with a cement or sand-based mortar. It is easy to mix on site, can readily be made as required, and is inexpensive. Such convenience comes at the expense of consistency. Small batches, variations in laying conditions and temperature, for instance, can all result in a mix that is inappropriate and unsuitable. The result of poor workmanship may not be evident for several weeks, months or even years.

Mortars should never be stronger than the stone on which they are used. A stone supplier will be able to give advice on the most appropriate mortar mix for any given paving material (Table 2.5). The sand may be a mixture of soft and grit sand to add texture and workability.

Road salt, in particular, can be very aggressive towards cement-based products and their mortars. This can reduce the effectiveness of traditional pointing used on driveways. It is possible to partially fill joints with a cement mortar and to finish the joint to paving level with a bespoke sealant, usually applied with a 'gun'. Gun point mortars (GPM) are a simple solution for grouting paving and setts. They attempt to introduce a more consistent approach, both to workmanship and to the products used. Designed to be applied using a mortar gun, the products create a consistent colour and an extremely durable paving joint. They are manufactured from a blend of specially selected aggregates, cements and additives. Only the addition of water is required to produce a high quality pointing mortar, suitable for natural stone paving, setts and brickwork and available

A paving pattern generated without consideration of joints. Note that this paving plan is idealised and not a true reflection of the final dimensions when joints are added

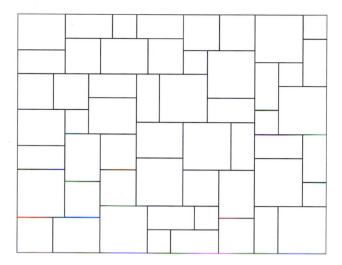

All joints opened up to a uniform gauge, e.g. 6mm. To maintain a uniform gap, some joints must remain fully closed, which is impractical and likely to cause the paving to fail. Note the width of the paving has increased by 7 x 6mm (=42mm) once joints are applied.

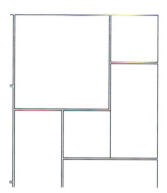

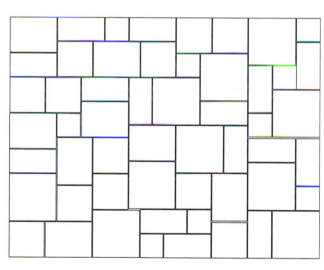

Joints should be adjusted, visually so that there is a random distribution of both wide (+10mm) and narrow (4mm) to facilitate a joint at every junction. The overall dimensions may increase again once joint widths have been balanced.

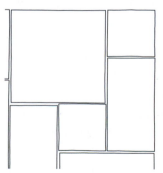

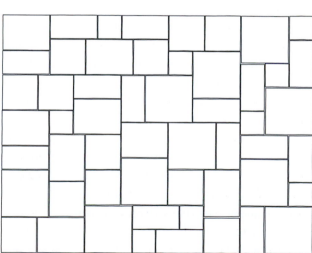

Figure 2.13 Balancing paving joints
Source: Adapted from www.pavingexpert.com/random03.htm

Table 2.5 Bedding cement mix ratios

Material	Paving flexural strength	Mortar ratio sand: cement
Limestone (e.g. Portland)	Weak	7:1–9:1
Sandstones	Medium	5:1–7:1
Granites	Strong	4:1–5:1
Slates	Strong	4:1–5:1

in a range of colours. GPM systems reduce labour and staining, which can be a problem in more traditional grouting methods. Such systems are initially more expensive but with reduced installation times and less waste through accurate and consistent application, they can prove valuable and durable.

Sweep-in mortars are two-part, epoxy resin-based powders or resins. They are ideal for jointing riven stone paving and setts. Applied in the form of a powder over the area to be pointed, a brushing action (sometimes with a specialist tool) forces the product into the joints. On exposure to air and UV, it cures, typically achieving a set within 24 hrs. It can withstand jet-washing, frost, salt, abrasion, and inhibits weed growth. The product does not rely on the addition of water, making it suitable for application in most weather conditions. A range of colours to complement paving ranges are available. As with all such products, a small test area should be tried in advance to determine if the resin causes any form of staining or changes to the character of a stone surface, creating a 'wet' look, for instance, which might not be desirable. Porous versions of these pointing compounds are available. Table 2.6 presents a summary of jointing methods.

Joint maintenance

Once laid, the paving should to be swept occasionally to remove dust and detritus.

Any vegetation will have germinated from seeds and is unlikely to have grown through the sub-surface layers.

It is easily removed. To keep paving units secure, joints need to be maintained, cracked mortar replaced, and dry sand joints topped up.

SPECIAL PAVING

Pedestrian access to areas that are restricted or considered a danger can be discouraged by the installation of **deterrent paving**. More typically found at pedestrian crossings and in urban landscapes, these types of aggressive surface units also suit divisions at boundaries or between drives, where a larger structure is unacceptable, but vehicular or pedestrian traffic needs to be contained.

Deterrent paving comes in a variety of types, some more severe than others. Basic solutions can be as simple as large cobbles set into a thick mortar bed. Those units designed for urban or trafficked areas are usually available in the British Standard module sizes. Special shaped bricks are available or created by using standard paving blocks in a creative fashion.

Tactile paving

Tactile paving with specific textures and patterns can be used to assist the visually impaired to navigate their environment. It can be used to give directional guidance, or warn of an impending hazard or the location of an amenity.

'When moving around the pedestrian environment, visually impaired people will actively seek and make use of tactile information underfoot, particularly detectable contrasts in surface texture' (DTR, 2007). The Department of Transport and the Regions sets out the correct use of textured paving to aid the navigation and improve the safety of the visually impaired.

A range of standard tactile paving with rigorous textures has been developed for specific applications. It is critical that tactile paving should be used only for its intended use and in accordance with the installation guidelines. With the exception

Table 2.6 Jointing methods

Jointing technique	Pros	Cons	Notes
Mortar pointing or wet grout	Cheap	Limited working life	Most common
	Readily available materials	Can be messy, create stains	Complete within 4hrs of laid paving
			Class II
Dry grouting	Cheap	Short time to complete	Used on decorative paving
	Readily available materials	Apply only in dry conditions	Works best on joints partially filled from laying (buttered)
	Can be quick		
Dry sand	Cheap	Apply only in dry conditions	Used on small format paving
	Readily available materials	Sand needs to be dry	Specific sand should be used (BS 7533)
	Quick	Joints require top-up within 4–6 wks, then annually	No cement added to the sand
Resin mortar dry	Permeable versions available	Lower strength than liquid systems	Brush-in type
	Supplied ready to use	Considerable variation between brands	Suitable for low traffic areas (patios)
	'Wash-in' types of products not limited to application in the dry	Can stain or bond to paving surface if not removed	Resin-coated sand
		Can have short working life	Cure in atmospheric conditions >0.7N/mm^2 is a reasonable strength product
Resin mortar liquid grout	Very high strength	Can be difficult to repair	Suitable for high traffic areas, including highways
	Flexible joints created	Can be messy and stain	May require special application equipment
	Difficult to damage	Skill required in its application	

of delineation strips used for shared routes, none of the tactile paving units or installations are treated as traffic signs. They are not included in the Traffic Signs Regulations and General Directions (TSRGD) and may not require authorisation. The design of tactile paving is controlled and the shape, style and height of the features must comply with the standard. There are many versions available, ranging from hydraulically pressed concrete, surfaces machined from natural stone, such as granite and even paving where the texture has been created by insetting metal components. Tactile paving units are 400mm × 400mm to allow them to be readily included in paved schemes using other standardised materials.

Blister paving

Blister paving is used to identify the presence of a dropped kerb at both controlled and uncontrolled pedestrian road crossings. Kerbs are used by the visually impaired to identify the presence of a road or sudden change in level. The grid pattern blister paving is essential to warn of the presence of a crossing point and that kerbs may not be present.

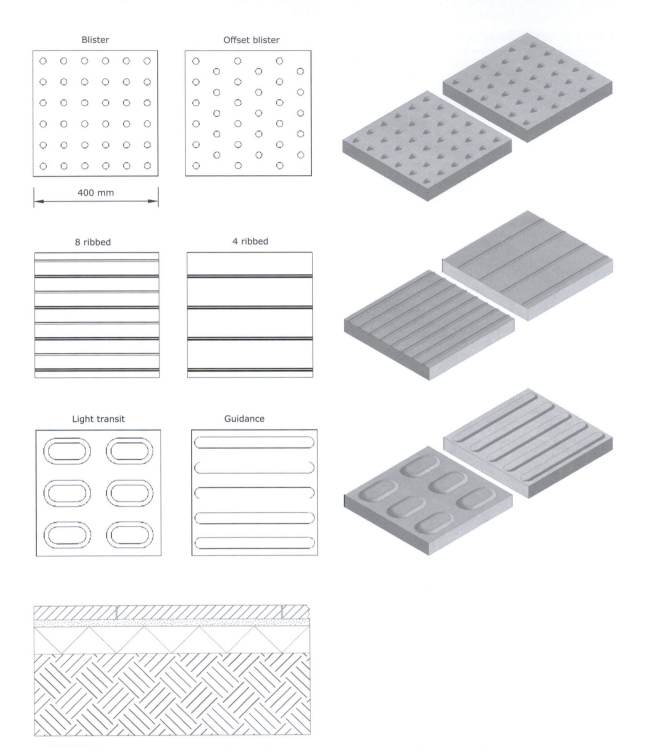

Blister

Offset blister

400 mm

8 ribbed

4 ribbed

Light transit

Guidance

Figure 2.14 Tactile paving

It is recommended that the paving is selected to visually contrast with adjacent materials. At **controlled crossings** only, the blister paving should be red, at **uncontrolled crossings** the paving should be a buff colour or such that it is in sharp contrast to surrounding surfaces.

The layout and extent of blister paving can be quite complex, especially where crossings are present on corners or are not perpendicular to the kerb edge. The *Guidance on the Use of Tactile Paving Surfaces* (DTR, 2007) includes several sample design layouts. Where the edge of a blister paving scheme ends at or over a building line that is formed by a forecourt or other private vehicular access, the local authority may seek permission to extend the tactile surface to its completion and into the private forecourt.

Hazard warning paving

Known as **corduroy** pattern pavings (8 ribbed) they are specifically used at level crossings, the approach to on-street **light rapid transport** platforms and at the top and bottom of steps (see Chapter 5, Steps and ramps). It is laid so that the bars are set perpendicular or across the direction of travel.

Cycleway paving

Paving to indicate a cycle track or shared footway is formed of four rectangular section bars. On the footpath side, they are set to run transversely to the direction of pedestrian traffic, while on the cycleway

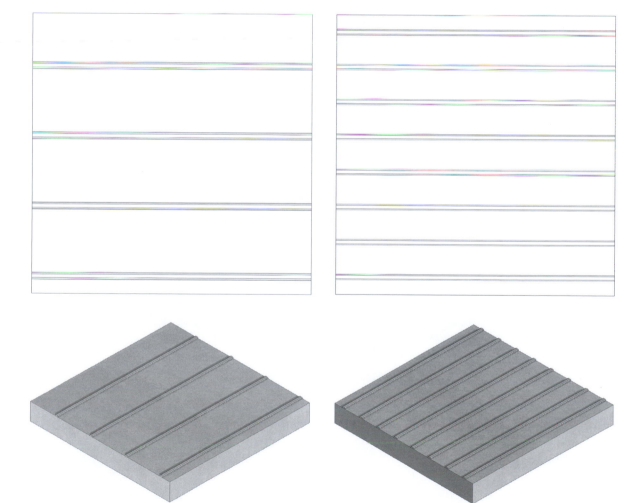

Figure 2.15 Cycleway plan

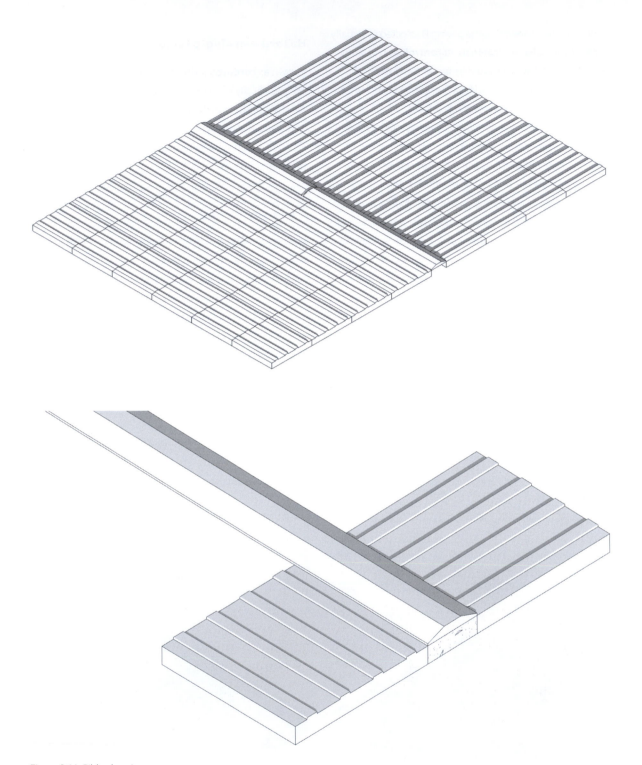

Figure 2.16 Ribbed paving

side, they run parallel to the direction of travel. Where cyclists and pedestrians share the same route, a central delineation strip is required to segregate the two paths. They are laid at the start and end of a path. The central delineation strip runs the full length of the shared pathway to maintain the separation of pedestrians from cycles.

Where there are junctions with other cycle tracks, footways and crossings, there are recommended arrangements for the installation of all required paving types.

Offset blister paving

Offset blister paving indicates the presence of a platform edge for underground, light rapid transport and heavy rail services. It is set back by 500–700mm from the platform edge and installed to a depth of 400mm (×1 paving unit). Light rapid transport platforms may also employ a specific paving design, know as a lozenge. It is installed in the same way as offset blister paving.

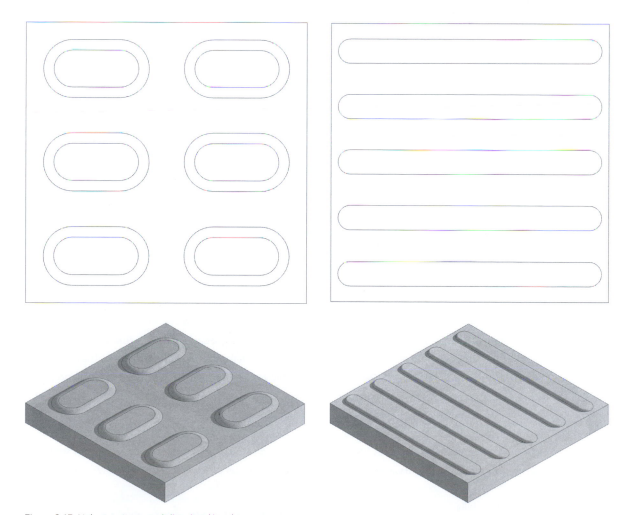

Figure 2.17 Light transit use and directional/guidance paving

Directional or guidance paving

In large public spaces such as squares and precincts, these paving units, usually laid in single rows, guide the visually impaired. The bars follow the line of travel or show a change of direction when laid at right angles. They are also used to draw attention to amenities such as post boxes, toilets, or cash dispensers.

Barface paving

This paving has a subtle ribbed pattern, designed to improve grip on inclined surfaces, such as footbridges, ramps or routes into and out of subways and underpasses, improving traction in damp conditions.

GRADIENT AND DRAINAGE

Paved surfaces are invariably treated as if they are two-dimensional. While the fall necessary to give adequate drainage is only barely perceivable, it does mean that the surface becomes something that requires careful consideration and, with attention to detail, can make it a success. Gradients, or falls, are necessary to direct and manage surface water run-off in the most effective and safest way possible. Excessive surface water build-up can create problems of access and mobility, can be problematic and a potential slip hazard as either water run-off or in winter as sheet ice.

Falls to paved areas are specified in BS 7533, Part 4. Typically 1:80 longitudinally and 1:40 (25mm per meter) transversely. However, for domestic areas, a combined fall of 1:50–1:60 is typical (Table 2.7). Large areas that are laid with block or brick paving can drain at up to 1:80 whereas bitumen-type materials will hold water and

are best laid to a steeper gradient such as 1:40, or more. The introduction of a gradient will require levels to be adjusted elsewhere in the scheme, for instance, at the top of a flight of steps. These levels should be checked before the design is finalised. Falls are best directed away from property and shed into open ground. Water should never be directed or allowed to drain onto steps, ramps or paved slopes.

Pavements should be drained in the preferred hierarchy:

- adjacent open ground (if suitable);
- SUDS specific structure (soak-away, attenuation cells, etc.);
- permeable paving.

It is not permissible to drain onto land belonging to a third party, and if an area is more than 1.5m wide, it can be advantageous to divert run-off in two directions.

Large flat areas can use a series of 'summits and valleys' to create the necessary falls. The summits should be a minimum 150mm below the damp-proof course level.

Paths and pedestrian areas adjacent to buildings should be sloped away wherever possible. Run-off should not be directed to planted areas, rain gardens or soak-aways that are close to buildings. If the path must slope towards the building, a drainage channel should be used to collect any excess water and direct it to the drains that take the surface water. **Linear drains** (Aco type) work well and are relatively discreet. They should be installed at a minimum of 150mm below the damp-proof course and 150mm away from the property, with a 20mm fall/metre.

It is essential that a survey is undertaken of the area to be paved to locate the presence of any utility or service ducts (e.g. water pipes, cable TV, electricity cables).

SUDS (sustainable urban drainage systems)

Most wearing courses have been designed to shed surface water to prevent penetration and thereby avoid

Table 2.7 Natural stone falls

Material	Fall
Natural stone riven	1:60 min
Natural stone sawn	1:80

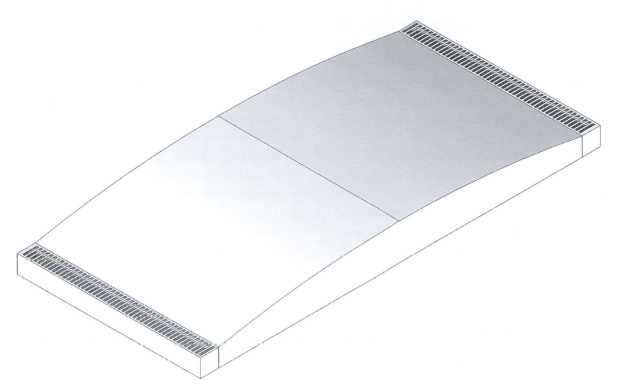

Figure 2.18 Camber

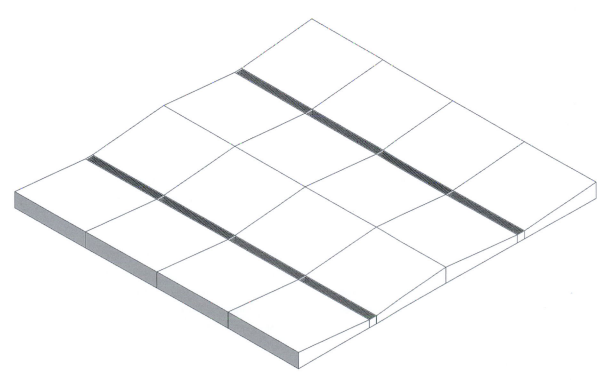

Figure 2.19 Peaks and troughs

the freeze–thaw action to both the surface and sub-base layers. Such concentrated dissipation of surface water can create a surge as it enters an urban drainage system, potentially contributing to flooding. While some surfaces such as roads and highways need to shed surface water as quickly as possible, areas for pedestrian and very light vehicular use are not so critical.

In the UK, planning permission is required to construct any surface that has an open boundary with a highway or footway that is impermeable, resulting in uncontrolled rainwater run-off from a front garden onto a highway. This invariably concerns the development of front gardens into hard-standing and vehicular parking areas. This also applies where existing hard-standing is being replaced, and for hard surfaces exceeding 5 square metres in area. It does not apply retrospectively to existing surfaces, even if they do not comply with the new legislation.

In the UK, planning permission is not required if the surface is less than 5sqm or is permeable (porous) or if an impermeable construction is used but run-off is directed away from the edge of the property into a drainage channel, soak-away or planted bed. Sites prone to waterlogging are unsuitable for permeable surfaces and are best drained in a more traditional manner. If a new drive or hard-standing area is constructed using permeable surfaces such as concrete block paving or porous resin bound gravel, or if the water is permitted to soak directly into (infiltrate) the ground, planning permission is not required in England and Wales. When constructing a new access into a garden across the footway, permission will be required from the local authority. Advice will be given on the extent of the drop kerbs required and if the public footpath needs strengthening over any buried services. The work may have to be carried out by approved contractors.

SUDS schemes are designed to attenuate surface water, releasing it back into the ground or a drainage system, in a controlled manner. Pollution is controlled and even reduced, aquifers and water courses are replenished naturally and at source. The maintenance cost of drainage systems is also reduced in line with the reduced demand on the infrastructure. Rainwater can be controlled in SUDS-compliant schemes through the use of:

- permeable paving;
- porous or pervious materials such as gravels;
- cellular systems;
- ponds, wetlands and swales;
- **infiltration**, collection, or distribution systems;
- filter drains;
- impermeable surfaces incorporating managed run-off.

Water retained within the ground (as in an infiltration system), or stored in a sub-base structure (as in an **attenuation** system) is slowly released into the water-table or retained for other uses, such as irrigation, long after the surge has passed. A combination of systems is typical. Most systems will have a capacity limit after which additional water is directed through an overflow to a suitable soak-away or drain.

Permeable solutions may not be suitable on steeply sloping (greater than 1 in 20) sites. In these cases, an impermeable surface could be used and, if possible, the water directed to a soak-away, rain garden or, as a last resort, directly to the drains. Where water is fed into permeable paving (e.g. from a downpipe), attenuation systems are preferred, where a typical ratio of 2:1 can be used between impermeable and permeable areas. Where buildings and gardens have been built over previously contaminated ground, the existing soil may be impermeable by design and necessity. Permeable paving may be possible but a more specialist construction is required, allowing the attenuated water to migrate from the sub-base to the surface water drains.

While conventional paving systems divert rainwater towards the perimeter of the path or hard-standing and then to the surface water drains, a permeable paving driveway deliberately retains the water within the paving structure, thereby allowing a controlled release of rainwater into the environment. Porous paving has been developed for both unit and resin bound pavements. Most permeable surfaces are either variations of block paving, bound gravel or open structure units. The unit materials, jointing, laying course and bedding materials used in permeable systems differ from their conventional counterparts, and the manufacturers' advice and recommendations should be followed.

In unit paving, water is permitted to percolate between individual pieces, integral features such as ribs maintain a uniform gap between adjoining units. Any material used to fill between units should be the same as the bedding layer, rather than a kiln-dried sand.

Resin bound macadams are available as open grade porous asphalts, they require specific construction, and systems vary between manufacturers. Often the inclusion of specialist membranes or retaining substrates are required.

Types of permeable paving systems

There are three types of permeable paving design (as defined in *The SUDS Manual* by CIRIA). These are:

- *System A: full infiltration*: where water percolates through the surface, the laying course and the sub-base, returning water eventually into the ground and water-table. The water is not directed into the drains so no pipes or gullies are required, this is the simplest and most economical of the permeable systems. The ground may not be suitable for a full infiltration system if a 300mm × 300mm × 300mm test hole, filled with water, takes more than 11 hours to empty.
- *System B: partial infiltration*: this system is preferred where the ground may not be capable or not have the capacity to absorb water. Rainwater which has percolated into the sub-base is diverted through pipes or gullies into other water management features such as **swales**, ponds and sewers. Directly connecting to the surface water drainage system is permitted only as a last resort.
- *System C: no infiltration* (also known as attenuation systems): this is suitable for contaminated or capped land. The sub-base is effectively isolated, through the use of impermeable membranes, below and up the sides of the attenuated area, from the surrounding land and water-table. This creates

an effective water storage device. Rainwater entering the sub-base is retained and excess, via an overflow pipe is passed onto other drainage systems such as swales, ponds and sewers. Containments are prevented from entering the water-table, making this a suitable solution for areas likely to suffer from pollution and chemical waste, if there is suitable downstream management of such pollutants. Attenuation systems act as huge soak-aways and require a substantial excavation. They are designed to protect against sudden surges, slowly releasing the captivated water and are frequently located under drives or large hard paved areas.

Improvement layers can be constructed below the permeable paving to ensure the system can meet the required structural load for the project.

The two commonest types of improvement layers are: dense bitumen **macadam** (DBM) and cement stabilised coarse graded aggregate (CSCGA). Such improvement is only required where limited or infrequent vehicular incursions have been anticipated and designed for.

Successful permeable paving relies on using the recommended aggregates. Incorrect use or specification of aggregates and the sub-base is the most common reason for failure. All paving joints should be filled with 6.3–2mm jointing grit. Poorly filled joints may allow blocks to move. The joints of permeable paving must not become contaminated, such as with soil, as work on the scheme is completed. Joints may need to be topped up with grit sand after two or three months due to settlement.

Whatever the specified wearing course, the sub-base needs to have an open structure to permit the infiltration of water. The thicknesses of coarse graded aggregate must be suitable for the traffic conditions it was designed for, and, in the case of attenuation systems, be sufficiently thick to store the amount of water necessary. Conventional **hardcore** (DTp Type 1) is unsuitable as a sub-base material for permeable paved areas. Type 3 (4/20) should be used as it is open-graded, consisting of larger stone particles, creating larger voids for the infiltration of water. The sub-base material should be compacted as for conventional construction.

A hydraulic analysis should be conducted at the intended site using the method set out in the Interpave Guidelines (see Guidance and Advisory publications, p. 98). Where an infiltration system is designed, capacity is not required but the porosity of the ground must be established. The ground must accept 20mm of water in one hour, this capability will have to be scaled up if the pavement is receiving run-off water from surrounding impermeable paving or from downpipes.

For the sub-base and laying base:

- for 60mm permeable paving, use 200mm deep sub-base;
- for 80mm permeable paving, use 275mm deep sub-base;
- if the sub-base is 10–20mm, use angular clean Type 3 material;
- if a 50mm layer of Type 3, 6mm open graded (no fines) gravel is used as the laying surface for the blocks;
- the permeable paving blocks are then laid in situ and an angular 2–4mm grit is brushed across the surface and into the voids between the blocks. As with conventional paving, the jointing used between the individual blocks is critical to the stability and strength of the driveway as a whole.
- Do not use dry kiln sand in between the blocks as this will severely restrict the rainwater flow. Consequently, a course of 2–4mm angular, no-fines aggregate is used as a jointing medium.

Maintaining permeable paving

Permeable paving systems require minimal maintenance if contamination during construction has been avoided. Permeable surfaces should be kept free of soil and detritus which will clog the gaps between blocks. Chemical cleaners and weed killers should be avoided, these will contaminate water as it enters the permeable system and subsequent water-table. Despite being permeable, any vegetative growth will be due to opportunistic germination of windblown seeds and not from below the paved area if built correctly.

Note: In the case of attenuation designs, sub-grade CBR values are equilibrium moisture content values. In the case of infiltration designs, sub-grade CBR values are soaked values.

Due to the wide and expanding variety of products and systems being developed, advice on the construction details/sub-base structure for specific products should be obtained from the manufacturer/supplier.

Drainage

Most modern properties have a dual drainage system. Such systems have multiple manhole covers in close proximity, typically foul water is always deeper than surface systems. Access chambers (ACs) are located on drain spurs and used for infrequent inspection and maintenance; they are rarely more than 600mm deep, and up to 300mm in diameter. Inspection chambers (ICs) are larger, up to 600mm diameter and 1m deep and typically located at the junction of drains. Manholes (MH) are the largest chambers and may permit manual/equipment access to a drain or sewer system. Sewer/drainage work is dangerous and specialist contractors should be used.

Soak-aways

Soak-aways rarely work on heavy clay soils, or when the water-table is very high. The success of a soak-away or rain/storm water garden is determined by the size of the area to be drained and the rate water percolates through the soil and the level of the water-table. Soak-aways must be at the lowest point of a drain system and a minimum distance of 5m away from a building and 2.5m from a boundary so as not to saturate the foundations of any structure, but ground conditions may require this to be increased. The local Building Control Department will be able to offer site-specific advice. Rainwater gardens or open planted areas that are used to divert rainwater should not use mulch as this will get washed away. Rather, use a decorative gravel which will remain in place and reduce soil transpiration.

They should be constructed so that the base of the soak-away is permanently above the water-table and causes no risk of contamination to surrounding land and vegetation from pollutants carried by run-off water, such as fuel and oil spills on a driveway.

A trial pit is useful to determine if a site is suitable. After 24hrs any water will have stabilised at the water-table level, this should be measured from ground level and used to determine whether the site is practical. If there is no water present, the location is likely to be suitable for a soak-away. If there is a high water-table, the required volume might be met by using a shallow but wide soak-away or even multiple, connected chambers. Guidance on the design of soak-aways and infiltration drainage systems is given in Building Regulations (UK) Part H, Drainage and Waste Disposal, Part 2, Surface water drainage, as well as BRE Digest 365, Soak-away Design.

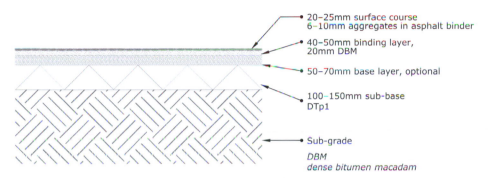

20–25mm surface course
6–10mm aggregates in asphalt binder

40–50mm binding layer, 20mm DBM

50–70mm base layer, optional

100–150mm sub-base DTp1

Sub-grade

DBM
dense bitumen macadam

Asphalt is a structurally weak material. As such, it must have restrained edges, whether formed by a structure, such as a wall or treated as a kerb. Open edges will collapse and degrade the path edge quickly. An alternative to a fine aggregate finish is to lay the surface course to 40mm thick and scatter and roll precoated chippings (10–20mm). This can give a more decorative finish. Not all aggregates are suitable and they must be precoated to form an effective wearing surface.

The surface should ideally be laid to 1:40–1:60.

Figure 2.20 Asphalt footpath: impermeable

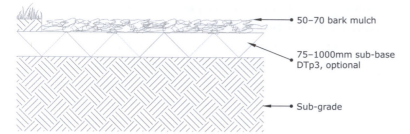

50–70 bark mulch

75–1000mm sub-base
DTp3, optional

Sub-grade

Bark paths are simple, inexpensive and quick to construct. The installation of a sub-base is not always necessary, only required where the ground is damp or waterlogged. A geotextile should be used in such conditions to maintain the integrity of the sub-base.

There are many types of bark/wood chips available. For long paths or through woodlands, a simple utility bark is sufficient. Where the path is decorative as well as functional, processed wood chips offer a more consistent alternative and are less prone to degradation.

There are grades of bark available for use around children's play equipment, where the depth should be increased to 300mm.

Figure 2.21 Bark footpath: permeable

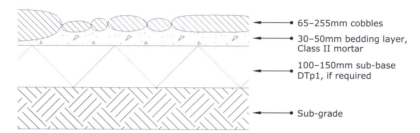

65–255mm cobbles

30–50mm bedding layer,
Class II mortar

100–150mm sub-base
DTp1, if required

Sub-grade

Cobbles (unworked rounded stones 65–255mm) can be used for pavements, surfaces or as an effective deterrent to discourage both pedestrian and light vehicular incursion.

As a paved, pedestrian surface, its use is usually determined by the context of the scheme; reflecting a traditional local style for instance. The materials and laying pattern used should reflect the local context.

Simplistically cobbles are laid as:
• random
• roughly parallel, required some sorting
• coursed, requiring the cobbles to be graded
• patterns where colour and size are used for mosaics, etc.

Deterrent paving uses cobbles 'on end' to create as rough and impassable surface as possible. The cobbles should be set to at least 50% of their length in a class II mortar.

For pathways, cobbles should be laid with the smoothest surface uppermost and as tight as possible. Small cobbles/pebbles are used to fill gaps. The stones can be laid into a bedding mortar (class II) or directly into a concrete bed (C20–35).

A sub-base is not required for pedestrian paths, only where there is intermittent loading or infrequent vehicle intrusion/crossing, e.g. driveway. The sub-base may be a separate DTp1 or a full concrete bed (min. 100mm). While cobbles can be laid directly into a concrete sub-base, a separate mortar bed allows work to progress slowly and for cobbles to be laid with care.

While an edge is not always required, where a concrete sub-base is installed, perimeter cobbles are less likely to be dislodged where a restraint is used.

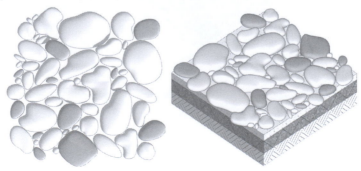

Figure 2.22 Cobbles as paving: impermeable

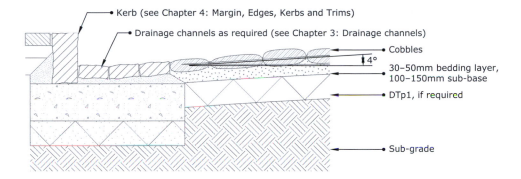

- Kerb (see Chapter 4: Margin, Edges, Kerbs and Trims)
- Drainage channels as required (see Chapter 3: Drainage channels)
- Cobbles
- 4°
- 30–50mm bedding layer, 100–150mm sub-base
- DTp1, if required
- Sub-grade

Where drainage is required to the path edges, a kerbstone or edge stone detail will be necessary. The foundation and sub-base for the margin and kerb should be a separate construction to that used for the main pathway.

This will create a pocket where water is readily retained. A camber to the paved surface of 4° will be sufficient to dissipate rainfall away from all but the deepest cavities.

Transverse section through pathway

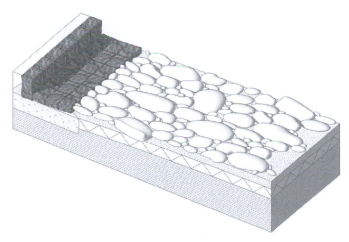

Figure 2.23 Cobbles laid with a camber, as paving: impermeable

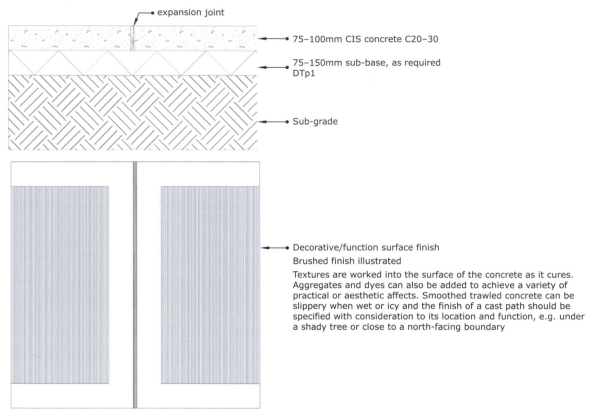

expansion joint

75–100mm CIS concrete C20–30

75–150mm sub-base, as required
DTp1

Sub-grade

Decorative/function surface finish

Brushed finish illustrated

Textures are worked into the surface of the concrete as it cures. Aggregates and dyes can also be added to achieve a variety of practical or aesthetic affects. Smoothed trawled concrete can be slippery when wet or icy and the finish of a cast path should be specified with consideration to its location and function, e.g. under a shady tree or close to a north-facing boundary

CIS (cast in situ) concrete does not require a sub-base; a **DPC** (e.g. Visaeen or PIFGA 1200) over a compacted sub-grade is sufficient for pedestrian pathways if the ground conditions are good. Regardless of conditions, the excavation trench should be to the sub-grade and never within the top-soil layer. Where the ground is uneven, the sub-grade is of poor quality or there is more than 100mm of top soil, a sub-base should be used. The edges of the path will need to be constrained, whether with temporary shuttering or with a permanent edge.

Concrete slabs up to 100mm thick will require a single layer of reinforcement mesh (A142), all edges 50mm or greater from the external surfaces of the concrete slab. Alternatively, polythene fibre reinforcement can be used.

The edges of the cast slab should be **arrised** (**chamfered**) to prevent **spalling** and damage. A path cannot be cast as a continuous surface. The concrete should be subdivided into smaller sections, not more than 18–20m². In practice for a 1.2m wide path, joints should be spaced at 4–6m intervals.

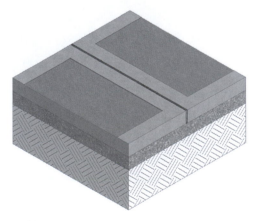

Figure 2.24 Cast in situ concrete: impermeable

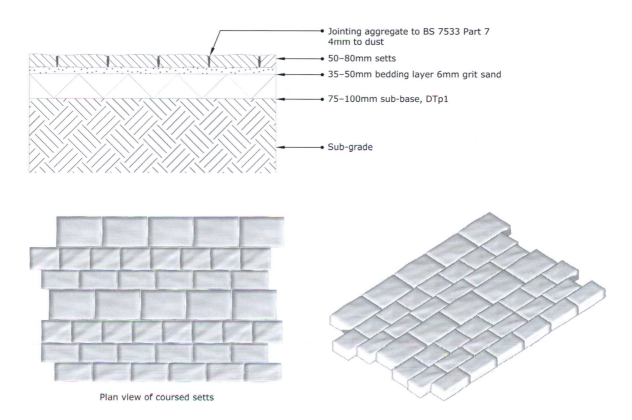

Jointing aggregate to BS 7533 Part 7
4mm to dust

50–80mm setts

35–50mm bedding layer 6mm grit sand

75–100mm sub-base, DTp1

Sub-grade

Plan view of coursed setts

The laying of setts is similar to the techniques developed for flexible concrete block paving. Joints should ideally be 3–6mm, but as setts have natural variation, wider joints may be required (10mm max.). Joints can be filled with a variety of materials: 4mm to dust hard aggregate is the easiest and cheapest, while flexible resin mortars are expensive but relatively easy to apply. Setts do not lend themselves to mortar pointed joints. It is time-consuming and any movement will result in the joint failing, whereas sand and resin accommodate some joint movement. Mortar pointed joints should only be used where a rigid bedding layer (concrete or mortar) has been used. Setts require edge constraint, ideally set in a concrete haunch, whether flush or proud of the paved surface.

Setts can be laid as staggered (stack) bond or coursed. Coursed offers the strongest bond, but, for pedestrian paving, the final aesthetic is more important than the resistance to loading. If the path is to be cambered, it should be created at the sub-grade layer. This will ensure that all subsequent courses are of uniform thickness.

Figure 2.25 Natural stone setts

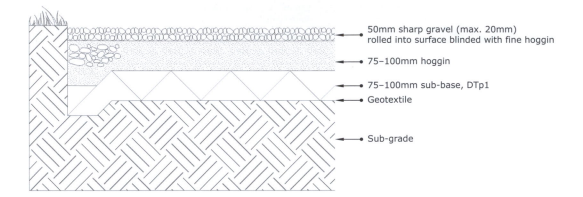

50mm sharp gravel (max. 20mm) rolled into surface blinded with fine hoggin

75–100mm hoggin

75–100mm sub-base, DTp1

Geotextile

Sub-grade

Hoggin is a mixture of gravels, clay and sand, traditionally obtained from the site excavations. It is traditionally found in the south of England, but is available nationwide. Whereas self-binding gravels are sourced locally across the UK, this is a blend of snaps, fines and gravel in a specific ratio (with up to 30% fines) that permits the creation of a smooth and hard wearing surface, when compacted. Both materials are applied in layers and compacted between applications. The surface can be left as a compacted, smooth surface or an optional layer of large (20mm) aggregate applied to aid traction and improve wear. The exposed surface can be virtually impermeable as the clay fines consolidate. A camber to the path greatly improves drainage.

An advantage of hoggin and self-binding gravels is that they can be easily and inexpensively repaired. Self-binding materials should not be laid to a gradient greater than 1:12 to prevent excessive material migration. Self-binding paths require edge construction. This can be as simple as an earth, timber or steel edge or a more constructed solution such as a sett or kerb restraint set in concrete. Edges, whether earth or kerbs, should be a min. of 10mm above the gravel surface to prevent excessive material migration off the path edges.

Self-binding gravel path

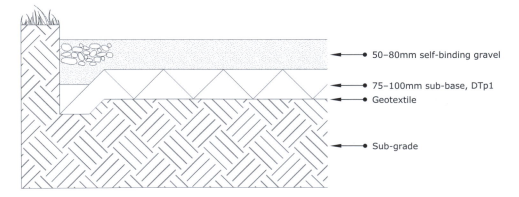

50–80mm self-binding gravel

75–100mm sub-base, DTp1

Geotextile

Sub-grade

Figure 2.26 Hoggin path: impermeable

Natural, random-sized stone paving laid to an irregular pattern ('crazy' paving)
Should be treated as regular-sized paving units. The joints should be as tight as
possible and ideally balanced so that they are uniform.

Figure 2.27 Natural stone irregular paving

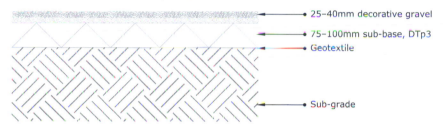

25–40mm decorative gravel

75–100mm sub-base, DTp3

Geotextile

Sub-grade

Gravels are an inexpensive and easy method to create a decorative path. Some gravels are not suitable, i.e. the rounded 'pea' gravels and small flints. Angular or sharp gravels (6–10mm) are self-binding and less prone to migration. The gravel depth is typically x3 the size of the largest aggregate used, e.g. 10mm x 3 = 30mm depth. If laid deeper, the gravel will drift and move underfoot.

The sub-base lends the path its strength, a Type 3 will ensure that rainfall passes through these bases quickly. A geotextile is essential for the success of a gravel path, lending support to the sub-base. Edge restraints are necessary and ideally raised 50–100mm above the gravel surface to prevent pushed or kicked gravel from migrating.

Gravel should not be laid on inclines or gradients over 1:12, ideally 1:15. Gravel-retaining structures (similar to grass-retaining structures) can be used or the gradient should have steps.

Figure 2.28 Loose gravel paving: permeable

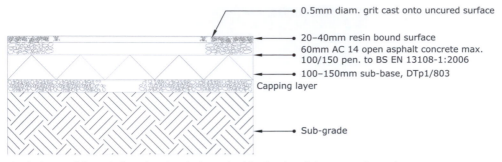

0.5mm diam. grit cast onto uncured surface

20–40mm resin bound surface

60mm AC 14 open asphalt concrete max. 100/150 pen. to BS EN 13108-1:2006

100–150mm sub-base, DTp1/803

Capping layer

Sub-grade

The thickness of the resin bound surface is determined by the size of the aggregate used:

- 3mm aggregate requires min. 16mm
- 6mm aggregate requires min. 18mm
- 10mm aggregate requires min. 24mm

The supporting layer may be an existing asphalt macadam surface. This should be tested to ensure it is fit for purpose, i.e. AC14 close surface asphalt concrete (max. 160/220 pen.). If there is any doubt about the integrity of an existing surface, it should be removed and replaced.

The thickness of the sub-base is dependent on the sub-grade soil conditions. If there is a poor sub-grade dispersant (CBR <2%), a granular capping layer may be required.

min. fall 1.5%

20–40mm resin bound surface

60mm AC 14 open asphalt concrete max. 100/150 pen. to BS EN 13108-1:2006

Geotextile to prevent downward migration of fine soil particles (optional)

150mm min., well-compacted type 3 granular sub-base to SHW (Specification for Highway Works) clause 805 or 4/40, 4/20mm graded crushed concrete aggregate to BS EN 12620

Terram 900/1000/Advantage geotextile membrane or equivalent to prevent upward migration of fine soil particle (optional)

Figure 2.29 Resin bound surfaces

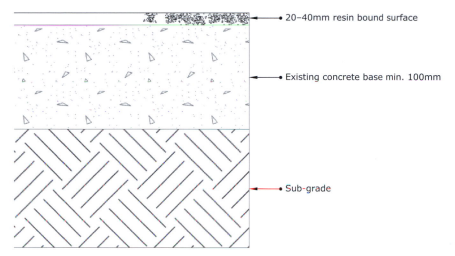

• 20–40mm resin bound surface

• Existing concrete base min. 100mm

• Sub-grade

Can be overlaid onto existing asphalt or concrete surfaces of suitable construction for the traffic expected.

Movement joints/construction joints in concrete should be extended up to the surface. Cracks in the existing surface should be broken out if necessary and filled with a polymer/cement crack-filling material.

It is advised that concrete bases are primed with a prepared, approved by the resin bound aggregate supplier, prior to installation.

If there is the risk of vehicular incursion, the integrity of the concrete base should be inspected and tested to ensure it meets Highway Agency requirements.

The maximum deviation of the binder course should not exceed 3mm under a 1 metre straight edge.

Figure 2.29 (Continued)

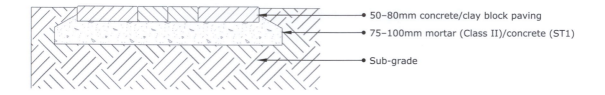

- 50–80mm concrete/clay block paving
- 75–100mm mortar (Class II)/concrete (ST1)
- Sub-grade

Setts

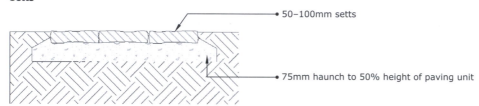

- 50–100mm setts
- 75mm haunch to 50% height of paving unit

Stepping stones are a decorative alternative to a continuous path. They are not intended for anything other than low frequency pedestrian use and as such the construction can be simplified considerably. Stones or pads can be set on individual beds of mortar or on a continuous bed (race) with stones spaced to give the illusion of stepping stones. Where a continuous bed is used, there should be a drainage hole to the sub-grade at each gap. A sub-base and edging are not necessary for such low impact paving. Mortar (Class II) 75mm min., can be laid over a DPC onto the excavated and compacted sub-grade. Concrete can also be used (ST1 or C30).

The blocks or setts should be bedded to at least 50% of their thickness and haunched at the perimeter. The supporting mortar bed should extend 75mm beyond the final paved area.

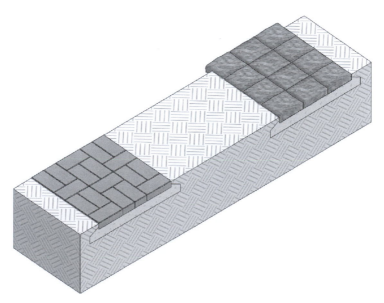

Figure 2.30 Stepping stones (ground-based)

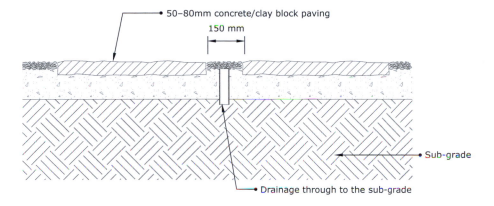

The spacing of stepping stones is subjective. The gap between the stones and the size of the stones should be laid out to suit the gait of those who will use the path. The stride length will be different between adults and children and between tall and shorter people. 150mm is a reasonable gap to start, but the best way to determine the placement of stones is by placing them in position to establish their best position, before being set in mortar. The minimum stone or pattern of setts/blocks is 450mm. Small stones force pedestrians to match their steps to the positions of the stones which can be uncomfortable. Larger stones can allow the pedestrian space to adjust their stride subtlely without feeling uncomfortable.

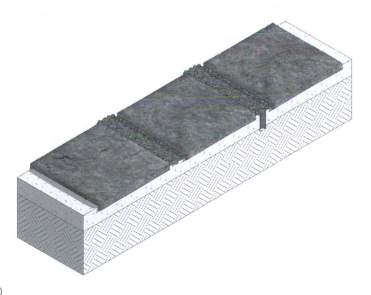

Figure 2.30 (Continued)

(Continued)

Paving slabs on hardcore

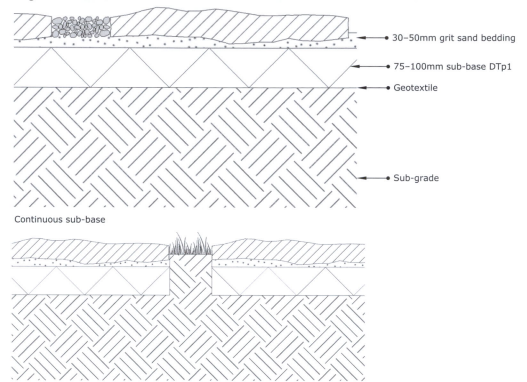

• 30–50mm grit sand bedding

• 75–100mm sub-base DTp1

• Geotextile

• Sub-grade

Continuous sub-base

Localised sub-base support

In practice, it is easier and more economical to build off a continuous sub-base rather than have localised support. A single excavation is easier to make and paving levels are readily adjusted.

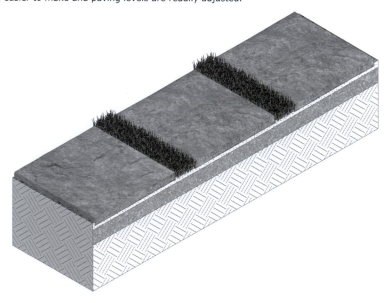

Figure 2.30 (Continued)

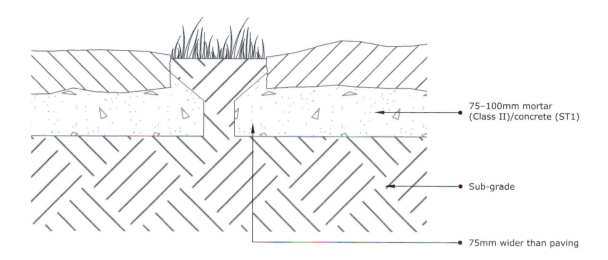

75–100mm mortar (Class II)/concrete (ST1)

Sub-grade

75mm wider than paving

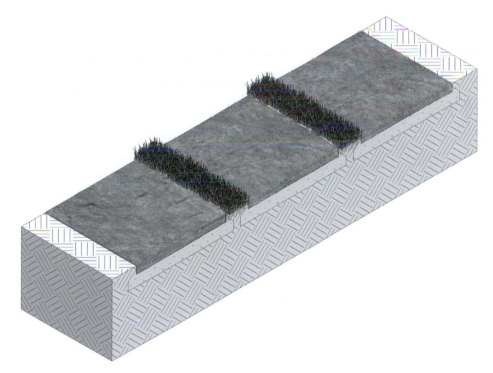

Figure 2.30 (Continued)

(Continued)

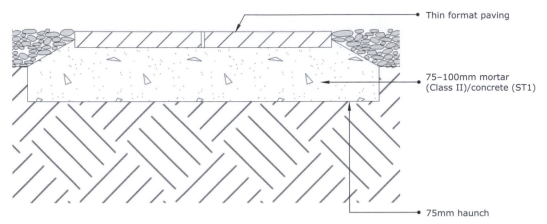

Thin format paving

75–100mm mortar
(Class II)/concrete (ST1)

75mm haunch

Decorative paving is supplied in a wide range of style and formats. Narrow, thin or small format paving is best laid onto a mortar (Class II) or concrete (ST1/C30) bed.

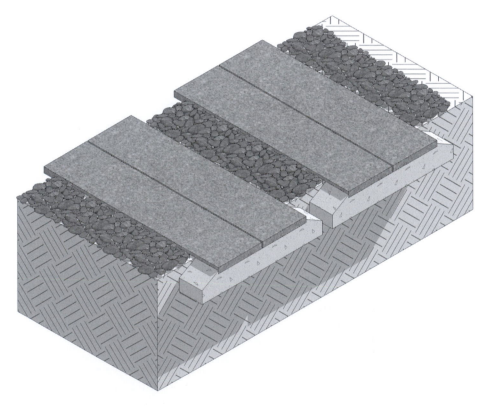

Figure 2.30 (Continued)

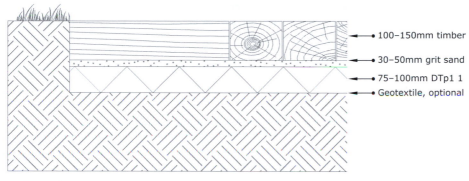

→ 100–150mm timber

→ 30–50mm grit sand

→ 75–100mm DTp1 1

→ Geotextile, optional

Timber can be used as a paving surface, with care. In the right location a timber pavement can weather and wear well, but placed in a damp or shady location, it can be a hazard.

A well-prepared sub-base is essential to keep the timber level and to dissipate rainfall so that the timber has the opportunity to dry out. A basket weave bond reduces the risk of slipping by introducing cross-grain.

A 3–5mm gap, filled with grit sand, will help water drainage as well as timber expansion. Joints will need to be recharged as the timber weathers.

Figure 2.31 Timber block paving

References

Standards and regulations

BS 1339:2003 Concrete paving flags

BS 1377:4 Soils for civil engineering purposes

BS 6297 Method for digging trial pits to access percolation rate of ground

BS 7533-13:2009 Pavements constructed with clay, natural stone or concrete pavers. Guide for the design of permeable pavements constructed with concrete paving blocks and flags, natural stone slabs and setts and clay pavers

BS 7997 Construction standards for tactile paving in clay, concrete and stone

BS 8301:1985 Code of Practice for Building Drainage

BS EN 752:2008 Surface water drainage and soak-aways

BS EN 1338:2003 Concrete paving blocks: Requirements and test methods

BS EN 1339 Tactile paving

BS EN 1341:2012 Slabs of natural stone for external paving

Building Regulations, Part H, 2002

DIN 19580 European standard for linear drains

Books

Dunnett, N. and Clayden, A. (2007) *Rain Gardens: Managing Water Sustainably in the Garden and Designed Landscape*. Portland, OR: Timber Press,

McCormack, T. (2011) *Driveways, Paths and Patios*. Ramsbury: Crowood Press.

Guidance and advisory publications

BRE Digest 365, DG 365, 'Soak-aways, drainage, rainwater'. Available at: www.eden.gov.uk

CIRIA, *SUDS Manual*. Available at: www.ciria.org/Resources/Free_ publications/the_suds_manual/aspx; www.ciria.com/suds/ ciria_publications.htm#C697

Department of Communities and Local Government (2009) *Guidance on the Permeable Surfacing of Front Gardens*. Available at: www.gov.uk

Department of the Environment and Regions, *Design Manual for Roads and Bridges*, vol. 7, *Pavement Design and Construction* HD 39/01. Available at: www.standardsforhighways.co.uk

Department of Transport (2006) *Practical Guide to Streets Works*. London: TSO.

Department of Transport and Regions (2007) *Guidance on the Use of Tactile Paving Surfaces*. London: TSO.

Disabled Persons Act 1981

Local Transport Note 2/95 *The Design of Pedestrian Crossings*. Available at: www.gov.uk

Planning Policy Guidance Note 25 (PPG25) SUDTraffic Advisory Leaflet, 'Audible and Tactile Signals', 491 and 5/91.

Traffic Measures in Historic Towns. Available at: www. historictownsforum.org

Traffic Signs Regulations and General Directions. Available at: www.tsrgd.co.uk (there is a free multi-platform App of this document)

Suppliers

www.breedon-special-aggregates.co.uk   self binding gravel

www.drainageonline.co.uk   drainage materials

www.marshalls .co.uk   paving materials

www.stowellconcrete.co.uk   concrete products

www.thomasarmstrong.co.uk   permeable paving solutions

www.tobermore.co.uk   paving materials

www.ultrascape.co.uk   rigid and flexible paving

Online resources

www.pathsforall.org.uk/pfa/glossary-of-path-construction-terminology/glossary-of-path-www.construction-terminology-a-z.html   A useful glossary of paving terms

www.pavingexpert.com   Probably the best practical guide to the construction of paths, drives and roads

www.paving.org.uk   Interpave, precast concrete paving and kerb association, permeable paving guidance

Trade bodies and associations

www.bali.co.uk   British Association of Landscape Industries

www.ciria.org/suds   CIRIA independent research on permeable paving

www.environment-agency.gov.uk/ppg   Government advice on water and environmental issues

www.environment-agency.gov.uk/suds   Government advice on SUDS

www.interlay.org.uk   Independent association of block paving contractors

www.paving.org   Trade association for block paving manufacturers

www.planningportal.gov.uk/house   Planning permission guidance

www.qpa.org   Quarry Products Association

www.rhs.org.uk   Royal Horticultural Society

www.sepa.org.uk   Scottish Environment Agency

www.susdrain.org   Community for sustainable drainage

www.ukrha.org   Rain Water Management Association

Addresses

Joint Mobility Unit
Royal National Institute for the Blind
224 Great Portland Street
London W1N 6AA
www.rnib.org.uk

Mobility and Inclusion Unit
Department for Transport
Great Minster House
76 Marsham Street
London SW1P 4DR

CHAPTER 3

Drainage channels

INTRODUCTION

Drainage is used to expedite the removal of surface water that might otherwise accumulate causing standing water and the inherent, associated problems of staining, surface damage and algae growth. Standing may percolate through a paved surface and accumulate in the construction courses below. Aggregates may be washed out, creating voids as well as the potential for damage through seasonal freezing. Legislation gives guidance on the removal and dispersal of surface and sub-surface water and these directives are listed in the resources at the end of this chapter. Knowledge of the correct drainage systems, materials and techniques is an essential skill for designers. Products for **civils** (i.e. public) and private/landscape use vary; what might suit a driveway will not necessarily be adequate for higher frequency use or larger catchment areas.

There are three classifications of drained water:

- foul (kitchen and bathroom);
- surface (roof and paved areas);
- combined.

In the UK, modern properties typically have separate foul and surface drainage systems but older properties, or where drainage systems are shared, may use combined systems. It is acceptable to connect a drainage outlet to a shared system but not to either a foul or surface drain, where they are separate. The drainage of properties is a subject covered elsewhere and requires specialist knowledge of the types of materials, construction techniques and the applicable legislation and regulations.

It is important to set out channel lines/radii to be clear and unambiguous with easily obtained reference points.

The location of each drain must be accurately specified, along with the necessary fall/gradient. Interconnected drains must be accurately considered in terms of the direction of flow, gradients and accumulated water volumes. Having designed a drainage scheme, it may be necessary to amend the paving patterns or gradients in the wearing surfaces to suit the finalised locations of drains, channels and gullies. There is a wide variety of designs and styles available, whether open or enclosed, discreet or as a feature. It is easy to design or specify an inappropriate channel. Gradient references, datum points and the location of service ducting are necessary considerations.

Paved areas must be laid to a suitable fall to direct water to the surface drainage channel or gutter. In small areas, traditional open stone or sett channels can look good as well as being relatively easy and inexpensive to construct. For larger areas, the consequences of an ill-specified drain are considerable, and so care must be taken in the specification and design of a drain/gutter. Rough surface materials might not permit the required flow across larger surfaces and longer runs. Commercially produced systems are available that can have decorative materials included in their construction to disguise their presence or incorporate them into the surrounding scheme. Any channel can be adapted to form part of a trim or edge. Small areas of paving can be designed to shed water to the perimeters where channels and gullies can be discreet. Larger surfaces may require the incorporation of surface drains within the paved areas. The design of these features is critical so that there is no risk that users will fall or trip in the paved areas. Particular attention needs to be given to disabled and visually impaired users, even if the space is for private use. The good practice and design guidelines given by the

Building Regulations and other advisory bodies should be followed.

ANCILLARY FIXTURES

Channels, by necessity, must be interrupted and intersected and the connections to drain systems and **soak-aways** require detailed consideration. Drains and gullies, as supplied by manufacturers, almost always have a range of components that allow for connection or integration with other units and materials. When such a drainage system is specified, always specify any associated accessories. Most manufacturers have an NBS (National Building Specification or equivalent) document that will include a full list of any products associated with the principal drainage units. While the NBS reference number and sheets may not be pertinent for use in all landscaping specifications and in particular for small and domestic schemes, the information is easily adapted for inclusion into other specification documents (such as the Heather Model Specification for Garden Design).

MATERIALS

Concrete

Many products, such as **PCC (precast concrete)** units are available in several unit sizes. Small format paved surfaces can be complemented by the use of similar-sized drainage channels. These are laid in a similar fashion to the paved areas. For larger pedestrian or vehicular areas, yard-long units were traditionally used in the UK. These are now available in decimal equivalents (914 or 915mm), although most manufacturers additionally offer standard metric-sized units (e.g. 1000mm, 1500mm). Concrete products that are likely to be subject to de-icing salts should be **hydraulically** pressed. Some manufacturers make products that specifically resist de-icing salts and other aggressive surface treatments. Concrete blocks used in the sub-surface construction of drains should conform to BS EN 1338:2003.

Clay

Clay bricks for channels and water containment should be solid, with durability designation FL (under BS 3921) or F2/S2 under BS EN 771-4:2011, strength class 5. While impervious, clay can be fragile and limited in colour. Its use has become somewhat limited to civil applications or where a particular aesthetic is required.

Plastic

uPVC, in a range of colours is the predominant material used for sub-surface drainage systems. It is flexible and a cheap alternative to the historic use of clay and concrete. Drains laid in excess of 1.2m are likely to require the use of rigid plastic pipes to prevent the mass of backfill materials from causing collapse. While plastic is not used for surface drains, enclosed channels in concrete or composite stone can be lined with uPVC pipes.

Slot drains are usually formed from a metal (stainless steel or galvanised) cover which fits into a sub-surface channel. These channels are constructed from PCC, plastic composites or metal. Additional decorative grates are available in a range of materials, from weathered steel to composite stone in a range of styles and colours. The grating must comply with the required performance class (see **linear/slot drains**).

LINEAR OR SLOT DRAINS

Linear, or slot, drainage is frequently used in paved areas and may be discreet or decorative. There are two types of linear drain:

- Those that are laid flat, having no integral fall. These are best suited to small areas.

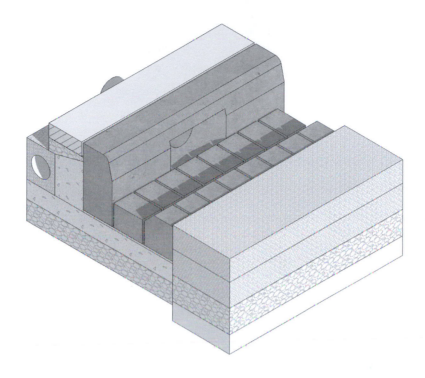

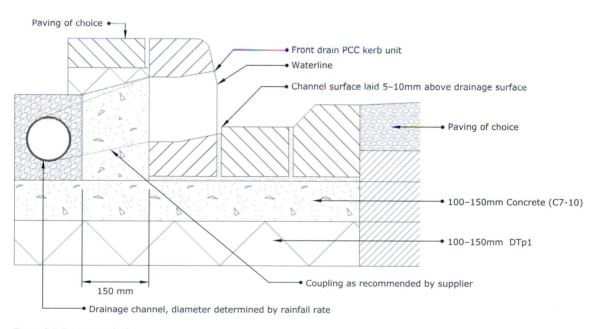

Paving of choice

Front drain PCC kerb unit

Waterline

Channel surface laid 5–10mm above drainage surface

Paving of choice

100–150mm Concrete (C7-10)

100–150mm DTp1

Coupling as recommended by supplier

150 mm

Drainage channel, diameter determined by rainfall rate

Figure 3.1 Drainage at kerbs

(Continued)

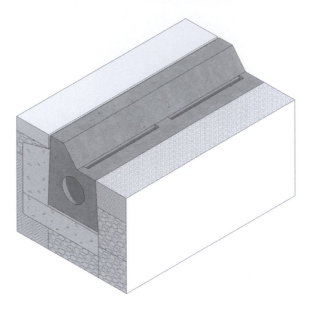

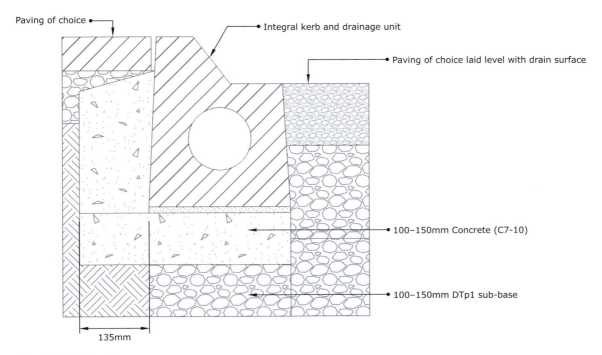

Paving of choice

Integral kerb and drainage unit

Paving of choice laid level with drain surface

100–150mm Concrete (C7-10)

100–150mm DTp1 sub-base

135mm

Figure 3.1 (Continued)

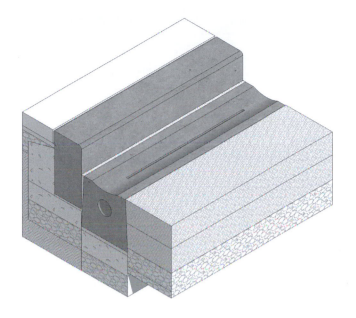

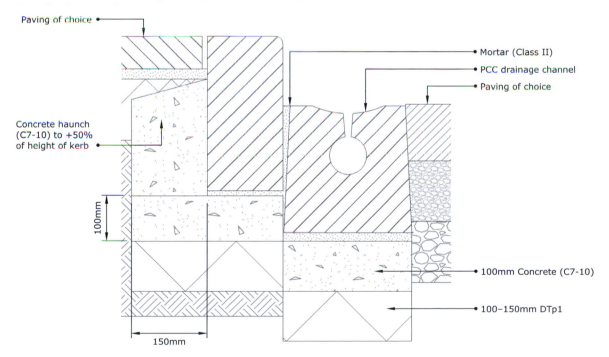

Paving of choice

Mortar (Class II)

PCC drainage channel

Paving of choice

Concrete haunch
(C7-10) to +50%
of height of kerb

100mm

150mm

100mm Concrete (C7-10)

100–150mm DTp1

Figure 3.1 (Continued)

Table 3.1 Strength classification of linear drains

Class	Load kN	Application
A	15	Pedestrians & cyclists
B	125	Car parks, driveways
C	250	Light industrial parks, service stations
D	400	All public highways
E	600	Heavy commercial
F	900	Exceptional loads, airports, freight yards

- Those laid to follow the fall of a paved area, thereby introducing a fall in the direction of flow. Drains with integral fall are designed for larger flat areas such as car parks.

Linear drains and gratings carry their own unique class rating (see Table 3.1) and the overall construction rating of a linear drain is determined by the loading class of the weakest component used, e.g. a C-rated grating used on a B-rated channel would give an overall B rating. While products may appear to be similar, they may have been manufactured to differing specifications to suit their intended applications. Linear drains usually are set on a concrete (C25) race. The bed thickness will be determined by the load class of the drain, and the manufacturer will be able to advise on this detail.

Drains have a flow capacity, using a typical rainfall intensity value for the UK of 50–75mm/hr. This capacity is quoted in litres/second (l/sec). Most standard (100mm diameter) landscape drains have a discharge rate of 5l/s (based on the UK typical rainfall intensity value) and are therefore more than adequate for paved areas up to 200msq. On larger areas, additional factors, such as the material roughness of the channel need to be accounted for. Catch pits and traps should be provided upstream of the main drain to prevent silt and grit from entering the system. All manufacturers will have technical support to assist in the selection of a drain with suitable capacity.

To calculate the linear drain requirements, the rainfall rates r (mm/hr), and area being drained A (m²) are required. The run-off capacity (Q) is measured in litres per second:

$$Q \text{ (run-off capacity)} = (A \times r)/3600$$

r = 75mm (UK rainfall intensity/hr)[1] or 0.014l/sec/msq[1] may be assumed for normal situations. Building Regulations, Part H, section 3 offers guidance on areas of high risk or in exposed locations.

A = area to be drained in M²

$$Q = (95 \times 75)/3600 = 2.0 \text{ litres per second}$$

Most slot drains have a run-off capacity of +2.5l/s. The drain must be laid to the manufacturers' recommended gradient. It is good practice to install a P-trap at the end of a linear drain to eliminate odours.

Covers and gratings for drainage channels can be problematic for blind people and visually impaired pedestrians as they may interpret the channels as a tactile surface. The recommended slot openings in a grating should be 13mm wide or less and 150mm long, ideally orientated at right angles to the direction of travel. Any grating should also be heel-safe. Channel covers and slot or linear drains should be positioned as far from main pedestrian flows as is practical. Most metal grating systems have a locking mechanism or use special headed fixings to prevent theft. Any inspection or service covers should be set flush to the adjoining paved surface. Channel gratings/covers should be installed approximately 5mm below the surrounding paved area to allow for settlement and prevent water accumulating at the interface of paving and drainage channels.

Pavements and surfaces should drain away from a building where possible. However, where necessary, a linear drain can be installed in close proximity to a building, 150mm or more, and at a minimum of 150mm below the damp-proof course.

Paving materials should be laid tight up to a drain with no mortar/concrete. Paving patterns against drains are frequently adjusted so that the drain is emphasised. This may be through the use of an alternative colour block or changing the bond around the drain, a soldier course, for instance. The use of highly textured material alongside a drainage channel can cause surface accumulation, unless the drainage channel is constructed from such materials (e.g. granite setts or natural split stone). Channels

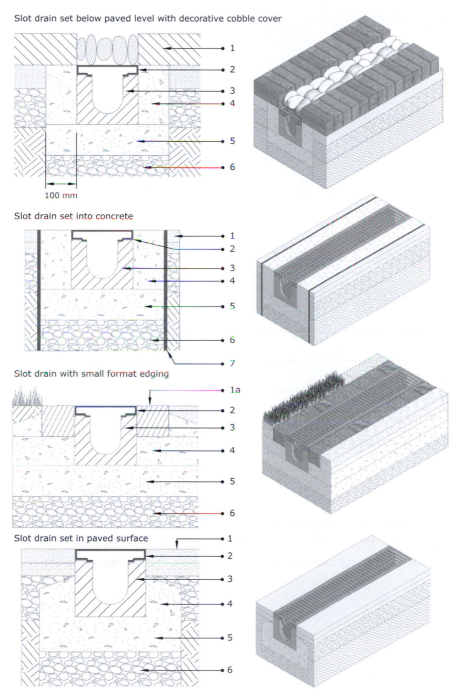

Slot drain set below paved level with decorative cobble cover

100 mm

Slot drain set into concrete

Slot drain with small format edging

Slot drain set in paved surface

1. Paving as selected (1a. sett 3–6mm above drain surface with +50% side haunch)
2. Slot drain cover, specify for applied load (see p. 104)
3. Slot drain channel, specify for applied load (see Table 3.1) and area to drain
4. Concrete (C20–30) haunch
5. C100–150mm concrete foundation (C20–30)
6. 100–150mm sub-base DTp1
7. Expansion joint 6–10mm

Figure 3.2 Slot drains

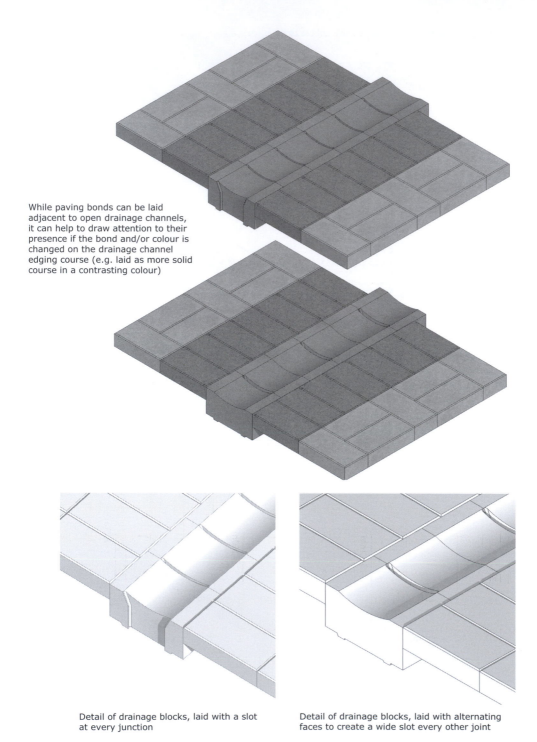

While paving bonds can be laid adjacent to open drainage channels, it can help to draw attention to their presence if the bond and/or colour is changed on the drainage channel edging course (e.g. laid as more solid course in a contrasting colour)

Detail of drainage blocks, laid with a slot at every junction

Detail of drainage blocks, laid with alternating faces to create a wide slot every other joint

Figure 3.3 Open slot drainage channels

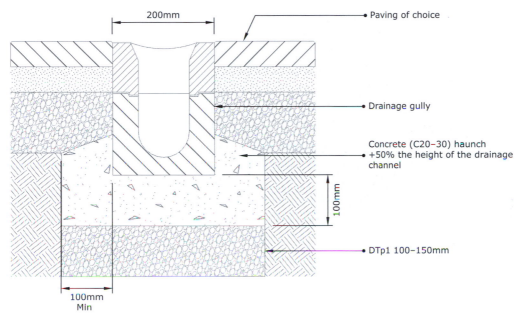

200mm

Paving of choice

Drainage gully

Concrete (C20–30) haunch
+50% the height of the drainage
channel

100mm

DTp1 100–150mm

100mm
Min

Illustrated: Marshalls Landscape drain linear drain system

The paving adjoining the drainage channel should be raised by about 6mm to allow surface water to 'fall' into the drain. The depth of the drainage gully will be determined by the size of the area served by the channel. A range of depths is available.

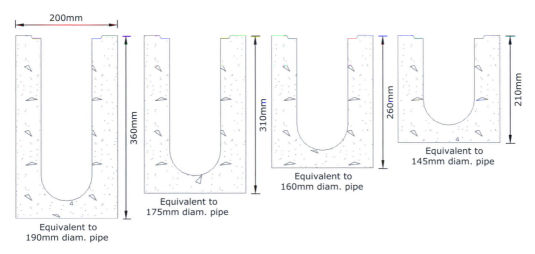

200mm

360mm

Equivalent to
190mm diam. pipe

310mm

Equivalent to
175mm diam. pipe

260mm

Equivalent to
160mm diam. pipe

210mm

Equivalent to
145mm diam. pipe

Figure 3.3 (Continued)

(Continued)

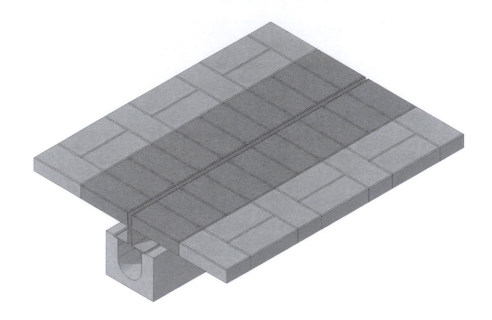

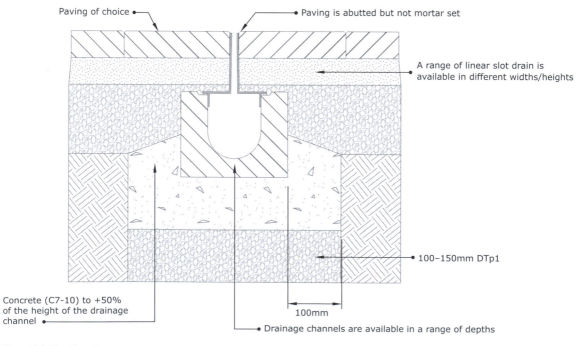

Paving of choice

Paving is abutted but not mortar set

A range of linear slot drain is available in different widths/heights

100–150mm DTp1

Concrete (C7-10) to +50% of the height of the drainage channel

100mm

Drainage channels are available in a range of depths

Figure 3.3 (Continued)

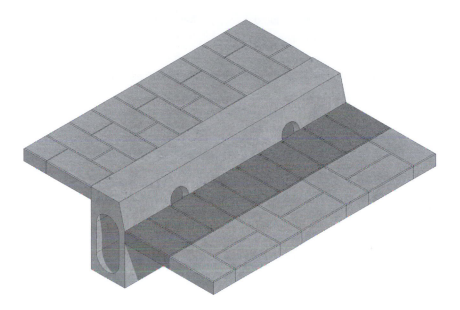

Units that are a combined drain and kerb are available in a range of sizes for use at the edges of carriageways. Often referred to as **Beany** blocks (or Mini Beanys), after the civil engineer who designed the first combined drains. Some designs separate the upper kerb section from the lower channel, allowing different capacity channels to be used.

The correct connection and interface components must also be specified, these can be advised by the manufacturer/supplier. Kerbs should comply with BS 1340 and be laid in accordance with BS 7533-6.

All highway works and construction should comply with the relevant local or national specification (UK Specification for Highway Works, vol. 1, Kerbs, Footways and Paved Areas), in addition (UK) Building Regulations Part H will apply to drainage and water management.

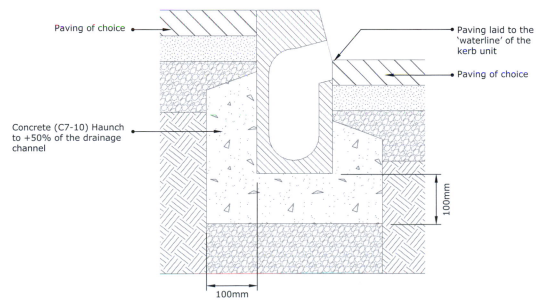

Figure 3.3 (Continued)

lined or constructed of rough surface materials should have an increased gradient to improve the discharge of surface water, 1:40 or greater.

Highway drainage should comply with BS EN 1433 (drainage channels for vehicular and pedestrian areas) and BS EN 752-4.

CHANNEL FREQUENCY

The spacing of **gullies**, drains and channels for public highways and pathways is determined by the local highway authority and is based on the highway camber, **gradient** and the area to be drained.

A simple formula for this is:

Gully spacing = (280 √s)/w

Where

s (%) = highway gradient
w = width (m)
Example: if s = 1.5%, w = 5.00m
Gully spacing = (280 × √1.5)/5 = 68.6m

For paved areas, one gully for every 200msq of surface catchment is a suitable starting point for any calculations. Additional gullies will be required where gradients are steeper than 1:20, flatter than 1:150 and where drainage from adjacent areas is introduced.

GRADIENT

The drainage gradient for a pavement is nominally 1:40 (25mm per metre). Large areas that are laid with block or brick paving can drain at up to 1:80 whereas **Tarmac** will hold water and a gradient of 1:40, or steeper will perform better.

A longitudinal fall of 1:40 and a transverse fall of 1:80 are typical for large areas. A combined fall of 1:60 would be adequate for smaller garden areas.

Minimum falls are:

- for footpath drainage 1:40;
- for road drainage (150mm drains) 1:60 (225mm drains) 1:90.

Gullies should always be positioned upstream of the tangent point at road junctions, where there is a low point and at obstacles, such as traffic calming structures. All drainage of or onto public carriageways will require the approval of the local highways authority.

Surfaces can be treated or finished in a way that encourages positive drainage:

- *Mono-pitch or sheet-like areas*: where the surface has a single slope, the drainage channel would be located at the lowest point of the slope.
- *Duo-pitch or double slope areas*: where two surfaces converge to form a valley with a natural location for a drainage channel. The drainage channel should be placed at the bottom of both slopes. The channels may be connected, as in the case of a valley, or separate if there is a sufficient distance between the bottom of both slopes.
- *Camber or crown drainage*: A raised surface encourages surface drainage down both sides and to edge/perimeter drains. This is a common treatment on roads and ramps where the kerb forms an upstand and the drainage is located there.

Large flat areas can use a series of 'valleys and troughs' to create a concave profile with the drain located at the junction, in the valley. This effectively directs water away from buildings but can create awkward changes in surface direction. The summits should be a minimum 150mm below the damp-proof course level.

Pavements should be drained in a preferred hierarchy:

- adjacent open ground (if suitable and not land belonging to a third party);
- **SUDS**-specific structure (soak-away, **attenuation** cells, etc.);
- **permeable** paving.

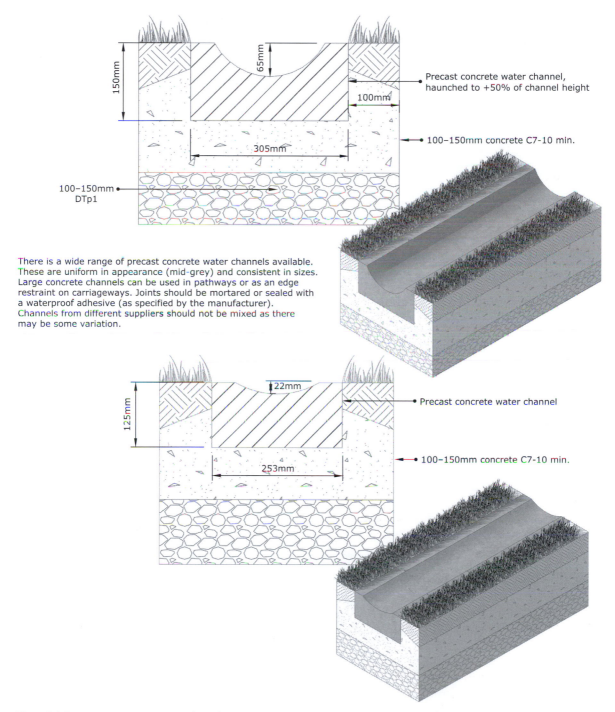

150mm

65mm

Precast concrete water channel, haunched to +50% of channel height

100mm

100–150mm concrete C7-10 min.

305mm

100–150mm DTp1

There is a wide range of precast concrete water channels available. These are uniform in appearance (mid-grey) and consistent in sizes. Large concrete channels can be used in pathways or as an edge restraint on carriageways. Joints should be mortared or sealed with a waterproof adhesive (as specified by the manufacturer). Channels from different suppliers should not be mixed as there may be some variation.

125mm

22mm

Precast concrete water channel

100–150mm concrete C7-10 min.

253mm

Figure 3.4 Precast concrete open water channels

(Continued)

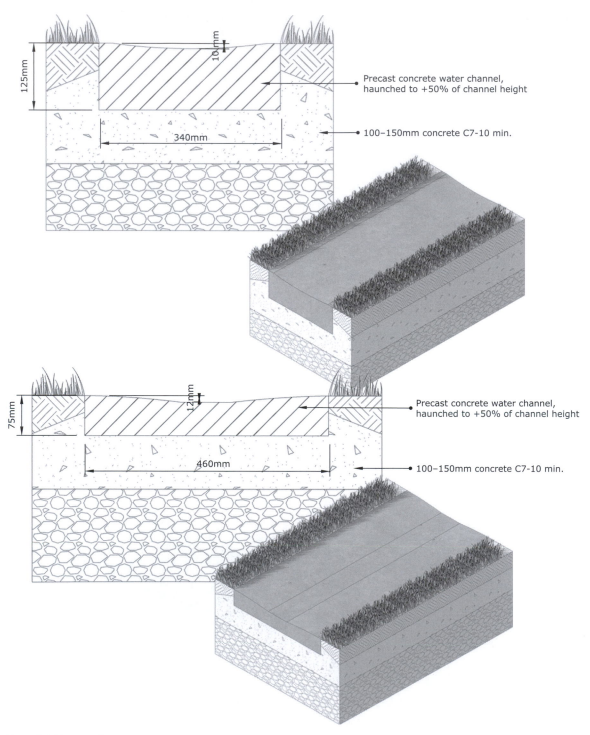

125mm

10mm

Precast concrete water channel, haunched to +50% of channel height

340mm

100–150mm concrete C7-10 min.

75mm

12mm

Precast concrete water channel, haunched to +50% of channel height

460mm

100–150mm concrete C7-10 min.

Figure 3.4 (Continued)

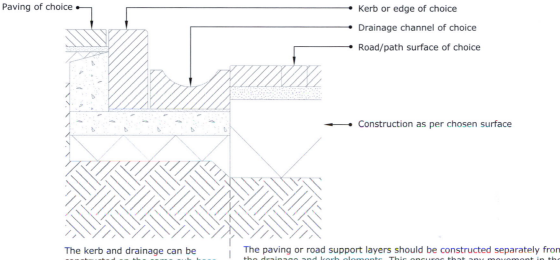

Paving of choice —•

Kerb or edge of choice

Drainage channel of choice

Road/path surface of choice

Construction as per chosen surface

The kerb and drainage can be constructed on the same sub-base and concrete foundation.

The paving or road support layers should be constructed separately from the drainage and kerb elements. This ensures that any movement in the paved area is constrained by the edging structures, that it does not flatten or fail.

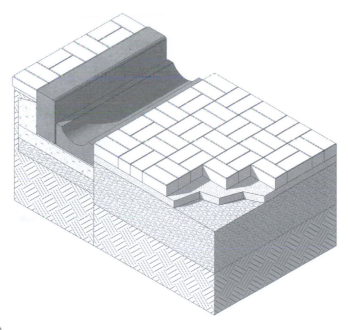

Figure 3.4 (Continued)

(Continued)

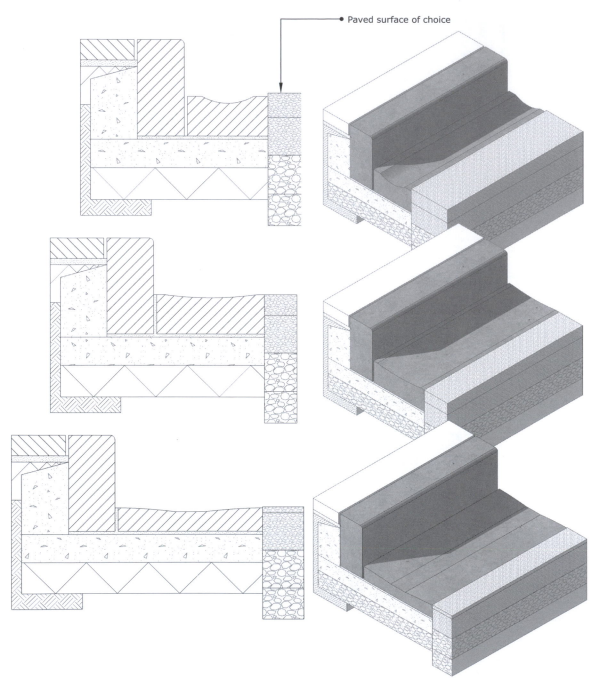

Paved surface of choice

Figure 3.4 (Continued)

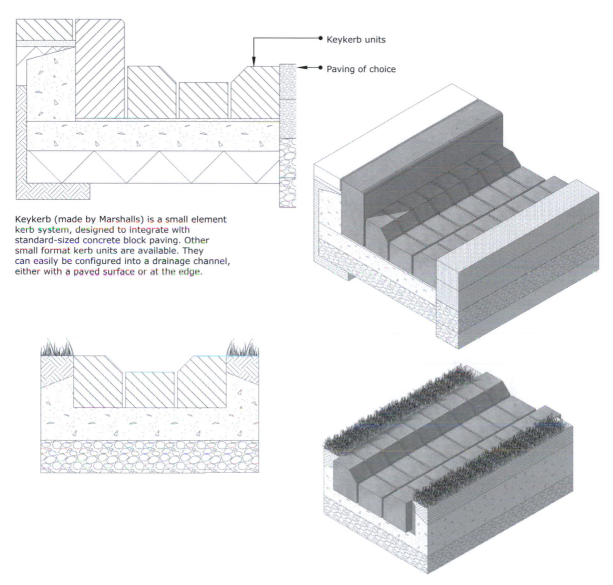

Keykerb units

Paving of choice

Keykerb (made by Marshalls) is a small element kerb system, designed to integrate with standard-sized concrete block paving. Other small format kerb units are available. They can easily be configured into a drainage channel, either with a paved surface or at the edge.

Figure 3.4 (Continued)

It is not permissible to drain onto land belonging to a third party, and if an area is more than 1.5m wide, consider diverting run-off in two directions.

SUDS

SUDS (sustainable urban drainage systems) are designed to manage rainfall and surface water accumulation close to the area that receives the rainfall. Water is slowed or attenuated as it tries to enter the natural water-table or water courses, thereby reducing the immediate impact on the urban drainage systems.

Permeable paving typically uses modified block paving to create a drive or path, but recently porous asphalt and resin bonded products have become available. Sites prone to waterlogging are unsuitable for permeable surfaces and are best drained in a more traditional manner.

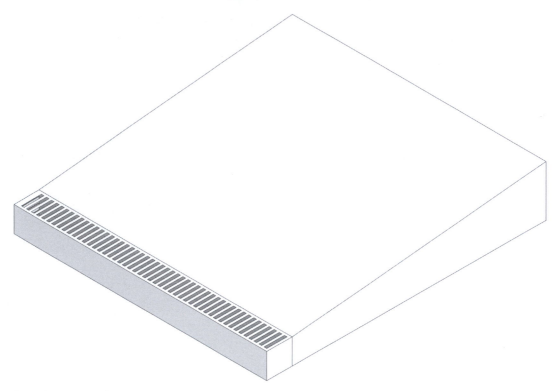

Figure 3.5 Mono-pitch

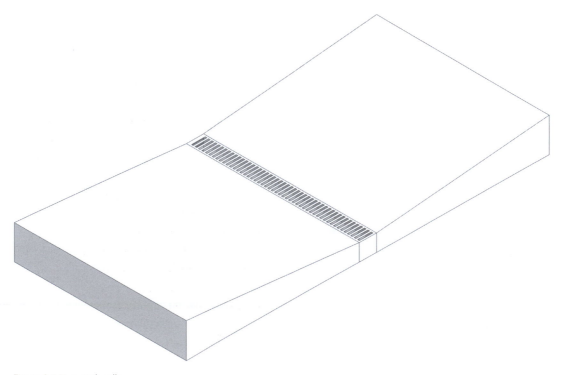

Figure 3.6 Duo-pitch valley

SOAK-AWAYS

Soak-aways were discussed in Chapter 2 and are not of use in heavy clay soils, or when the water-table is very high. It is pointless specifying a soak-away where it will not work. The success of a soak-away is determined by the environment, the type of soil/sub-grade, the size of the area to be drained, the rate water percolates through the soil and the level of the existing water-table.

Soak-aways must do the following:

- be at the lowest point of a drain system;
- be at least 5 metres away from any building (BS EN 7521-4);
- not saturate the foundations of any structure;
- be constructed so that the base is permanently above the water-table;
- not cause any risk of contamination from pollutants.

A basic formula to determine soak-away volume is:

$$Vol = \text{area drained(msq)} \times \text{(storm rainfall rate (mm)}/3000)$$

In the UK, the storm rainfall rate is 50–75mm/h.[1] For example:

$$\text{Volume required} = 75\text{msq} \times (50/3000) = 1.25\text{m}^3$$

It is not acceptable to tap into a soak-away located on adjoining land/in another property. Traditional soak-aways are filled with large bits of rubble and clean granular material (no fines); there is usually 30–50% void. Such material will settle, and soak-aways made this way should not be located under patios or driveways. A modern equivalent are crate-type systems; these have up to 95% void and are designed to be structural. They can be located under patios and driveways and have a much longer life in service.

Construction Products Regulation (CPR), which came into effect in 2013, is a European-wide standard that requires construction products, as listed in the standard, to have clear information and comply to a minimum safety and performance regulation. Such products will have full documentation and specifications available and carry a CE mark.

An integral part of EN 1433 is the installation requirements and concrete surround (haunch). All combined kerb and drainage units must be tested for watertightness, being sealed and attached to one another with a proprietary adhesive or mastic, as specified by the manufacturer and laid to their recommendations. As with **kerbs** and edging, the rear haunch is critical for the longevity and performance of a drainage channel or combined kerb; the height, strength and slump of the concrete required will vary between manufacturers and should not be assumed to be compatible.

All drainage must be tested prior to final haunching and again before project completion, to ensure no leakage or ponding water. Drainage channels must run clean and be free from debris before the project is signed off.

SUB-SURFACE DRAINS

The stability of the drains in any paved area relies on the strength and durability of both the wearing surface and that of the sub-grade. Sub-grades can be adversely affected by water and it may be necessary to install two drainage systems; a surface water drain and a subsoil drain. The ground excavation, compaction and the grade of materials used in sub-grade structures should be specified. A subsoil/grade drain, typically called a French drain, is a generic term for a perforated/slotted pipe encased in a gravel-filled trench.

Such land drainage can be used to collect and disperse excess sub-surface water. Drains are typically installed with a minimum slope of 1:100 to 1:200 towards the outfall. Land drains are best constructed from the outfall point, i.e. 'uphill'. Excess surface water can be discharged to a suitable area, called a 'leach field'. The area over which the dispersal system must be laid is determined by the percolation rate of the soil and the size of the septic tank. Such a tank is necessary to collect and retain particulates and contaminants prior to dispersal. Dispersal systems are invariably 'closed systems' with no outlet point, designed so that the water is evenly distributed throughout the land drain system.

A modern and more effective version of the French drain is the Fin drain. These are comprised of a rigid 'geo-grid' or corrugated sheet, between bonded layers of **geotextile**. They act as an industrial-scale slot drain. This collection drain directs water to a subsoil perforated pipe, embedded in gravel. The corrugated core comes in a range of widths and therefore capacities. The membranes block the soil particles from entering the drain while allowing water through. Fin drains can reduce the need for backfill in a trench and, with the right trenching equipment, can reduce excavation time and costs. Fin drains are very discreet, they can be located along the edge of a path, between the paving and the soil and used to capture and disperse run-off from a path where it would otherwise sit in the margin and form ponds.

On a domestic scale, such a collection or interceptor drain should be located to collect groundwater or surface run-off before it enters a garden. Typically these are laid just inside a boundary fence, where the surrounding land is higher or there is evidence of the direction of ground water travel, occasional flooding from a field, for instance. The capacity of a 250–300mm-wide trench is more than adequate for most situations, an over-wide trench will give little advantage.

Trenches should preferably be lined with a geotextile; while not essential, it will prolong the life of the drain. An exception is where such drains are installed in hard water areas. The calcium carbonate dissolved in the water will be deposited onto the geotexile and quickly will reduce the effectiveness of the drain. The drainage pipe should be checked for gradient before the side and backfill are added. Limestone chippings are not suitable as the aggregate trench fill, as the calcium carbonate can block pipe perforations. Where a geotextile has not been used, a catch-pit should be considered to remove sediments. The depth of an interceptor drain will be determined by the depth of the water-table present. A test hole will help establish this (see discussion of trial pits in Chapter 2). Excavations deeper than 1m must be protected and, where required, covered by a **CDM** risk assessment.

The colour of a drainage pipe is only important for commercial work. Rigid plastic or clay pipes should always be used at depths greater than 1.2m and where the weight of the surface material or traffic would crush a flexible or perforated plastic pipe.

It can be useful to establish if existing drains are present and functioning. Any existing drains should be traced, if possible, to determine if they might be ignored or can be repaired, with perforated pipe or filter drain.

Outfalls

Discharge should, ideally, be to a soak-away or other infiltration system where practicable. Discharge into a water course may require the consent of the Local Authority or the Environment Agency in the UK, who can impose a limit on the rate of any discharge. Where other forms of discharge are not possible, the Local Authority and Building Inspector should be consulted. It is almost never permitted for land drainage to discharge into a combined or a foul water system although connection to the surface water system may be permitted in some circumstances. Water authorities will have recommended specifications for outfalls and regulations on discharge and must be consulted before commencing work.

Surfaces located around buildings and in public spaces are usually impermeable. Water landing on these surfaces has to be accommodated and managed so as not to cause a problem, inconvenience or hazard. Constructed areas should be developed in such a way as to maximise the use of existing permeable areas, attenuating surface water run-off.

Where free draining or porous paved surfaces are not possible, impervious materials should be used with gullies and channels discharging into a drainage system. Gullies should be provided at the low points where water would otherwise accumulate. Intermediate channels should be installed at intervals close enough to ensure that channels do not become overloaded and that the depth of flow does not exceed the channel capacity. The size of the channels should be designed to accommodate both typical and surge rainfall. The hazards associated with open channels, and the mobility of pedestrians and

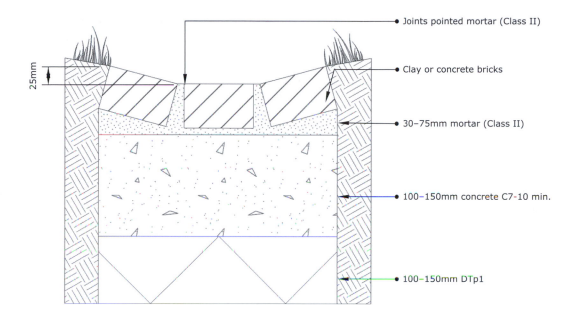

25mm

- Joints pointed mortar (Class II)
- Clay or concrete bricks
- 30–75mm mortar (Class II)
- 100–150mm concrete C7-10 min.
- 100–150mm DTp1

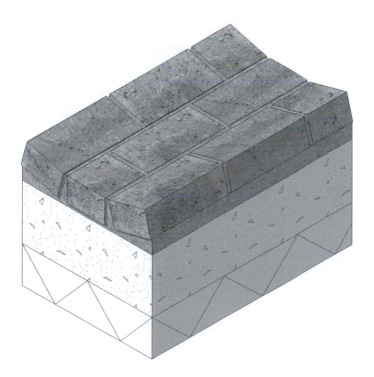

Figure 3.7 Brick-lined open channel

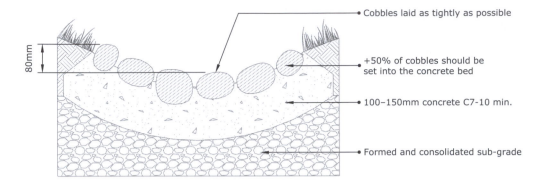

Cobbles laid as tightly as possible

+50% of cobbles should be set into the concrete bed

100–150mm concrete C7-10 min.

Formed and consolidated sub-grade

80mm

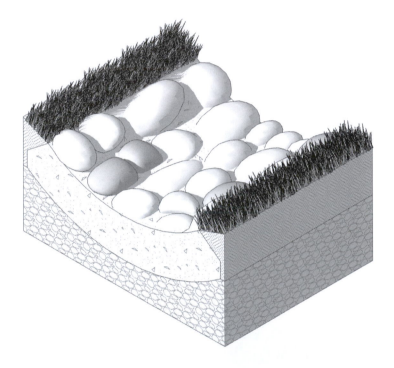

Cobbles and other irregular, natural materials lend a particular aesthetic to a space. The colour and size of the stones should be selected to complement the adjoining pavements and other constructed details. The stones are set into a wet concrete bed and pointing is not necessary. Stones that are elongated should be laid parallel to the direction of the channel. Adjoining land or surfaces should be higher than the drainage channel to allow the movement of surface water into the drain.

Figure 3.8 Cobble-lined open drainage channel

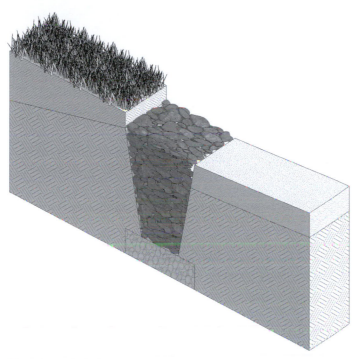

The drainage ditch shown provides catchment from one direction only. The position of the geotextile can be arranged symmetrically to provide catchment from both sides of the trench.

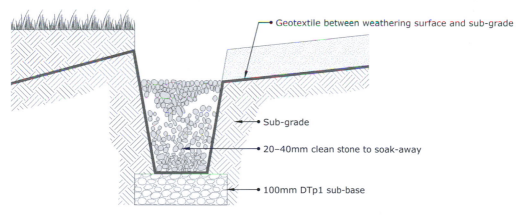

Geotextile between weathering surface and sub-grade

Sub-grade

20–40mm clean stone to soak-away

100mm DTp1 sub-base

Figure 3.9 Open gravel drain

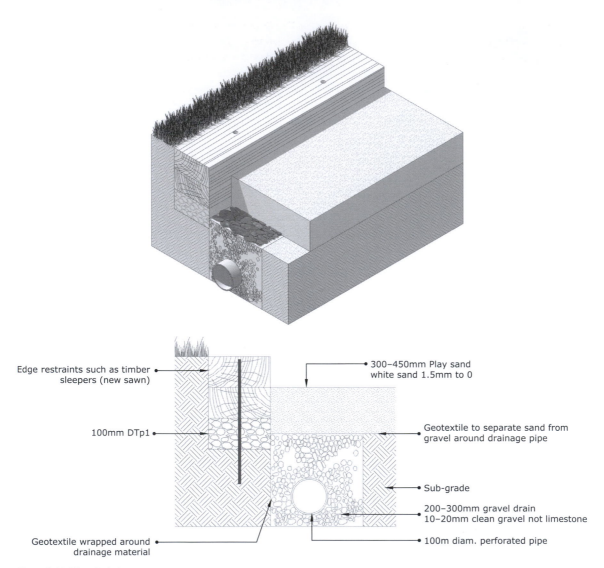

Edge restraints such as timber
sleepers (new sawn)

300–450mm Play sand
white sand 1.5mm to 0

100mm DTp1

Geotextile to separate sand from
gravel around drainage pipe

Sub-grade

200–300mm gravel drain
10–20mm clean gravel not limestone

Geotextile wrapped around
drainage material

100m diam. perforated pipe

Figure 3.10 Play pit drainage

traffic, will require careful consideration and detailing. Additionally, the risks associated with blocked channels, such as slip hazards from damp areas, algae growth or frozen standing water, should be minimised through good design detailing. Drains should have sufficient capacity to cope with the predicted flow. Drains should have a diameter of not less than 75mm for surface water ducts and 100mm, if serving more than one building. Both 75mm and 100mm drains should be laid at not less than 1:100, gradients for larger pipes are given in BS EN 752-4.

NOTE

1   UK stormwater rate (50–75mm is used in practice to accommodate infrequent deluges). Source: Building Regulations, Part H, 2013, section 3.

REFERENCES

Building regulations and advisory documents

BRE Digest 365, DG365, Soak-aways, drainage, rainwater
BRE Digest 365, DG365, Soak-aways design updated, 2003
Building Regulations, Part H, 2002, with 2010 amendments, Drainage and waste disposal
Building Regulations, Part M, 2013, Access to and use of buildings
CIRIA publication C522. Sustainable urban drainage systems design manual, 2000
Good Building Guide, GBG 42, Part 1, Reed bed design and construction, 2000
Highway Agency IAN117/8, Combined drainage
Planning Policy Guidance Note 25 (PPG25), SUDS
Scottish Building Regulations, Section 4

British (BS) and Combined European (BS EN) Standards

BS 65:1991 Specification for vitrified clay pipes, fittings and ducts, also flexible mechanical joints for use solely with surface water pipes and fittings

BS 1196:1989 Specification for clay-ware field drain pipes and junctions
BS 1339:2003 concrete paving flags requirements
BS 3921 designation and selection of bricks
BS 4660:2000 Thermoplastics ancillary fittings of nominal sizes 110 and 160 for below ground gravity drainage and sewerage
BS 4962:1989 Specification for plastics pipes and fittings for use as subsoil field drains
BS 5328-1 and 2 and 5 Concrete guide to specifications
BS 5911 Precast concrete pipes
BS 5911 Concrete pipes and ancillary concrete products:
   Part 1: 2002+A2:2010: Specification for unreinforced and reinforced concrete pipes and fittings with flexible joints (complementary to BS EN 1916:2002)
   Part 3: Specification for unreinforced and reinforced concrete manholes and soak-aways (complementary to BS EN 1917:2002)
   Part 4: Specification for unreinforced and reinforced concrete inspection chambers (complementary to BS EN 1917:2002)
   Part 5: 2004+A1:2010 Specification for prestressed non-pressure pipes and fittings with flexible joints
   Part 6: 2004+A1:2010 Concrete pipes and ancillary concrete products. Specification for road gullies and gully cover slabs
BS 6297: 2007 +A1: 2008 Code of practice for the design and installation of drainage fields for use in wastewater treatment
BS 7158 Plastics inspection chambers for drains and sewers
BS 8000-13 Workmanship on building sites for above ground drainage
BS 8000-14 workmanship on buildings sites for below ground drainage
BS 8110 structural use of concrete
BS EN 295-1 to 6:1991 Requirements for vitrified clay pipes and fittings and pipe joints for drains and sewers:
BS EN 752:2008 Drain and sewer systems outside buildings
BS EN 7521-4 Drain and sewer systems outside buildings
BS EN 771-4 2011 Specification for masonry units
BS EN 12056-3:2000 Gravity drainage systems inside buildings. Roof drainage, layout and calculation
BS EN 124:1994 Gully tops and manhole tops for vehicular and pedestrian areas. Design requirements, type testing, marking, quality control (was BS 497)
BS EN 1253-1:2003 Gullies for buildings
BS EN 1338:2003 Concrete paving blocks
BS EN 13476-3:2007+A1:2009 Plastics piping systems for non-pressure underground drainage and sewerage. Structured-wall piping systems of unplasticized poly(vinyl chloride) (PVC-U), polypropylene (PP) and polyethylene (PE). Specifications for pipes and fittings with smooth internal and profiled external surface and the system, Type B

BS EN 13508-1:2012 Investigation and assessment of drain and sewer systems outside buildings. General Requirements

BS EN 13508-2:2003+A1:2011 Investigation and assessment of drain and sewer systems outside buildings. Visual inspection coding system

BS EN 13598-1:2010 Plastics piping systems for non-pressure underground drainage and sewerage. Unplasticized poly(vinyl chloride) (PVC-U), polypropylene (PP) and polyethylene (PE). Specifications for ancillary fittings including shallow inspection chambers

BS EN 13598-2:2009 Plastics piping systems for non-pressure underground drainage and sewerage. Unplasticized poly(vinyl chloride) (PVC-U), polypropylene (PP) and polyethylene (PE). Specifications for manholes and inspection chambers in traffic areas and deep underground installations

BS EN 1401-1:2009 Plastic piping systems for non-pressure underground drainage and sewerage. Unplasticized poly(vinyl chloride) (PVC-U). Specifications for pipes, fittings and the system

BS EN 1433:2002 Drainage channels for vehicular and pedestrian areas. Classification, design and testing requirements, marking and evaluation of conformity

BS EN 1610:1998 Construction and testing of drains and sewers

BS EN 1852-1:2009 Plastics piping systems for non-pressure underground drainage and sewerage. Polypropylene (PP). Specifications for pipes, fittings and the system

BS EN 1916:2002 Concrete pipes and fittings, unreinforced, steel fibre and reinforced

BS EN 1917:2002 Concrete manholes and inspection chambers

DD CEN/TS 1852-3:2003 Plastics piping systems for non-pressure underground drainage and sewerage. Polypropylene (PP). Guidance for installation

DD ENV 1401-3:2001 Plastics piping systems for non-pressure underground drainage and sewerage. Unplasticized poly(vinylchloride) (PVC-U). Guidance for installation

DIN 19580 European standard for linear drains

Suppliers

www.aco.co.uk   Aco
www.Althon.co.uk   Althon
www.drainageonline.co.uk   Drainage materials
www.graf-water.com/   Rainwater harvesting
www.hauraton.com   Hauraton (lots of construction drawings)
www.lateraldesignstudio.co.uk   Decorative slot drain covers
www.marshalls.co.uk   Marshalls
www.pds-plc.com   Pipeline and drainage systems
www.wadedrainage.co.uk/   Drainage products

Online resources

www.constructionproducts.org.uk   Construction Products Regulation (CPR) July 2013. CE marking and harmonised Standard application for Europe-wide construction products
www.environment-agency.gov.uk   UK Environment Agency
www.lbstock.com/pdfs/portfolio/16-17european.pdf   Bricks: European Standard notes
www.sepa.org.uk   Scottish Environment Agency
www.sfa.wrcplc.co.uk/ceswi-7th-edition.aspx   Sewers for Adoption, 7th Edition
www.susdrain.org   Community for sustainable drainage
www.wras.co.uk   Water regulation advisory scheme (WRAS) Note 09-02-05 identification of pipework for reclaimed water systems

CHAPTER 4

Margins, edges, kerbs and trims

INTRODUCTION

The edge structure is a critical element of any path, road or paved surface. Loose materials will migrate with constant traffic and a surface without an edge support, no matter how well compacted, will sink or locally collapse. An appropriate edge will both retain and maintain the consolidated paving materials and its **sub-base**, across the entire paved surface.

Both flexible and loose paved surfaces require edge restraints. Edge construction is not essential for rigid structures, such as cast concrete, for instance, but often is desirable; adding an aesthetic coherence to a space as well as a convenient location for drainage channels. A change in level will naturally create a point of transition from one surface to another. The resulting structure should be detailed in such a way that the separated areas ensure structural integrity, safety and longevity of use. Some edges require less stability than others, the edge to a lawn, for instance, whereas many must comply with specific criteria for strength and wear, such as a highway **kerb**. While edges and trims in a domestic or private space may not be subject to as much wear as those in more public areas, the detail of the construction remains essential to the integrity of the retained paved space. The transition between materials, levels and surfaces requires that edges and trims are frequently required to announce hazards and direct traffic, vehicular or pedestrian. While the choice of material is important, it is vital that edges and trims offer protection from hazards (such as drops and changes in level) and maintenance requirements. The approach to a pool or water feature, edging to a ramp or a deck will all require the appropriate selection of a material, its orientation and installation to specific requirements.

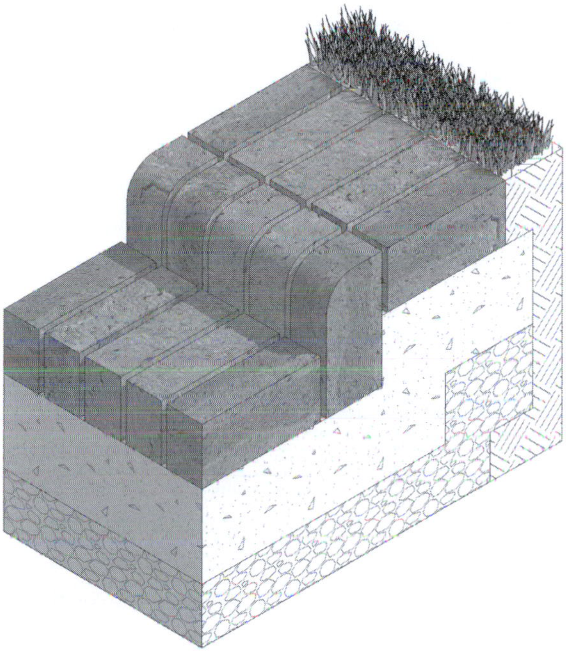

Figure 4.1 Brick edge, bullnosed

Most edging details are constructed from small unit materials, such as bricks, pin kerbs (narrow kerb pieces set on edge) or **setts**; these are usually laid on a compacted sub-base and set in place with haunched concrete, usually over a CIS concrete foundation. Strip edges can be used to create a range of effects, where there is either a transition in levels or between materials.

Timber strips, attached to driven stakes, are the simplest form of edge, used where the budget is a constraint, such as supporting long paths or expansive areas of gravel and **hoggin**. Often these are laid to ground level so that they remain as discreet as possible These are easily damaged and subject to deterioration from the surrounding ground conditions.

With the introduction of modern alloys, metal is a viable alternative to timber. While it can be similarly used to create a subtle demarcation, decorative finishes and an inherent strength give it considerably expanded functionality over timber. Plastic lacks such inherent stiffness and has limited application.

complementary coloured face. Curved edges are ideally suited to thin metal edge systems. Units designed to bend may require specific installation or modification and advice should be sought from the supplier. Like concrete, purpose-made units are available in specific and set radii.

METAL EDGES

Metal edges are available in steel or aluminium. They are designed to give a neat, sharp edge at the junction between one material and another. Commonly used at the edge of lawns, a metal strip provides a convenient mowing strip. Where the lawn is raised above the surrounding path, then an extra long edge is required as it will need to be supported below ground to retain its vertical face. The height of the lawn above the ground will also require a thicker edging material than that used for areas where the levels are equal. Typically, edges are 3mm thick but edges up to 10mm are available. Metal edge systems can be installed dry, without the need for haunching or concrete set posts. The coupling devices and retaining pins are usually supplied with the edging runs. Certain applications, such as road and driveway edges, may require a more resilient restraint, with the poles, pins or support pegs being set in a concrete race.

Metal edging is effectively used to delineate between other unlike (particularly loose laid), materials, such as soil and resin bound gravel, or gravel and soils where it acts as a retaining edge as well as a convenient edge to indicate where to stop trimming the grass. Fixings are usually completely concealed, presenting a thin and uninterrupted edge. Some profiles are reversible, allowing either a square or round top edge to be used.

Steel edging works better than other materials where the edge is raised above the ground, or the edge is subject to high levels of pedestrian and vehicular traffic. **COR-TEN**® and equivalent finishes are popular, requiring no surface treatment while presenting an attractive and

PLASTIC EDGES

Plastic can make a viable alternative to metal edging. Usually supplied for use on smaller projects, to act as edge restraints on paths and paved surfaces, where small format materials have been specified: block pavers, cobbles and setts. Typically laid to just below the level of the paving, such edges are almost unnoticeable once installed and will significantly reduce the incidence of damage and collapse at the paving edge. They are discreetly coloured and, unlike metal, minor damage and scratches will remain unnoticed. They are not as stiff as their metal counterparts and are unlikely to work as well for heavy duty areas.

Lawns that are intended for play areas or likely to be used by children should have an appropriate safe edge, narrow profile metal or plastic will not be suitable. Moulded in blacks, browns or greens, plastic edges with large, safe, rounded edges are available for such installations.

ABUTMENTS

Edging that abuts a building must lie a minimum of 150mm below any damp-proof course (DPC). If the edge of the surface cannot be constructed at this level or if the paved or lawn or soil level must remain at the DPC or even higher, then a local channel or recess adjoining the building is typically constructed.

Irregular unit materials such as cobbles and gravel are frequently used as margin fill or treatments. They add contrast and texture to the perimeter of an area and are

Metal edges are available in many styles and sizes. The specific installation requirements will be provided by the product supplier. Some edges can be formed into curves, or have preformed curved sections added. The size and frequency of ground pins will depend on the materials retained and the size of the edge. The support base of the edging strip is usually set under the paved area (i.e. not on the soil side).

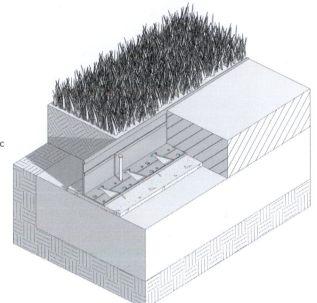

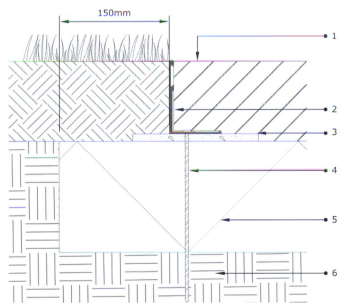

1. Paving of choice
2. Metal edge
3. 10–20mm mortar strip (Class II) as specified by edge supplier
4. Metal pin (supplied by edge supplier)
5. Sub-base DTp1 100–150mm
6. Sub-grade

Figure 4.2 Aluminium or steel edging

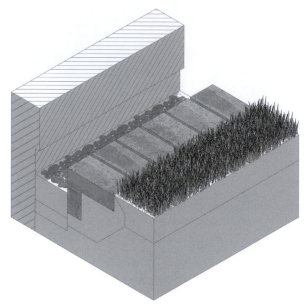

Where the ground level is to be raised close to or above the DPC

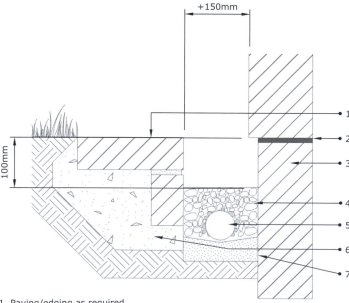

1. Paving/edging as required
2. DPC
3. House or building wall
4. 10–20mm clean stone (not limestone). If litter or debris collection is a problem, the gravel level can be brought to 30mm below the DPC. A waterproof membrane against the build to the top of the gravel may be required
5. 60–80mm perforated land drain to surface water outlet
6. Concrete foundation C7-10
7. PCC concrete open drainage channel on a C7-10 bed

Figure 4.3 Edge detailing against a building

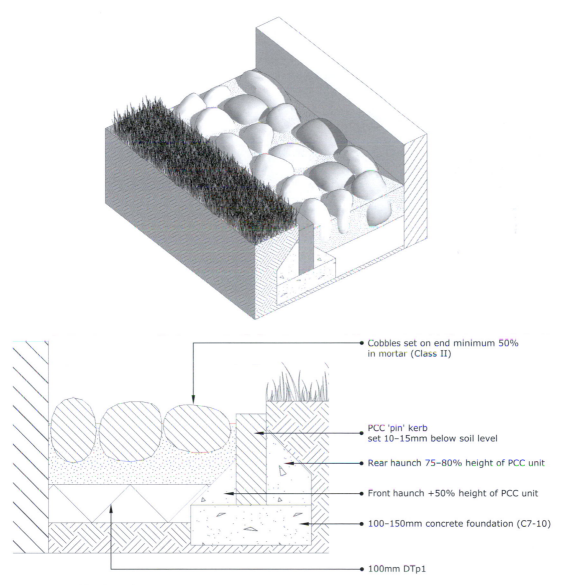

Cobbles set on end minimum 50% in mortar (Class II)

PCC 'pin' kerb set 10–15mm below soil level

Rear haunch 75–80% height of PCC unit

Front haunch +50% height of PCC unit

100–150mm concrete foundation (C7-10)

100mm DTp1

Figure 4.4 Cobble edge with PCC narrow concrete support

less expensive than other materials. Loose laid materials are best laid over a suitable sub-base, and the use of appropriate landscape membranes will prevent the growth and penetration from below of persistent and existing vegetation. Airborne seedlings will naturally accumulate and graveled areas will require frequent maintenance to keep clean. Where such materials are laid loose, rather than bound or set into a mortar bed, there must still be a constraining edge to prevent the migration of material.

LAWN LEVELS

Any edge that borders a lawn should be set 20–30mm below the required lawn level, when it is freshly laid, as this allows for settlement. Edges set above a lawn will create difficulties when mowing and for maintenance.

Where gravel or cobbles border an area of lawn, the edge should be set at a height that permits a mower to trim all of the grass without disrupting the material or causing the mower to foul. A 'mowing strip' to a width of

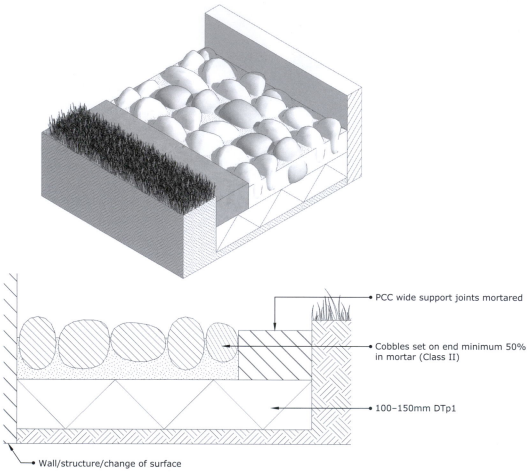

PCC wide support joints mortared

Cobbles set on end minimum 50% in mortar (Class II)

100–150mm DTp1

Wall/structure/change of surface

Where a large PCC unit is used, it can be set directly on the sub-base. Side haunching may not be necessary if the unit is sufficiently wide (+200mm). The PCC unit may be set on a 50mm bed of mortar (Class II) if required. The PCC edge should be set 10–15mm below the soil level if a mowing strip is required.

This detail is a decorative edge and not suitable as a pedestrian or vehicular surface.

Figure 4.5 Cobble edge with PCC wide concrete support

at least 225mm is best constructed from materials laid flat and to the level of the lawn or just below it. Such mowing strips allow access for grass cutting, especially against vertical surfaces, where it can be difficult to mechanically mow and intervention by hand is required. They can be set over relatively thin foundations, although the size and weight of the mowing equipment may require a deeper sub-base and continuous concrete race. Planted areas, including lawns, should not abut buildings or walls, even where the soil is isolated from the wall surface and below the DPC. It is good practice to step the soil margin

at least the length of a brick (225mm) away from the vertical surface.

CAST IN SITU (CIS) CONCRETE EDGES

CIS concrete margins will require the use of a concrete mixture with a relatively high slump. Such a fluid mix will have some capacity to self-level and create a cleaner and smoother surface than a standard ready

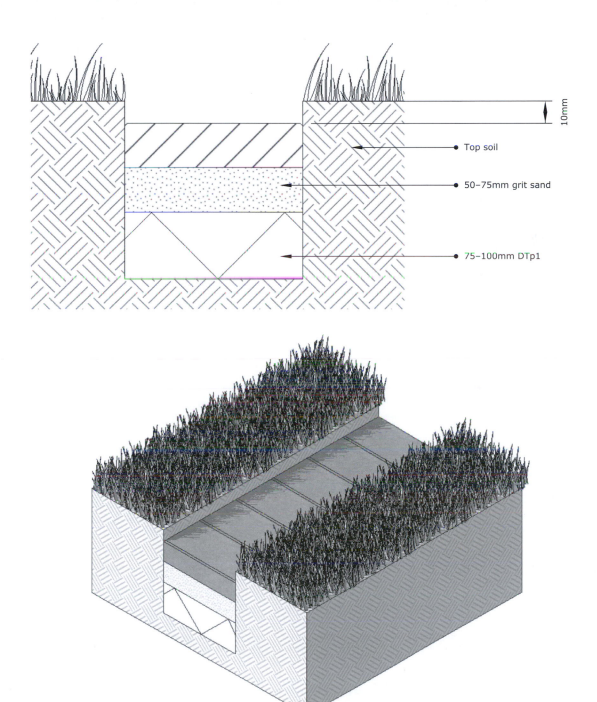

10mm

Top soil

50–75mm grit sand

75–100mm DTp1

Figure 4.6 Brick/block edge to a lawn

or on-site mix would achieve. As such, there may be a requirement for shuttering (formwork) to retain the mix and maintain the required level. **Precast concrete (PCC)** units are available, sometimes incorporating a detail that permits integral drainage. There are many sizes of unit available with a wide range of colours and finishes. Cheap, easy and fast to lay, they can be used effectively in combination with other materials, e.g. granite setts.

Large radius curves can use standard straight PCC units, either at their full or a cut length. Laid to tight curves, PCC units can result in expanded and unsightly joints. Curves should be laid dry to determine the best method and location for cutting.

BRICK

While most bricks and paving blocks can be used to create an edge detail, clay bricks (calcium silicate strength Class V), are designed to perform in damp, ground conditions and will give a better life in service. Clay bricks do not always fire evenly and where there is considerable mismatch or some minor distortion, these are often sold as seconds. While unsuitable for general building work or façades, they can be used advantageously in simple non-structural strips at edges and trims. Bricks and blocks set vertical or on edge perform better if mortared and pointed. The mortared joints prevent water ingress to the foundations and prevent freeze–thaw action and damage. Mortar dabs are not recommended to secure edge detailing in place. Bricks, blocks and setts laid horizontally can have sand-filled joints. Edges and trims can be exposed and suffer damage from impacts and spillages; all joints, whether sand or mortared, will require annual inspection and minor remedial work.

KERBS

A kerb (called a curb in the USA) is differentiated from an edge in that it performs the additional function

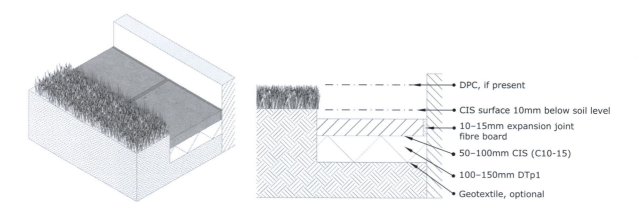

DPC, if present

CIS surface 10mm below soil level

10–15mm expansion joint fibre board

50–100mm CIS (C10-15)

100–150mm DTp1

Geotextile, optional

Where an edge or margin is required alongside or adjoining a vertical structure, expansion joints are required (at 3000mm centres). These accommodate any dimensional changes in the cast slab but, more importantly, protect the structure from any loads the slab may impose.

Where the margin is not a paved surface, for pedestrian or vehicular access, it can be laid over a simple light sub-base. The cast surface should be set a min. 150mm below a DPC, if one is present. The cast surface can be positioned to −75mm of the DPC if it is sloped away from the structure by a min. of 1:12.

Figure 4.7 CIS (cast in situ concrete) adjoining a structure/building

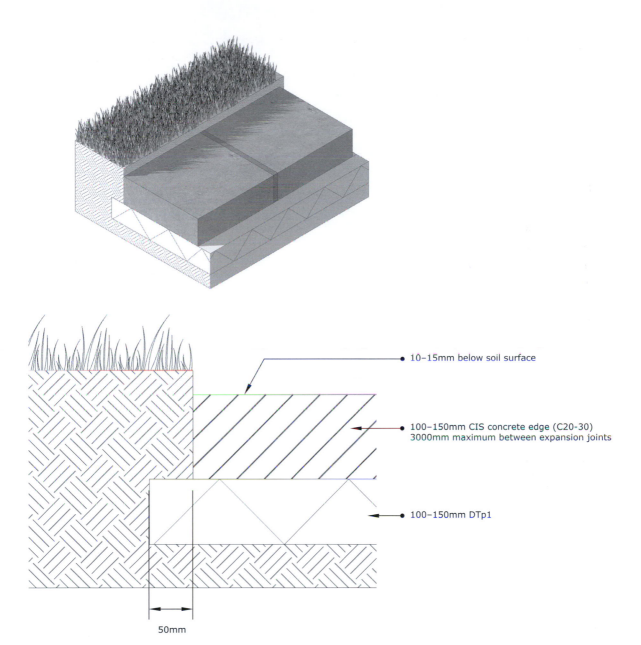

10–15mm below soil surface

100–150mm CIS concrete edge (C20-30)
3000mm maximum between expansion joints

100–150mm DTp1

50mm

Figure 4.7 (Continued)

(Continued)

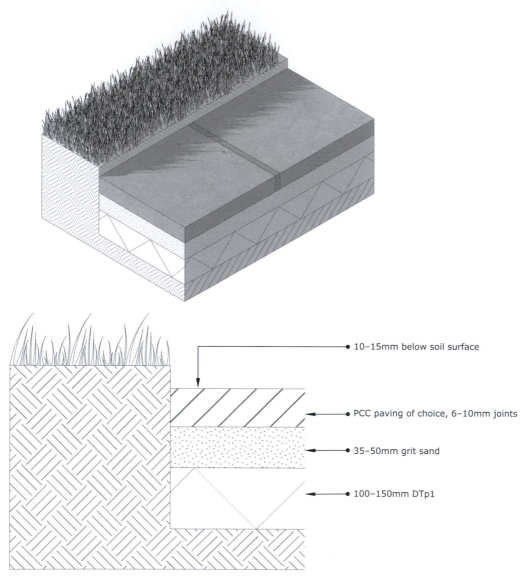

10–15mm below soil surface

PCC paving of choice, 6–10mm joints

35–50mm grit sand

100–150mm DTp1

Figure 4.7 (Continued)

of acting as a transition between two working paved surfaces. Flexible road surfaces require retention at their edges so that the wearing surface can be consolidated by compaction: rolled or vibrated. Typically these restraints are kerb stones. Modular lengths in either natural stone or precast concrete, set on a concrete bed (a race) and then haunched. In some minor constructions, such as footpaths other materials may be used, such as folded steel, bespoke aluminium edging or even plastic. Whether between pavements, carriageways or a combination, the constructed detail

needs to retain material as well as create an appropriate and safe transition between separated and often elevated surfaces.

Road kerbs serve a number of purposes:

- retaining the carriageway edge to prevent 'spreading' and loss of structural integrity;
- acting as a barrier or demarcation between road traffic and pedestrians or verges;
- providing a physical 'check' to prevent vehicles leaving the carriageway;

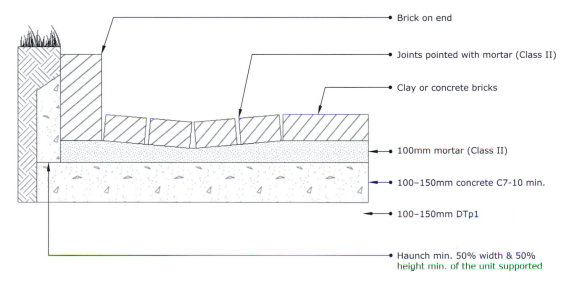

- Brick on end
- Joints pointed with mortar (Class II)
- Clay or concrete bricks
- 100mm mortar (Class II)
- 100–150mm concrete C7-10 min.
- 100–150mm DTp1
- Haunch min. 50% width & 50% height min. of the unit supported

For areas and paths less than 1.5m, a single drain is sufficient to cope with the run-off. Areas in excess of 1.5–2m will require a drainage channel on both sides.

The depth of the drainage channel should be 25–40mm.

Clay bricks for channels and water containment should be solid with durability designation FL (under BS 3921) or F2/S2 under BS EN 771-4:2011, strength Class V.

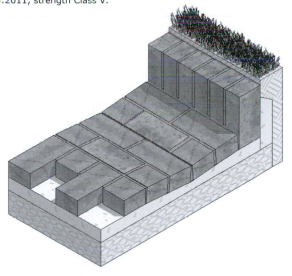

Figure 4.8 Brick-lined open drainage channel with upstand

- forming a channel along which surface water can be drained.

Kerbs are generally classified as either being 'barrier' or 'mountable' types. Barriers are designed to prevent or discourage incursions from vehicles, usually located at critical locations such as road corners where there is significant flow of pedestrian traffic, or pedestrian traffic is exposed. Usually over 150mm, there are a range of heights designed for specific locations. Mountable kerbs are designed so that vehicles can cross the threshold between two paved surfaces, such as driveway entrances or pedestrian areas where deliveries are permitted or emergency vehicle access is required. The local highways authority will have guidelines on which type is required or permitted.

Amendments or alterations to an existing line of road kerbs, forming part of a public highway, are not permitted

Brick edge with raised brick trim

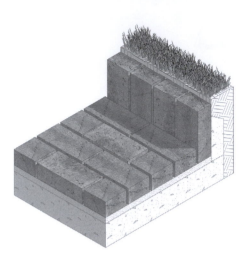

- 10–15mm below soil surface
- Concrete (C7-10) to +50% of brick
- Class II mortar
- 100–150mm concrete C15-20

100mm

Brick edge set into concrete

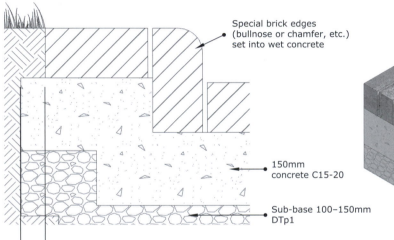
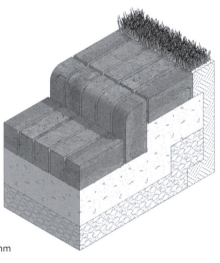

- Special brick edges (bullnose or chamfer, etc.) set into wet concrete
- 150mm concrete C15-20
- Sub-base 100–150mm DTp1

75–100mm

Brick on edge strip

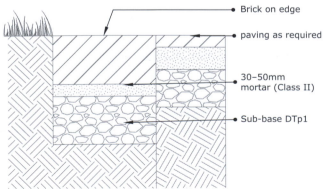
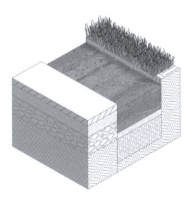

- Brick on edge
- paving as required
- 30–50mm mortar (Class II)
- Sub-base DTp1

Figure 4.9 Brick edges

Soldier course brick strip

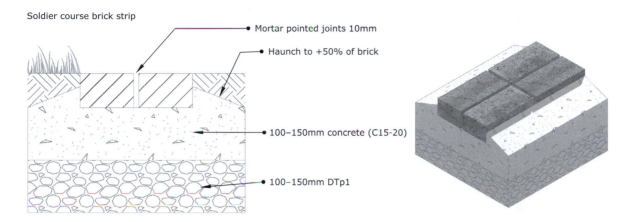

• Mortar pointed joints 10mm

• Haunch to +50% of brick

• 100–150mm concrete (C15-20)

• 100–150mm DTp1

Vertical soldier course brick strip

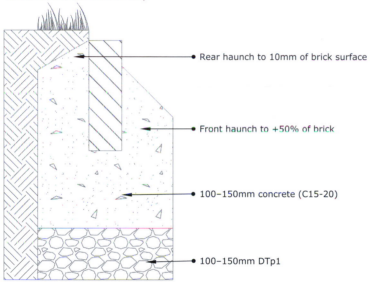
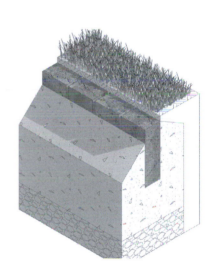

• Rear haunch to 10mm of brick surface

• Front haunch to +50% of brick

• 100–150mm concrete (C15-20)

• 100–150mm DTp1

Running/stacked bond brick strip

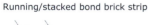
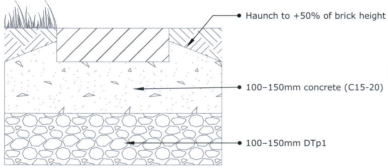
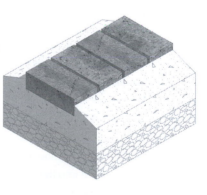

• Haunch to +50% of brick height

• 100–150mm concrete (C15-20)

• 100–150mm DTp1

Figure 4.9 (Continued)

(Continued)

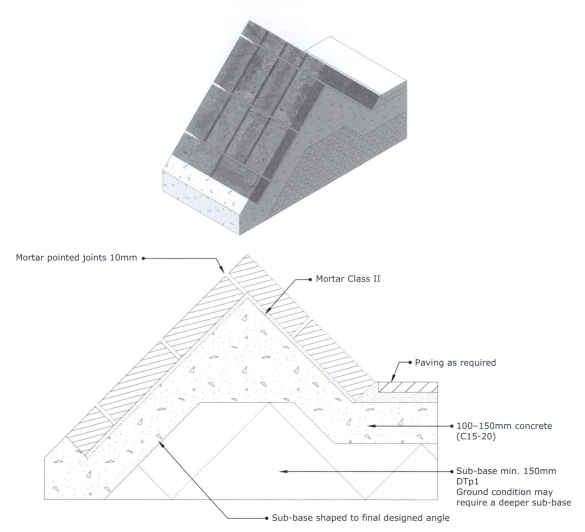

Mortar pointed joints 10mm

Mortar Class II

Paving as required

100–150mm concrete (C15-20)

Sub-base min. 150mm DTp1
Ground condition may require a deeper sub-base

Sub-base shaped to final designed angle

Figure 4.9 (Continued)

without the consent and approval of the local highways authority. This includes the footway and carriageway that adjoins or forms part of the drive to a private residence, for instance. The introduction of drop kerbs also requires the consent of the local highways authority.

Kerbs are supplied in a range of shapes and styles and these can be integrated into the structure of both flexible or rigid paved areas. Most modular building materials can be adapted to create a raised kerb.

The most popular are the precast (**hydraulically pressed**) concrete units. They are consistent, manufactured to tight **tolerances** and inexpensive. These

are generically referred to as BS sections/kerbs (BS EN 1340) or PCC (precast concrete). PCC units are almost always grey; this can be used effectively to highlight the expansive paving material. The range (BS EN 1340) includes quadrants, angles transitions, radii (internal and external) and a range of linear units with a variety of sectional profiles. Units are unpolished and have a low potential for slip.

The more popular sized units from the BS range of kerbs are available in alternative materials. Granite, both in a hammered or smooth machined finish, gives a decorative and very resilient alternative. Curved units are also produced to complement the more common profiles. Kerbstones can be very dense and of considerable weight, a 300 × 200mm 1m precast concrete unit might weigh +130kg, the same size in granite +160kg. Such units cannot be manually placed, so the design of the path or road must facilitate mechanical lifting and handling.

There are four basic kerb profiles available as PCC units commonly used throughout the UK:

- half-battered
- bullnosed
- splayed
- square.

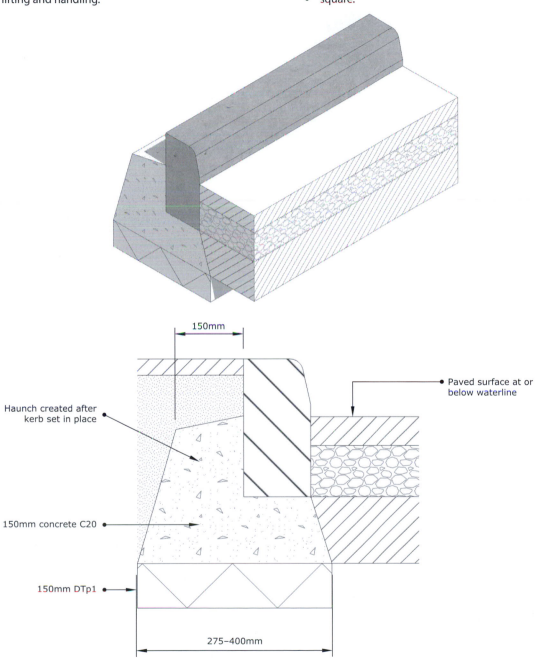

Figure 4.10 Standard PCC kerbs

(Continued)

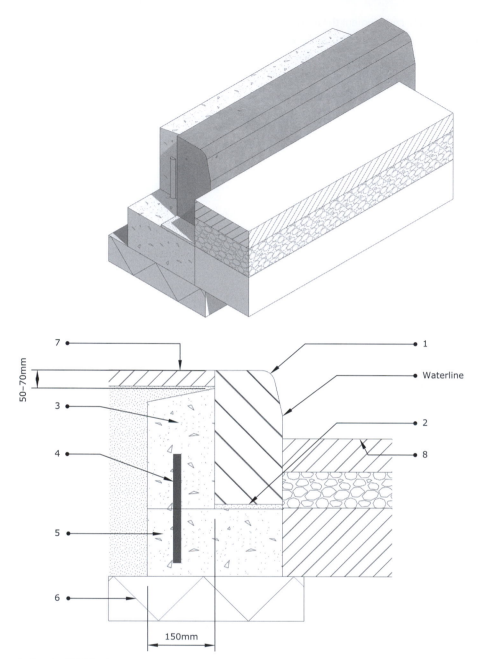

1. Standard PCC kerb
2. Mortar class II 12–15mm
3. Concrete C10 minimum
4. Rebar pins if required (high impact risk). Diam. 16mm, 350mm long at 450mm centres
5. 215mm minimum concrete C15-20
6. Sub-base DTp1 150mm min.
7. Pedestrian paving as required
8. Road surface laid to 25–75mm below waterline

Figure 4.10 (Continued)

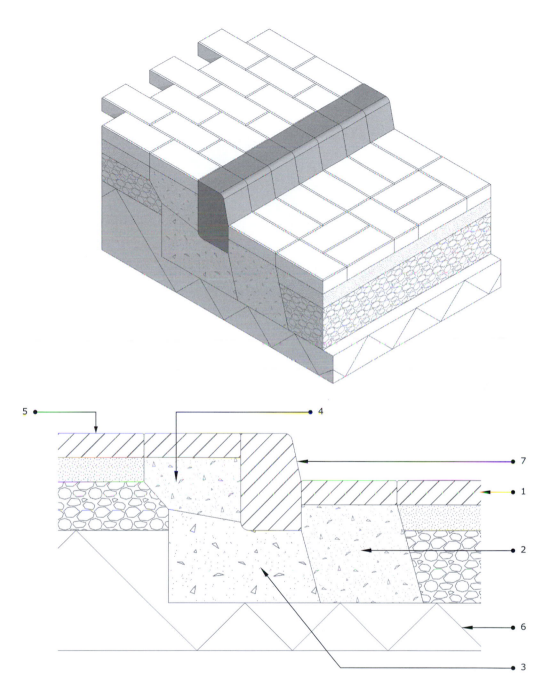

1. Paving as required, sub-base to be laid after kerb is laid
2. Concrete bedding C7-10
3. Concrete C20
4. Haunch C20
5. Pedestrian paving as required
6. DTp1 100–150mm
7. Exposed face of kerb 100–150mm

Figure 4.11 Concrete kerb alongside carriageway

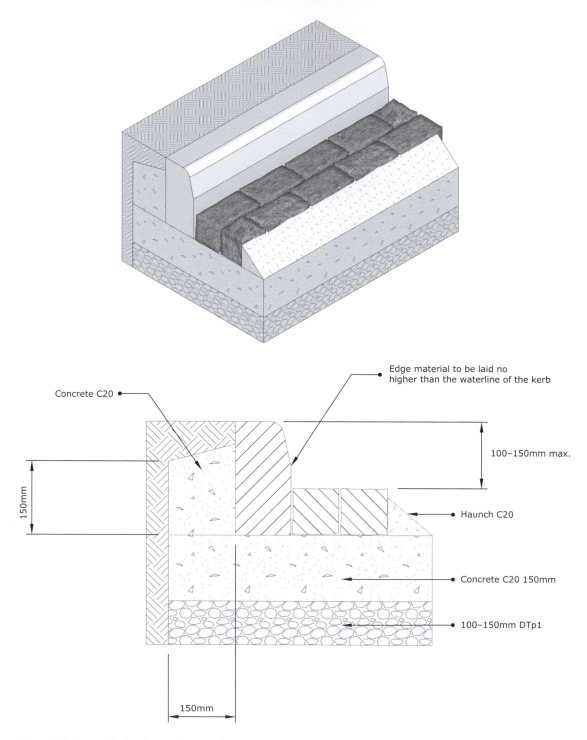

Figure 4.12 Concrete kerb with natural stone edge

Labels within figure:

Concrete C20

Edge material to be laid no
higher than the waterline of the kerb

100–150mm max.

150mm

Haunch C20

Concrete C20 150mm

100–150mm DTp1

150mm

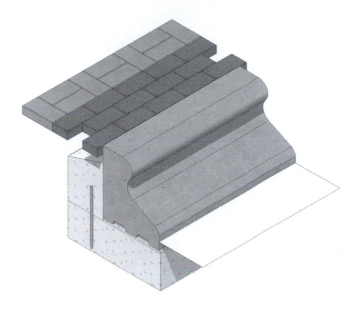

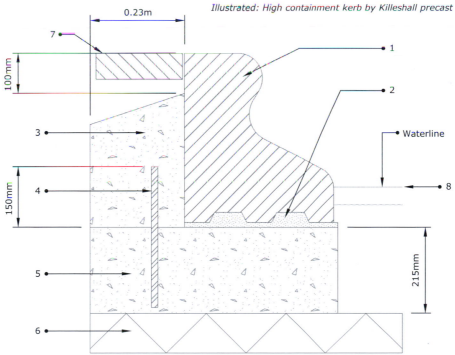

Illustrated: High containment kerb by Killeshall precast

1. High containment kerb
2. Mortar Class II 12–15mm
3. Concrete C10 min.
4. Rebar pins if required (high impact risk). Diam. 16mm, 350mm long at 450mm centres
5. 215mm min. concrete C15-20
6. Sub-base DTp1 150mm min.
7. Pedestrian paving as required
8. Road surface laid to 250–275mm below waterline

Figure 4.13 High containment carriageway kerb

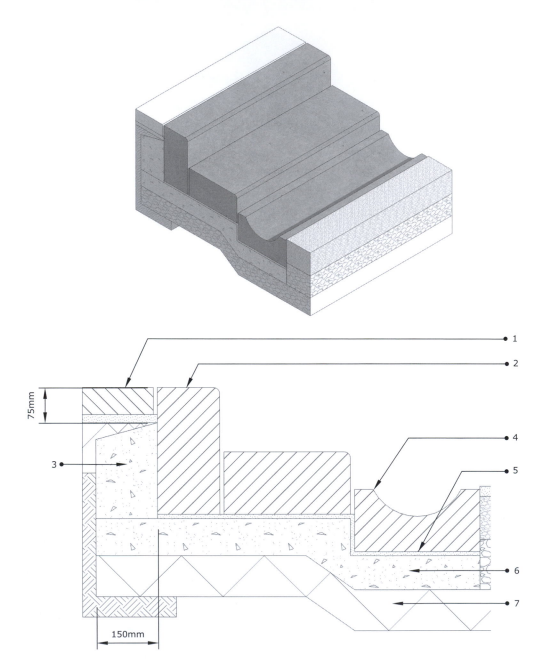

1. Pedestrian paving as required

2. PCC kerb

3. Haunch C15, kerb base set prior to laying haunch

4. PCC channel as required

5. 10–30mm mortar class II

6. Concrete C15-20 100–150mm

7. DTp1 100–150mm

Figure 4.14 Stepped PCC kerb with channel

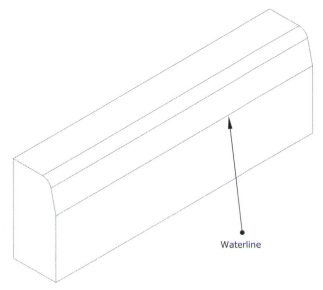

Figure 4.15 Waterline of kerbstone

Additional ranges to those in the standard are available. They are designed as modules of block paving and may have specific limitations on their application, for instance, not to be used for highway kerbs. The manufacturers' specifications should be consulted to determine if a kerb is appropriate for the intended application. These are frequently used in residential areas to improve the appearance of kerbs and integrate frequent drop kerbs where drives and crossings are much more common than on public highways.

All kerbs (other than those with a square profile) have a waterline or watermark. This is typically the lower edge of a chamfer or radius on the vertical roadside face, rather than an actual line and is the line above which surface water, when laid, should not extend. This line is usually kept 25mm above the road surface when the kerb is laid.

Half-battered kerbs are the most common in use and typically used where a footpath or pavement runs alongside a road. Splayed (chamfered) kerbs are used where a vehicle may be required to mount the verge in an emergency or in infrequent circumstances and as such are not suitable as a kerb where pavements are present. Local authority highways' consent is required to use a non-BS kerb on a public highway.

Lightweight versions of the BS kerbs are also available, usually in shorter lengths with some material removed,

for example, on the rear of the unit. Permission will be required to use these modified designs on public highways, as they may not satisfy local standards for impact resistance.

High containment kerbs are used to ensure traffic remains on the highway, protecting footpaths and equipment and structures that may be vulnerable from an impact (pedestrian islands, sharp bends and telecommunication junction boxes). There are several designs available and each has specific installation requirements and specifications for the size of the foundations and haunching required.

Kerb drain systems, generically known as 'Beanys' after the civil engineer who developed the system, are becoming more commonplace. A simple concept, whereby kerb units are formed hollow with large holes on the roadside face that straddles the waterline. Unlike standard kerb units, these are bonded together and create an internal drainage system.

Brick edges

Where a low rise kerb is required, for non-highway applications, bricks used on end can create attractive details. The style and colour can be selected to complement or even contrast existing structures such as driveways or walls. If used as an edge to a drive or path, brick kerbs should be constructed prior to the paved surface being constructed. Similar to the large BS kerbs, bricks require the support of a concrete race with side haunching to prevent lateral movement. Haunching should be to at least half the height of the brick. Brick edging can be laid without pointing, with units laid as tightly as possible. This may lead to problems with the haunching if rainwater freezes in colder months. Pointed joints would prevent this. Bricks used at or below ground level should be suitable for such applications (for clay: calcium silicate strength Class V), house or walling bricks are not suitable.

Timber kerbs

Raised timber edges are a cheap and simple solution to domestic kerbs. Timber that retains damp soil has a limited life in service and will require repair or replacement after 5–10 years. Timber upstands have little inherent strength and should not be used where there is a risk of impact. Timber upstands of 25mm × 100–150mm are typically attached to stakes 40 × 40mm minimum and approximately 450–600mm long. An alternative to rectangular board upstands is the use of machined timber rounds, +100mm diameter. These are attached to stakes in a similar fashion, from the rear of the log. Formed from an entire trunk, these have a respectable life in service of +10yrs although the fasteners and stakes will require inspection and replacement within a shorter timeframe. Log kerbs are suited to car parks and rural environments. They do not adapt to curved edging.

Larger square section timbers, +100 × 100mm, can be mounted on purpose-made upstands to form a rail. The upstands are available to suit standard section timbers and should be of either galvanised or stainless steel. The timbers are simply placed in the support bracket and secured by nails or screws. The height of the timber is determined by the bracket and several options are available. The brackets require a firm anchor. These might be set into a post hole and backfilled with a suitable 'post-crete' type concrete mix. Alternatively the demarcation between the materials and surfaces on either side of the rail can be emphasised by constructing a CIS concrete strip. Once cured, the timber support brackets are secured with mechanical anchors or bolts. If the concrete strip bisects a slope, a land drain on the upward side of the strip will be necessary and the CIS strip may require breaks to permit the passage of water or the drain at regular intervals.

Countryside kerbs

These are kerbs that have a rustic or 'natural texture' appearance which allows them to be used effectively in conservation and traditionally in locations where appearance is a critical factor. Manufacturers frequently offer wide top versions of this kerb style. They can be cut from natural stone, such as granite or manufactured from a combination of reclaimed materials and reconstituted stone, shot blasted after casting to create a hammered stone effect. As with all kerbs used on highways, installation instructions are supplied by the manufacturer and must comply with the local highways authority guidance and requirements.

Radius kerbs

Kerbs that form curves alongside highways are frequently classified as fast or slow, there is no demarcation between these descriptors but the tighter the radius, the faster the curve. Radial kerbs (BS) units are usually 780mm long. This ensures that ¼ circles can be constructed of whole units. These are formed into set radii layouts. A range of curved units is available and the correct units must be used as specified by the manufacturer to achieve the required arc. Arcs less than 12m radius should be constructed using the nearest equivalent PCC kerb and be cut to length. Intermediate radii can be created by altering the joints or cutting the ends to the required angle. Internal and external angles are available to suit all PCC kerbs, they eliminate the need to create mitred joints and therefore weaker pavement corners. The size of a radius

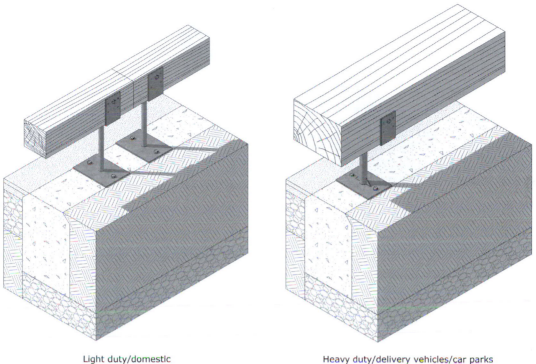

Light duty/domestic   Heavy duty/delivery vehicles/car parks

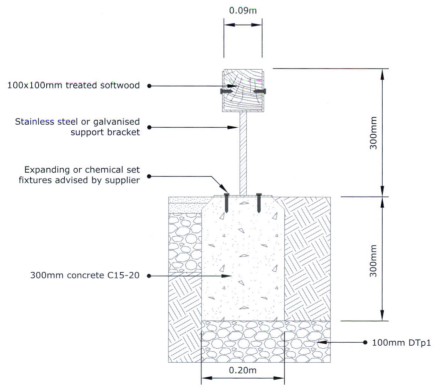

0.09m

100x100mm treated softwood

Stainless steel or galvanised
support bracket

Expanding or chemical set
fixtures advised by supplier

300mm concrete C15-20

300mm

300mm

100mm DTp1

0.20m

Figure 4.16 Raised timber wheel stop

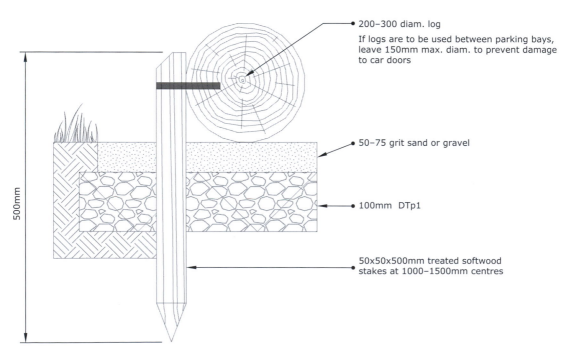

200–300 diam. log

If logs are to be used between parking bays, leave 150mm max. diam. to prevent damage to car doors

50–75 grit sand or gravel

100mm DTp1

50x50x500mm treated softwood stakes at 1000–1500mm centres

500mm

Figure 4.17 Timber log wheel stop

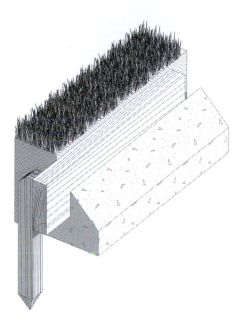

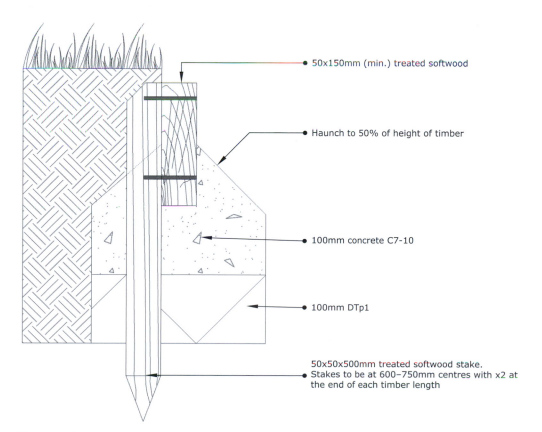

50x150mm (min.) treated softwood

Haunch to 50% of height of timber

100mm concrete C7-10

100mm DTp1

50x50x500mm treated softwood stake.
Stakes to be at 600–750mm centres with x2 at
the end of each timber length

Figure 4.18 Timber kerb/lawn edge

The 'countryside kerb' is a common term for kerbstones fashioned from natural stone. Typically they are mechanically split, leaving a rough surface. Countryside ranges are available from many suppliers, in a range of stone types and profiles, granite being the most durable.

Vertical countryside kerb

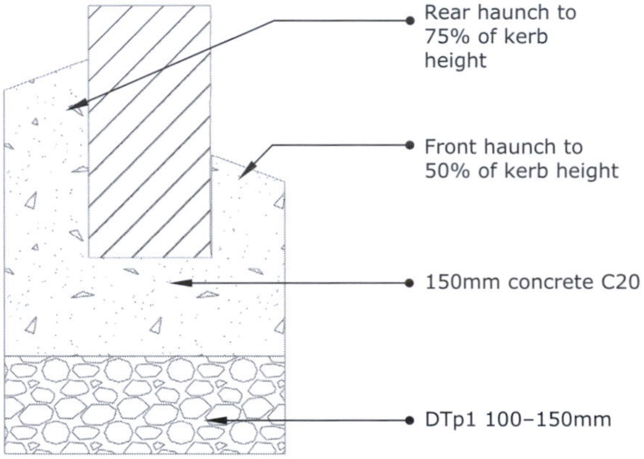

Rear haunch to 75% of kerb height

Front haunch to 50% of kerb height

150mm concrete C20

DTp1 100–150mm

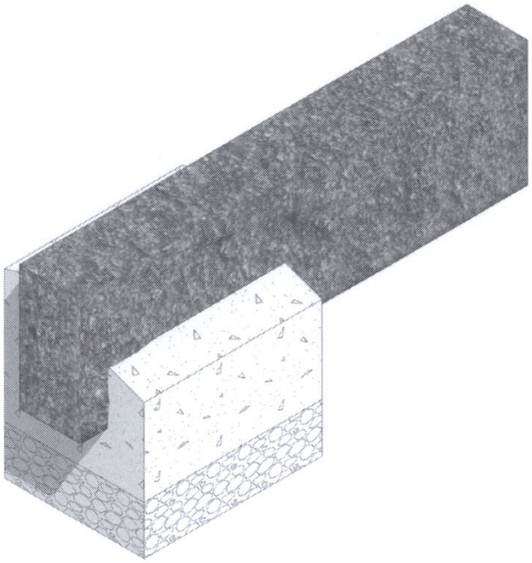

Cambered countryside kerb

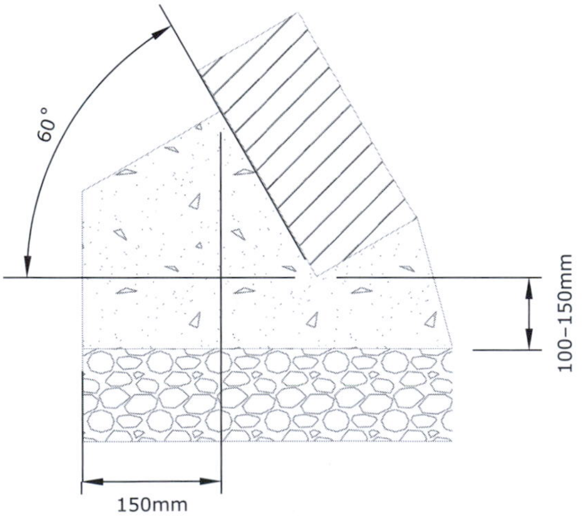

60°

100–150mm

150mm

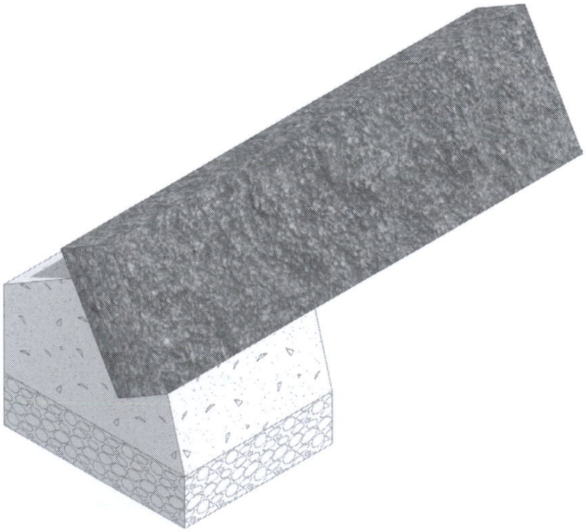

Illustrated: Charcon countryside kerb square section

Figure 4.19 Natural stone (countryside) kerbs

is always measured to the kerb line face, i.e. the face alongside the road.

Quadrants (sometimes called 'cheeses') are available in profiles to match the standard kerb ranges. They come in two sizes, 305mm and 455mm, and are used to create a solid curved section with a very tight radius, where a larger radius from the kerb range would take up too much space (e.g. the divider in a car park or a pedestrian island refuge).

All kerbs should be set in place prior to the laying of the base and the surface of a road or path and laid on a race of 100mm minimum thickness, haunched to a minimum of 150mm. Bedding to the front of a kerb should be removed or shuttering used to keep the race tight to the kerb position, this facilitates differential movement in the road bed from traffic vibration and ensures the kerb foundation is never subject to unnecessary loads. A kerb set on a rigid sub-base (concrete slab) is set directly on the slab, as its function is simply to prevent the loss of paving materials at the perimeter of the paved area.

Joints are often not mortared but laid tight. An exception is the use of integral drain kerbs such as the 'beany' style units that must be sealed to one another.

Typically, haunching extends to +2/3 the height of the kerb, although this may be altered if a deeper paving material abuts the kerb. Certain manufactured units have very specific haunching requirements and these should be investigated prior to specification.

Dowelled or pinned connections between the race and the haunch are used only on the largest sizes of kerbs. These add strength in case of a side impact. The material, diameter and frequency of these dowels will be advised by the kerb manufacturer.

Extruded kerbs (CIS) are becoming more popular in the UK, especially on large public road schemes. This technique does not successfully adapt to smaller schemes.

Dropped kerbs and raised crossings

It is frequently necessary to create an access point, such as a drive entrance or pedestrian crossing, and kerbs must be locally lowered, or dropped, to facilitate the movement of pedestrians or traffic. Drop sections are part of the BS range and available to suit all profiles. They are 'handed' units, but can be used in different orientations to achieve different drops or transitions to other kerb profiles. Some manufacturers produce transition units that adapt a BS profile to one of their own. This is frequently encountered in residential areas where public highways might merge with private access routes and driveways.

Level or flush access is essential for the majority of wheelchair users. Such access, by dropped kerb or raising a road section, must be provided at all pedestrian-controlled crossings. On longer, side and residential roads, dropped kerbs should, where possible, be provided every 100 metres to avoid the need for wheelchair users to make lengthy detours to cross.

Wherever possible, the dropped kerb should be flush with the carriageway (maximum 6mm proud for rounded bullnosed profiles) and have a maximum gradient of 8% (1 in 12) on the direct approach; 9% (1 in 11) on the flared sides. The minimum width of the area flush with the road should be 1200mm (up to 3000mm where there are heavy pedestrian flows), though 1000mm is acceptable adjacent to car parking reserved for disabled users. Where a dropped kerb is provided at a controlled road crossing, it should be the same width as the crossing itself (minimum 2400mm). At the foot of the dropped kerb, the camber of the road should be no more than 5% (1 in 20) to a distance approximately 600mm away from the kerb line. This avoids the wheelchair front wheels or a footrest being caught by an opposing upslope.

If the width of the footway is sufficient, there should be a level area, 900mm minimum width, along the rear side to allow easy passage for wheelchair users who are not crossing the road.

TOLERANCE

Construction and detailing with unit materials require an appreciation of the variations that are inherent in manufactured components. This variation is called **tolerance**. Over short areas and distances, the dimensional variations between supplied pieces will have little effect. However, on a long continuous run, e.g. a brick edge, small dimensional changes are compounded and may have an effect on the intended design.

Paving may be designed to neatly fit a defined area, based on the **nominal sizes** provided by the material suppliers (e.g. paving units at 300mm wide). The material specification may indicate 300mm +/– 5mm. This may lead to the possibility that ×6 paving

units are supplied at 305mm each, a total of 30mm accumulated laying width. The paving may now not fit the required space. Paving might be cut to suit or the designer can remove a whole paving unit and introduce a gravel strip or similar detail that will accommodate the paving variation, eliminating any cuts. The designer should appreciate that such dimensional fluctuations are inherent in all materials and design accordingly; anticipating where cut units might be placed, joints expanded to remove the need to cut to fit, or detailing added, such as gravel strips, to accommodate such variations.

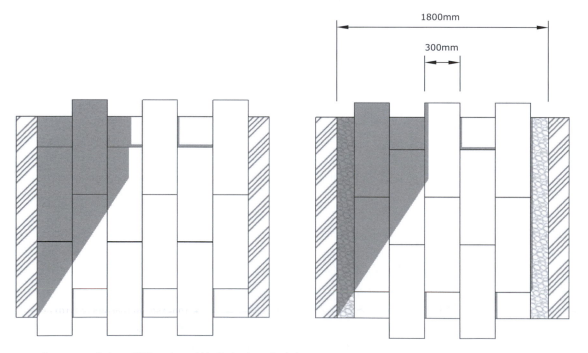

A gap between walls (e.g. 1800mm) would indicate that x6 whole paving units could be laid.

In reality, the space required to lay x6 300mm paving slabs is 6(300mm) + 7(10mm) = 1800 + 70 = 1870mm to allow 10mm for joints.

Paving can be supplied within a declared tolerance (typically +/–5mm). If the worst case is assumed (i.e. top tolerance = 305mm wide units) 6(305mm) + 7(10mm) = 1830 + 70 = 1900mm, paving will not fit without cutting.

It is better to design in a feature, such as a gravel strip, that can be flexible in its width to accommodate the paving as supplied. Laying x5 paving units, aligned centrally, ensures that full width paving is used and that there are no cuts.

Figure 4.20 Designing paved spaces to accommodate tolerance changes

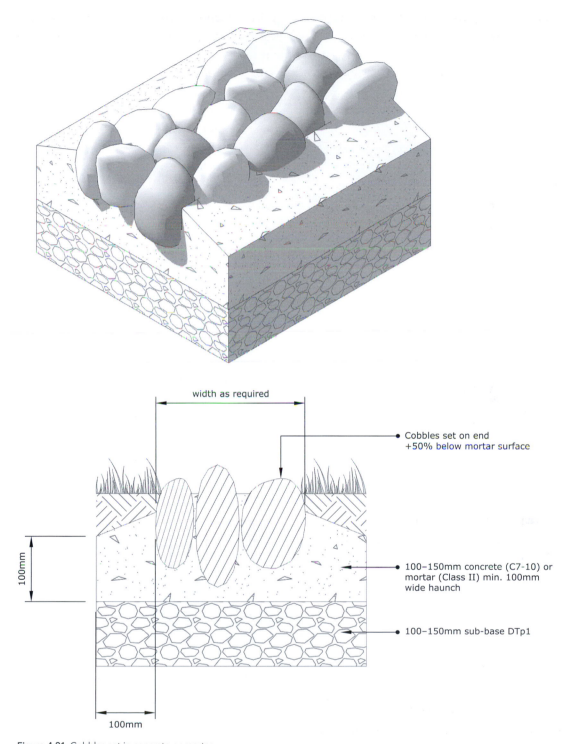

width as required

● Cobbles set on end
  +50% below mortar surface

100mm

100mm

● 100–150mm concrete (C7-10) or
  mortar (Class II) min. 100mm
  wide haunch

● 100–150mm sub-base DTp1

Figure 4.21 Cobbles set in concrete or mortar

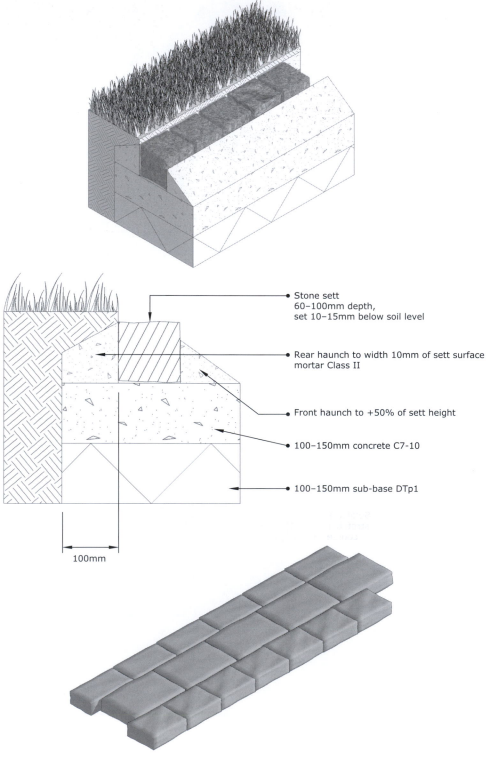

Stone sett
60–100mm depth,
set 10–15mm below soil level

Rear haunch to width 10mm of sett surface
mortar Class II

Front haunch to +50% of sett height

100–150mm concrete C7-10

100–150mm sub-base DTp1

100mm

Additional courses should be gauged and joints offset

Figure 4.22 Sett edge

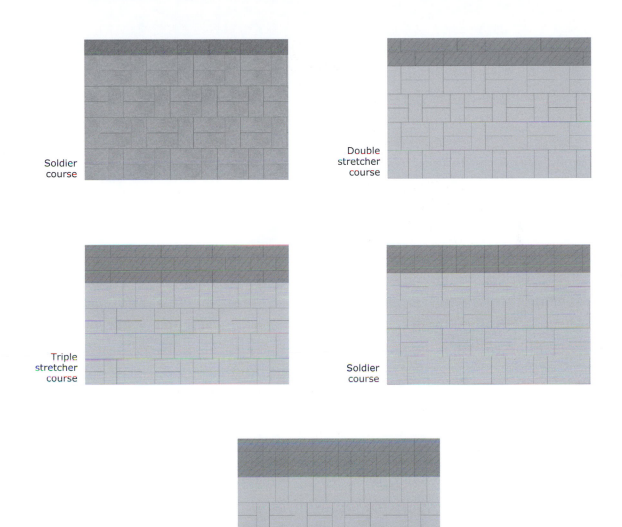

Figure 4.23 Typical edge patterns for block paving

(Continued)

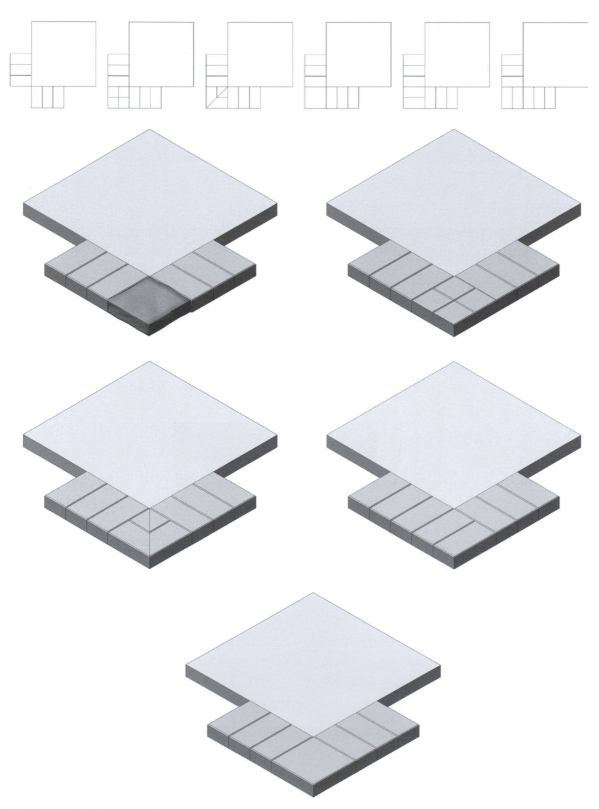

Figure 4.24 Block edge corners plan

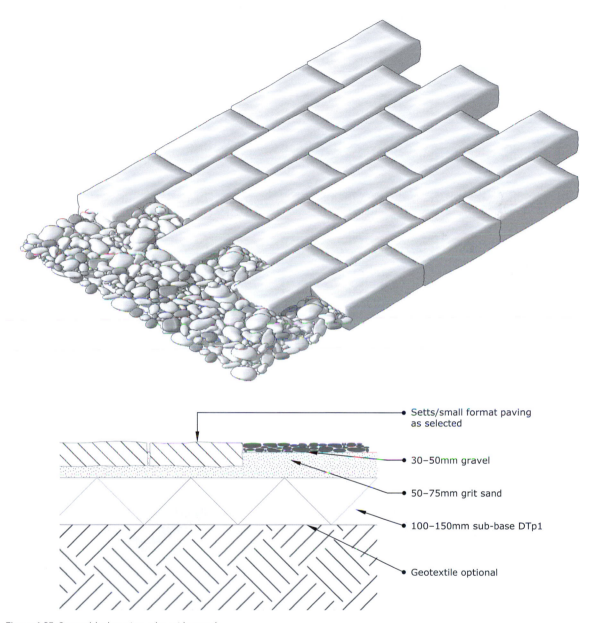

- Setts/small format paving as selected
- 30–50mm gravel
- 50–75mm grit sand
- 100–150mm sub-base DTp1
- Geotextile optional

Figure 4.25 Sett or block paving edge with gravel

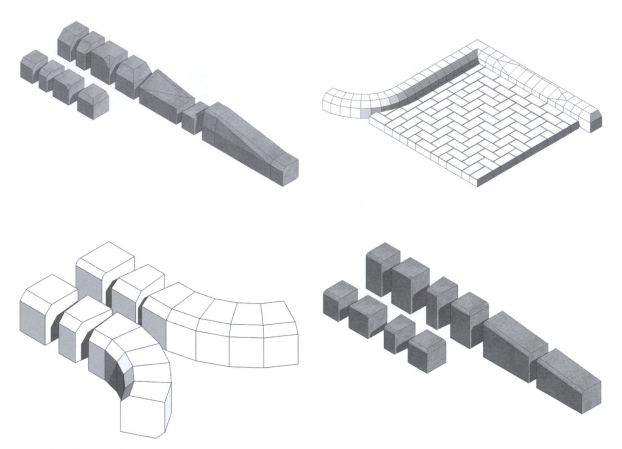

Figure 4.26 Keykerb splay range

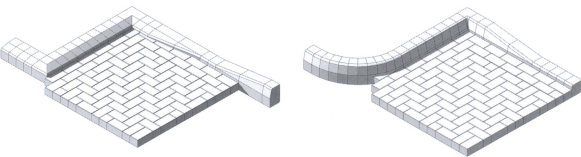

Figure 4.27 Keykerb half-battered short and long

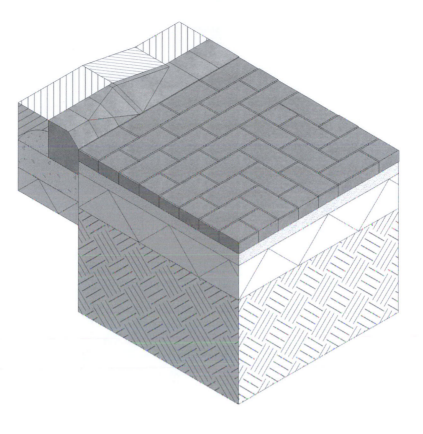

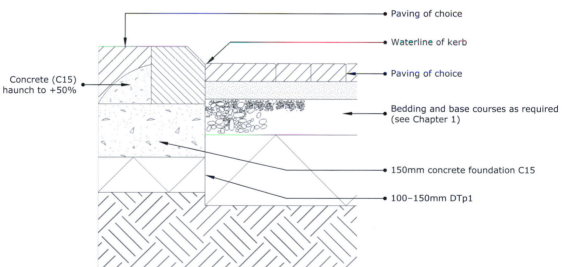

Paving of choice

Waterline of kerb

Paving of choice

Concrete (C15) haunch to +50%

Bedding and base courses as required (see Chapter 1)

150mm concrete foundation C15

100–150mm DTp1

Figure 4.28 Keykerb dropped kerb

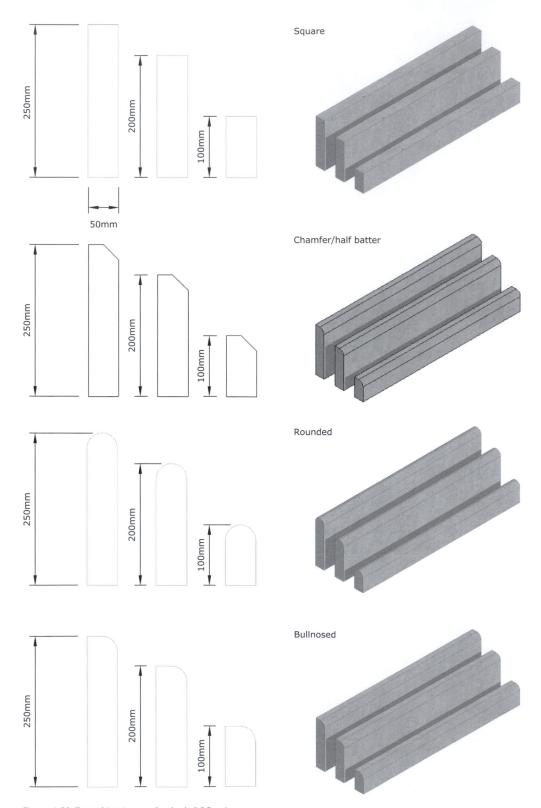

Square

Chamfer/half batter

Rounded

Bullnosed

250mm

200mm

100mm

50mm

Figure 4.29 Typical 'pin' or garden kerb PCC units

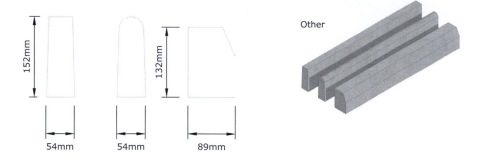

Other

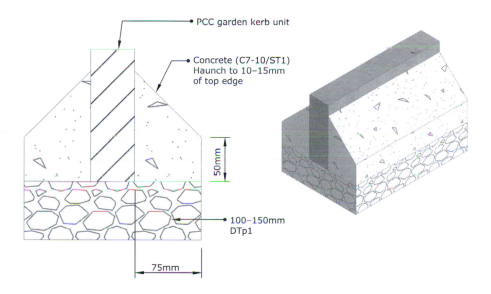

PCC garden kerb unit

Concrete (C7-10/ST1)
Haunch to 10–15mm
of top edge

50mm

100–150mm
DTp1

75mm

Care should be taken when designing or ordering PCC garden or pin kerbs. They can be supplied in the metric equivalent of 3ft (914mm) lengths. Many suppliers make a more convenient metric equivalent (1000/1200/1500mm).

Figure 4.29 (Continued)

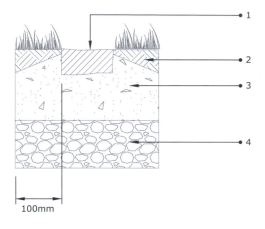

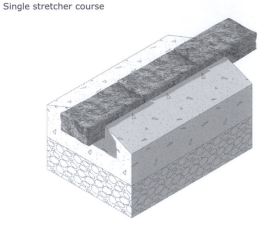

Single stretcher course

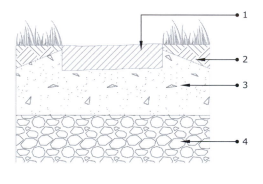

100mm

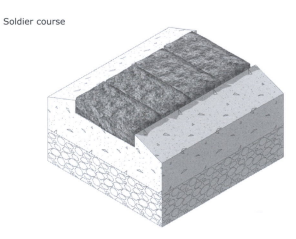

Soldier course

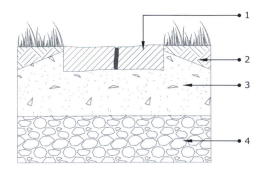

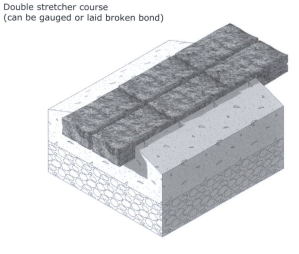

Double stretcher course
(can be gauged or laid broken bond)

1. Sett (60–100mm thick) as required
2. Top soil
3. Concrete haunch (C7-10/ST1) to within 10mm of sett surface
4. 100–150mm DTp1

Figure 4.30 Sett edges to planted or pedestrian areas

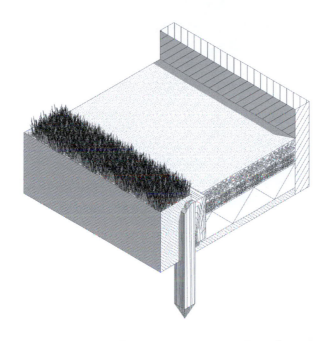

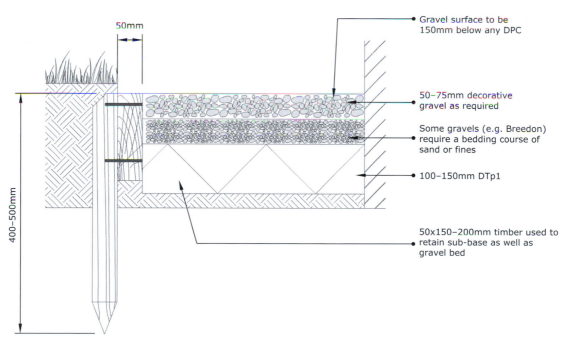

50mm

400–500mm

Gravel surface to be
150mm below any DPC

50–75mm decorative
gravel as required

Some gravels (e.g. Breedon)
require a bedding course of
sand or fines

100–150mm DTp1

50x150–200mm timber used to
retain sub-base as well as
gravel bed

Figure 4.31 Gravel with timber edge

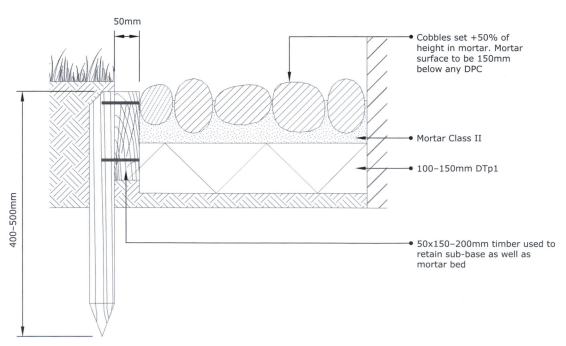

50mm

Cobbles set +50% of
height in mortar. Mortar
surface to be 150mm
below any DPC

Mortar Class II

100–150mm DTp1

400–500mm

50x150–200mm timber used to
retain sub-base as well as
mortar bed

Figure 4.32 Cobbles with timber edge

REFERENCES

Standards

BS 435:1975 Specification for dressed natural stone kerbs, channels, quadrants and setts

BS 7533 Part 6 installation of kerbs

BS EN 771-2:2003 Specification for masonry units. Calcium silicate masonry units

BS EN 772-7:1998 Clay masonry damp proof course units

BS EN 1340:2003 Concrete kerb units

BS EN 1342:2000 Setts of natural stone for external paving. Requirements and test methods

BS EN 1344:2002 Clay pavers

Books

Bannister, A., Raymond, S. and Baker, R. (1998) *Surveying*, 7th edn. Harlow: Longman.

Landphair, H.C. and Motloch, J.L. (1985) *Site Reconnaissance and Engineering: An Introduction for Architects, Landscape Architects and Planners*. New York: Elsevier.

Lynch, K. and Hack, G. (1984) *Site Planning*, Cambridge, MA: MIT Press.

Suppliers

www.aggregate.com   Durakerb, lightweight kerb system, also BS range and Charcon Access system.

www.brett.co.uk/landscaping   Kassel kerb system

www.burdens.co.uk   Kerbs and civils

www.civilsandlintels.co.uk   PCC kerbs and edging

www.exceledge.co.uk   Aluminium, plastic and COR-TEN® edging

www.everedge.co.uk   Steel edging

www.hauraton.com   Hauraton (lots of construction drawings)

CHAPTER 5

Steps and ramps

INTRODUCTION

Steps are both a functional necessity as a means of changing level but can also be a decorative addition to a garden or landscape. Given due consideration, they can form one of the principal elements of a garden. The transition between levels need not be mundane; there are many ways to design access over unlevel ground: ramps, steps and large terraces, for example. The context and scale of the space will be the influencing factor. Steps can add intrigue by subtly changing direction, inviting to a space as yet unseen, or drama by verging on being sculptural. Ramps and steps can work to unify areas rather than separate them and a well-designed

change in level will always look more interesting than a flat space. Vertical faces can be exaggerated and used to display plants, water or even the sculptural qualities of the materials used.

There are rules concerning the successful transition between levels, whether by steps or ramps. These apply in principle to areas used by the public or where large groups might congregate. Steps and ramps on land away from residential buildings and for private use are mostly uncontrolled and, as such, Building Regulations may not apply. While the guidance given by Building Regulations might appear prescriptive, they are based on sound research and guided principally for our health and safety, they should be adopted wherever possible.

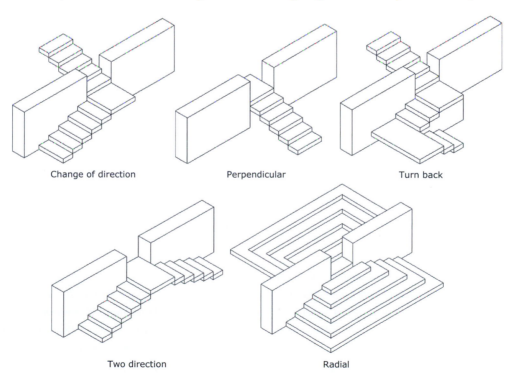

Change of direction   Perpendicular   Turn back

Two direction   Radial

Figure 5.1 Some typical step arrangements

There is no minimum width for a flight of stairs, guidance from the regulations is given for internal stairs or public access areas, however, they form a reasonable reference for private external use: minimum width of 900mm, ideally 1200mm, with at least 1000mm as measured between handrails.

If there is a possibility that steps might be used by disabled people, there should be a minimum width of 1000mm (between handrails). If stairs exceed 1800mm, a central handrail might be considered, thereby creating two routes.

A single step is considered a hazard, unless at a door or threshold. For flights between **landings**, a maximum of 16 **risers** is given by Approved Document K. Stairs intended for disabled access should have no more than 12 risers. Where stairs have more than 36 risers in total over consecutive flights, there should be at least one change of direction (min. 30 degrees in plan) to reduce the risk of injury from falls and fatigue.

Steps can be, and frequently are, constructed from a wide range of materials. It is essential that the material selection is appropriate to the location of the steps (e.g. is there constant overhead cover or shade?) and smooth materials are never used.

HANDRAILS

The use of handrails can be contentious. While the designer or client might feel that they spoil a vista or are unsightly, with careful, design they can become an integral part of the design. Building regulations (also called **Approved Documents** in the UK) are very explicit as to where handrails and **balustrades** must be used. The Part M and K documents place an obligation on the designer for internal stairs or public access, they are not obligatory for private garden spaces but do form a useful guide. The height a handrail should be set is identified in Approved Document K. Stair flights should have a handrail on at least one side if they are less than 1 meter wide and on both sides if they are wider than 1 meter. The minimum domestic handrail height, to the

top of the handrail above the pitch line of the stairs, or the **tread** surface, is 900 mm for both stairs and landings, while public handrail heights should be at a minimum of 900mm on stairs and 1100 mm on landings. Handrails should extend beyond the first and last riser by a minimum of 300mm. Looped or closed ends will prevent injury or snagging of clothes. The cross-section of a handrail is also included in the Approved Document, most manufacturers will comply with these sizes.

The removal or exclusion of these safety features, where required, is not acceptable.

LANDINGS

Landings are used to give relief from the effort of ascent. Landings at the top and bottom of a flight of steps should be a minimum 1200mm long and with 400mm clear of hazards, such as opening doors, etc. Intermediate landings should be a minimum 1500mm long.

Stairs flights should not exceed 12 risers (where the tread is less than 350mm) or 18 risers (where the tread is more than 350mm). Stairs with more than 36 risers in consecutive flights (i.e. even if landings are used to add relief) must make at least one change of direction of not less than 30 degrees. The landing width at the change of direction should be at least the width of the stairs. The Approved Documents give very clear guidance on access to public and commercial buildings regarding ramp lengths, landing frequency and gradients (Table 5.1). The designer should be familiar with this guidance before undertaking or advising on access issues.

If wheelchair users cannot see from one end of the ramp to the other or there are three or more flights, then intermediate landings are required that are a minimum 1800mm wide and minimum 1800mm long.

All landings are to be level or with a max. gradient of 1:60 along their length. Where landings are used to connect flights or at the top and bottom of steps, the maximum slope is 1:20.

Table 5.1 Recommended step rise and going

Category	Max. rise (mm)	Min. going (mm)	Notes
Private single dwelling	220	220	Max. pitch 42 deg
Institutional and for assemblies of people	180	280	Max. no. risers 16. For building less than 100m sq floor area going = 250mm
Others	190	250	
Disabled	170	250	Max. rise between landings of 1800 and clear flight of 1000mm

Source: Building Regulations, Part K (UK).

GRADIENTS

There are numerous formulas that provide a means of calculating the angle, step height (**rise**) and step length (tread or '**going**') for external stairs. Robert Holden and Jamie Liversedge (2011) have even measured this ratio on some of London's landmark buildings.

Steps are not definite in their design and the variation of riser, tread and the total height to be gained requires a flexible formula (Holden and Liversedge, 2011):

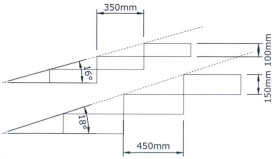

Step ratios
2R + G = 550–750mm

For external steps, a riser over 150mm can be tiring to negotiate
2 (150) + 450 = 750.
Given that 150mm is the ideal maximum riser, this gives a maximum tread (going) of 450mm.

Figure 5.2 Step ratios
Source: Holden and Liversedge (2011).

$$2R + G = 550\text{–}750mm$$

where

R = riser

G = going

Ideally the ratio should achieve 630mm

$$2R + G = 630mm$$

The Building Regulations, Part K, state:

$$2R + G = 550\text{–}700mm$$

although with the same ideal/target dimension of 630mm.

The increased latitude given by the Holden and Liversedge version of the formula makes it more useful and tolerant of material dimensions.

In practice, it is useful to start with riser height or tread length that are based on the units' size or modules of actual building materials, e.g. a brick on its edge (115mm).

While Building Regulations, for external steps, suggest risers be 150mm min. and 200mm max., with treads 250mm min. and a 450mm max., the generally accepted design criteria is:

Riser 150mm max. with tread 300mm min.

The resulting pitch (the notional line connecting **nosings** and the horizontal) or angles of a flight of steps with these combinations is between 18 and 39 degrees. As a comparison, the regulations for private, internal stairs, intended to be used for only one dwelling, recommend a maximum rise of 220mm and a minimum going of 220mm with a maximum pitch of 42 degrees. External steps are approximately 50% shallower than internal domestic flights.

Semi-public stairs, e.g. factories, offices and common stairs serving more than one dwelling are typically 38 degrees; and public stairs, 33 degrees.

Institutional and assembly area stairs, serving a place where a substantial number of people will gather, require

400mm slab, 25mm nosing brick riser on edge
5 risers = 853mm height gain x 1640mm going

400mm slab, 25mm nosing brick riser laid flat
6 risers = 800mm height gain x 1762mm going

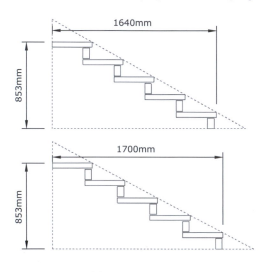

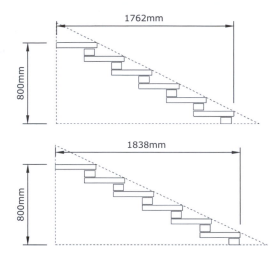

400mm slab, 10mm nosing brick riser on edge
5 risers = 853mm height gain x 1700mm going

400mm slab, 10mm nosing brick riser laid flat
6 risers = 800mm height gain x 1838mm going

450mm slab, 25mm nosing brick riser laid on edge
6 risers = 853mm height gain x 1890mm going

450mm slab, 25mm nosing brick riser laid flat
6 risers = 800mm height gain x 2063mm going

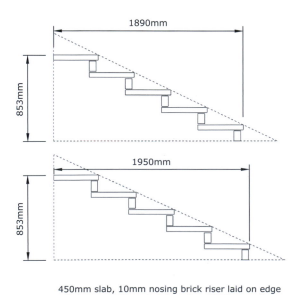

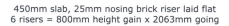

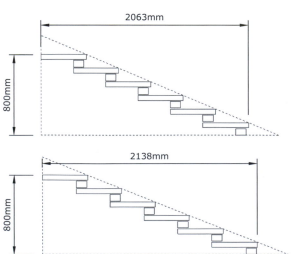

450mm slab, 10mm nosing brick riser laid on edge
6 risers = 853mm height gain x 1950mm going

450mm slab, 10mm nosing brick riser laid flat
6 risers = 800mm height gain x 2138mm going

Figure 5.3 Comparison of tread and nosing and riser configurations

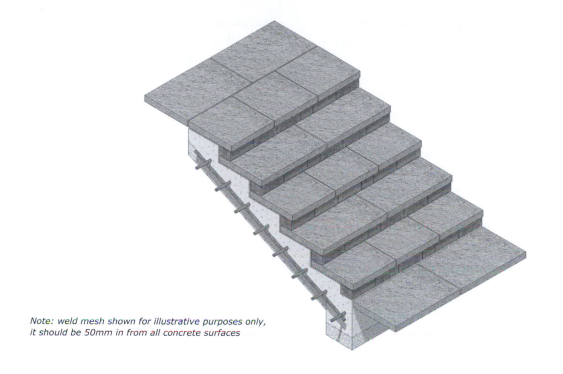

Note: weld mesh shown for illustrative purposes only,
it should be 50mm in from all concrete surfaces

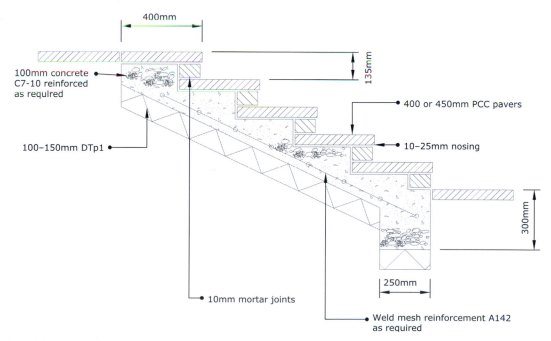

400mm

135mm

100mm concrete
C7-10 reinforced
as required

400 or 450mm PCC pavers

10–25mm nosing

100–150mm DTp1

300mm

250mm

10mm mortar joints

Weld mesh reinforcement A142
as required

Figure 5.3 (Continued)

a maximum rise of 150mm and a minimum going of 280mm, very similar to the generally accepted design criteria given above.

Riser heights should be constant throughout the flight, or consecutive flights. If there needs to be an adjustment in the riser height to accommodate any variation, then the bottom step should be the one that is changed (within building regulation guidance).

The regulations for stepped ramps are a little different to those for flights of steps: there should be a constant gradient of 1:12 (max.), where wheelchair users are expected to have access and 1:10 for pedestrians, any risers not exceeding 100mm. Water should be encouraged to shed across the ramp rather than down it (max. fall 1:60 and cross-fall 1:40) and it is good practice to have a drain at or close to the top of the ramp; this also applies to steps.

Ramps should be no longer than 10m per slope and intermediate landings a minimum of 1800mm × 1800mm to provide adequate space for passing. Hazards along the route of any ramp, such as window and door openers must be avoided. This also applies to landings. If absolutely necessary, doors and gates should open away from the landing and not into it.

STEPS: MATERIALS

Natural stone

Some natural stones should be used with caution for steps. Slate, for example, is impervious and with a hand riven surface, water may collect on the treads. Machined textures can be applied, flaming or sandblasting, that abrade the surface and enhance the grip. Granite and sandstones are naturally hard wearing with an inherent rough texture, making them well suited to stair treads and risers. Small format materials, such as **setts**, can create appealing flights of steps. The pieces used to form the risers should be a minimum of 250mm in height and supported by the lower tread units over at least half of their height.

Small unit materials introduce a risk of displacement when used as risers, larger format materials are easier to secure and less likely to be displaced. Cobbles make attractive treads to steps but should be used with care. River cobbles are extremely smooth and the area of contact with a foot is minimal. In wet conditions they can be extremely hazardous. Shallow and long steps, with a handrail, would help mitigate the risk.

Concrete

Interior flights of steps on modern properties are frequently formed of **precast concrete** units, often supplied as a single unit. Exterior grade precast step flights are available. These are useful in that they are manufactured to a tight **tolerance**, and are a quick and precise solution. They are only suitable for locations where installation by crane is possible. Foundation pads, location features and the preparation of the sub-base will be advised by the manufacturer.

Precast concrete units are also available as separate risers and treads, or as a combined riser + tread units. There is a small degree of flexibility in how these might be combined. If steps are to be built between two constructed walls, precast units are able to span the void without the need for any backfill or intermediate supports, making for a relatively inexpensive and quick construction. Set in place with a suitable mortar, they can be used as a replacement for cast in situ concrete and over-clad with the preferred paving material.

Reconstituted stone steps are available in similar sizes to precast concrete. reconstituted stone can be inherently decorative and over-cladding is not always necessary. Decorative edge details, curved steps and pilasters are available.

Steel

Steel has a long history of use in forming steps. It is predominantly used with an open tread design, weld mesh, for utility and service access such as fire escapes. Steel on its own will quickly corrode, usually starting

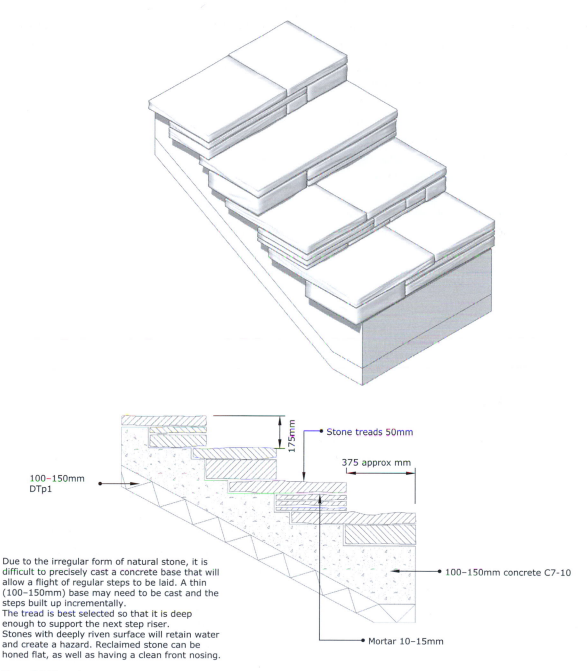

175mm

Stone treads 50mm

375 approx mm

100–150mm
DTp1

100–150mm concrete C7-10

Due to the irregular form of natural stone, it is difficult to precisely cast a concrete base that will allow a flight of regular steps to be laid. A thin (100–150mm) base may need to be cast and the steps built up incrementally.
The tread is best selected so that it is deep enough to support the next step riser.
Stones with deeply riven surface will retain water and create a hazard. Reclaimed stone can be honed flat, as well as having a clean front nosing.

Mortar 10–15mm

Figure 5.4 Natural stone steps

at joints and welds. Galvanising is by far the most effective coating that can be applied to steel to prevent corrosion. Galvanising is best applied after the steel has been cut, drilled and formed into the final components. Subsequent work to the steel will compromise the coating and corrosion will occur.

The introduction of weathered steels, also known as self-passivating, such as Cor-ten®, has introduced a new aesthetic for steel into landscapes, one that is more complementary to plants and other materials, than the initial silver-like appearance of galvanised steel. Weathered steels are expensive and require both careful

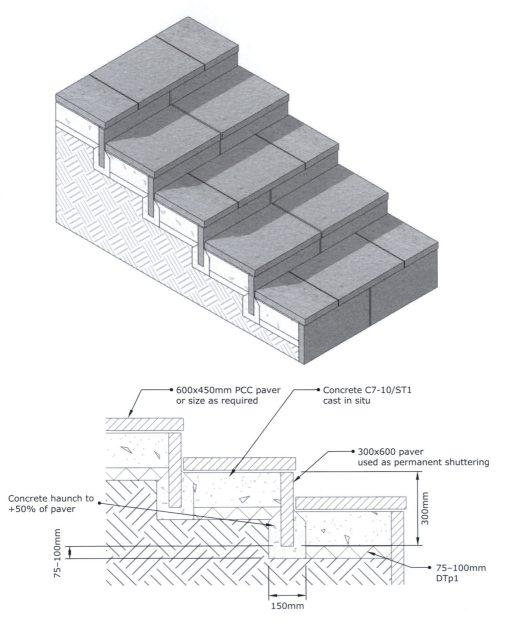

Figure 5.5 Steps with precast concrete paver treads and risers

manufacture and handling on site. The self-passivating surface stabilises after a few years, and no residue or run-off is likely. This will depend on the environmental conditions and the detailing around such steels should assume some run-off is likely. Steel placed directly onto a porous surface such as sandstone will result in some staining. Used to form steps, the bottom riser should be surrounded by a strip of gravel or non-porous material that can be cleaned or replaced. The passivated surfaces are initially rough but with use can become smooth and a hazard in wet conditions. While the steel surface will reach a point of equilibrium after a few years, this may not be the case in damp or humid environments. Exposed to a cycle of rain and dry spells, weathered steel

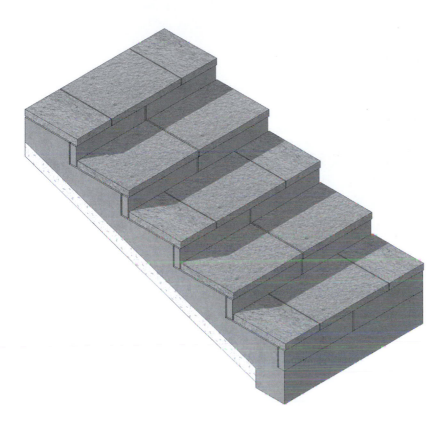

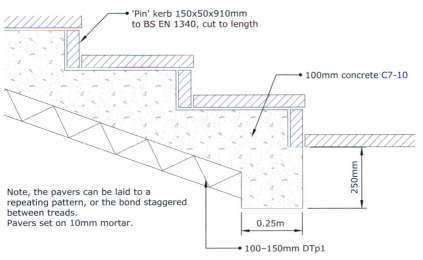

'Pin' kerb 150x50x910mm
to BS EN 1340, cut to length

100mm concrete C7-10

250mm

Note, the pavers can be laid to a
repeating pattern, or the bond staggered
between treads.
Pavers set on 10mm mortar.

0.25m

100–150mm DTp1

Figure 5.6 Steps with precast concrete paver treads and pin kerb risers

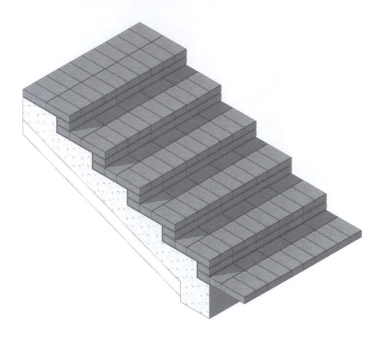

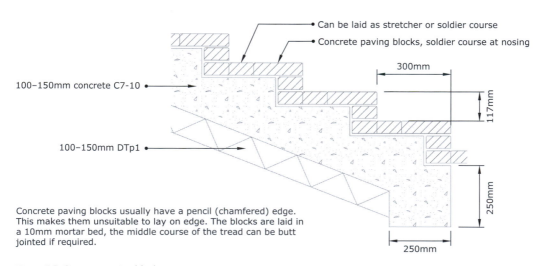

Can be laid as stretcher or soldier course

Concrete paving blocks, soldier course at nosing

300mm

117mm

100–150mm concrete C7-10

100–150mm DTp1

250mm

Concrete paving blocks usually have a pencil (chamfered) edge. This makes them unsuitable to lay on edge. The blocks are laid in a 10mm mortar bed, the middle course of the tread can be butt jointed if required.

250mm

Figure 5.7 Concrete paving block steps

can continue to passivate and produce a residue that can stain the surrounding surfaces.

Weathered steel for steps is likely to be constructed using grade Core-ten A 606. This is designed for 'thinner' sheets (up to 30mm thick). The thickness of the steps will depend on the design of the flight and the foundation or support system. Therefore, 5mm should be the minimum thickness although

8–10mm may be required for steps that must support their own form.

Steel steps, whether galvanised or weathered, are best attached and secured in position by mechanical fasteners. This requires that a suitably larger and stable foundation pad is created. Anchors to secure the steps are available as the expanding, mechanical type or chemical set. Expanding anchors introduce stress on the hole into

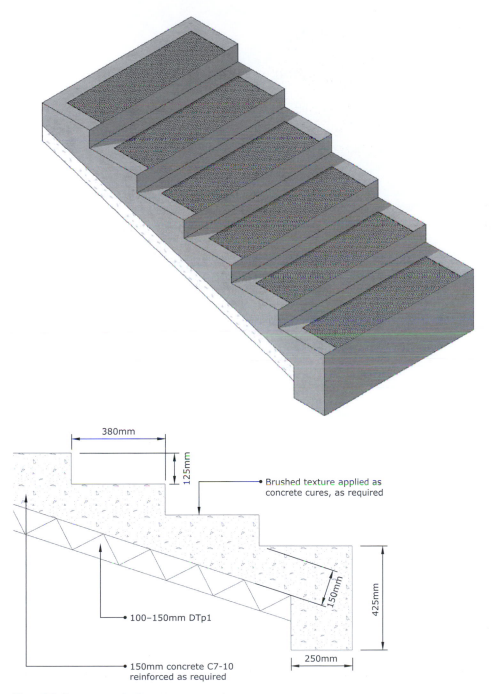

380mm

125mm

Brushed texture applied as
concrete cures, as required

100–150mm DTp1

150mm concrete C7-10
reinforced as required

150mm

425mm

250mm

Figure 5.8 Concrete cast in situ steps

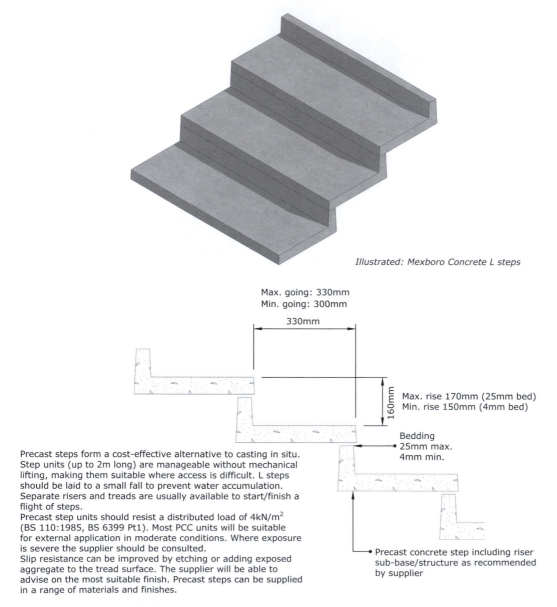

Illustrated: Mexboro Concrete L steps

Max. going: 330mm
Min. going: 300mm

330mm

160mm

Max. rise 170mm (25mm bed)
Min. rise 150mm (4mm bed)

Bedding
25mm max.
4mm min.

Precast steps form a cost-effective alternative to casting in situ. Step units (up to 2m long) are manageable without mechanical lifting, making them suitable where access is difficult. L steps should be laid to a small fall to prevent water accumulation. Separate risers and treads are usually available to start/finish a flight of steps.
Precast step units should resist a distributed load of 4kN/m^2 (BS 110:1985, BS 6399 Pt1). Most PCC units will be suitable for external application in moderate conditions. Where exposure is severe the supplier should be consulted.
Slip resistance can be improved by etching or adding exposed aggregate to the tread surface. The supplier will be able to advise on the most suitable finish. Precast steps can be supplied in a range of materials and finishes.

Precast concrete step including riser
sub-base/structure as recommended
by supplier

Figure 5.9 Precast concrete (PCC) steps

which they are set and can cause fracturing. This can lead to failure if the foundation is of an inferior material or poorly constructed. Chemical anchors are very similar, a bolt is set into a drilled hole, but a chemical adhesive is used to secure it in place. There is no inherent stress and the risk of failure is reduced.

Steps that traverse a wide area are well suited to weathered steel. Steel trim, designed for path edges, can be used successfully as step risers, with sufficient support. Typically edges are 3mm thick but material up to 10mm is available and in a range of metal types including weathered steel. On short tread widths, less than 1000mm, metal edge systems can be installed dry without the need for haunching or concrete set posts. For wider treads, the edging material will have to be set into a concrete race (bed) with haunching.

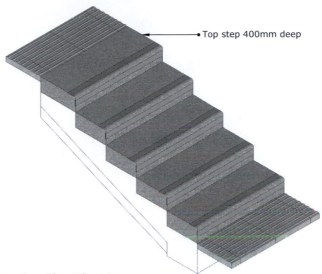

Illustrated: Marshalls Solid concrete step units, with antislip strip

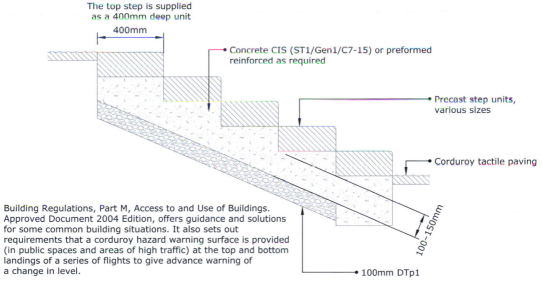

The top step is supplied as a 400mm deep unit

400mm

Concrete CIS (ST1/Gen1/C7-15) or preformed reinforced as required

Precast step units, various sizes

Corduroy tactile paving

Building Regulations, Part M, Access to and Use of Buildings. Approved Document 2004 Edition, offers guidance and solutions for some common building situations. It also sets out requirements that a corduroy hazard warning surface is provided (in public spaces and areas of high traffic) at the top and bottom landings of a series of flights to give advance warning of a change in level.

100–150mm

100mm DTp1

Figure 5.10 Precast concrete (PCC) steps

Wide treads with a concrete set edge will require a simple land drain behind the concrete foundation to relieve any hydroscopic pressure. Edge fixings are usually concealed, presenting a thin and uninterrupted line. Some profiles are reversible, allowing either a square or round edge to be uppermost. Curves are possible with most systems and suppliers will indicate which products are best suited to the proposed application.

Loose fill treads are inherently dangerous. The use of bark, **hoggin**, gravel and soil can result in differential settlement, leaving a trip hazard at the riser–tread interface. Loose material is also prone to movement and migration. Tread design and specification should be for a solid and immovable surface to ensure a firm landing platform for pedestrians, with no risk of trips or material movement which would lead to accidents.

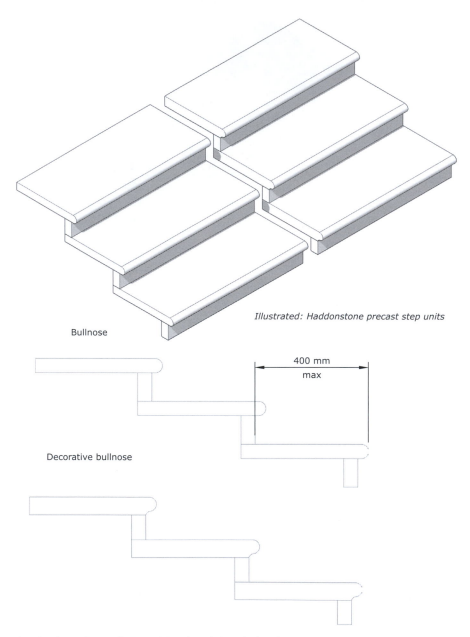

Bullnose

Illustrated: Haddonstone precast step units

Decorative bullnose

400 mm
max

An advantage of separate precast treads and risers is that the tread (going) length can be adjusted to the specific site requirements. Tread heights in various sizes may be available.

Precast pieces are available in a range of materials, from concrete to reconstituted stone (e.g. Haddonstone). Precast treads can be combined with other materials used as risers (e.g. natural stone/brick) and are a simple and effective method of renovating an existing flight of steps. Note that as Building Regulations (Part M) have developed, older flights of steps may not comply with the dimensions or current recommendations. If in doubt, advice from the local building control or planning department should be sought.

Figure 5.11 Precast concrete steps with individual treads and risers

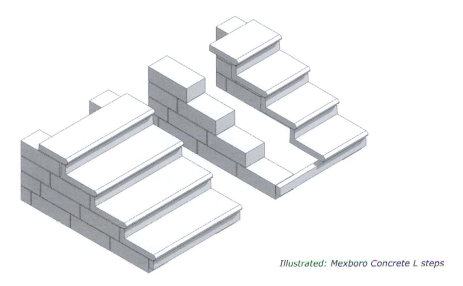

Illustrated: Mexboro Concrete L steps

Precast units can be constructed over a void, with suitable end supports. The effective span will be advised by the supplier. This is both cost-effective and an efficient use of labour. An overhang at the sides may be required to accommodate a decorative finish to the block walls (e.g. render/stone cladding)

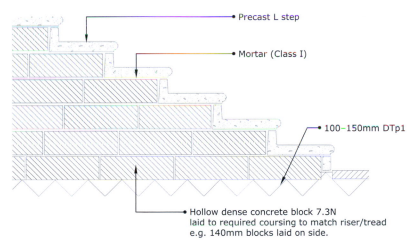

- Precast L step
- Mortar (Class I)
- 100–150mm DTp1
- Hollow dense concrete block 7.3N laid to required coursing to match riser/tread e.g. 140mm blocks laid on side.

Figure 5.12 Precast concrete steps with combined riser and tread

Timber

Steps made from timber are easy to construct and inexpensive. The grade of timber used should be suitable for exterior and subsoil use (e.g. C14). Steps with timber treads should have the lengths running across the width rather than parallel to the direction of the steps themselves. This gives some texture and resistance to slipping. In wet or damp conditions, such as under a perpetual tree canopy, timber can be a hazardous surface to navigate. Timber risers that retain gravel or hoggin loose fill material can wear quickly, the gravel migrates onto the riser and the timber can quickly splinter. As described above, the use of loose fill in step treads is inherently dangerous. Nails and even screw fasteners are unlikely to permanently anchor and fix timber, especially if it is damp for an extended period of time. Timber risers or stringers (retaining side panels) should be attached to stakes or pinned with 'road pins', into the sub-base and sub-grade. Specialist extended fasteners are available,

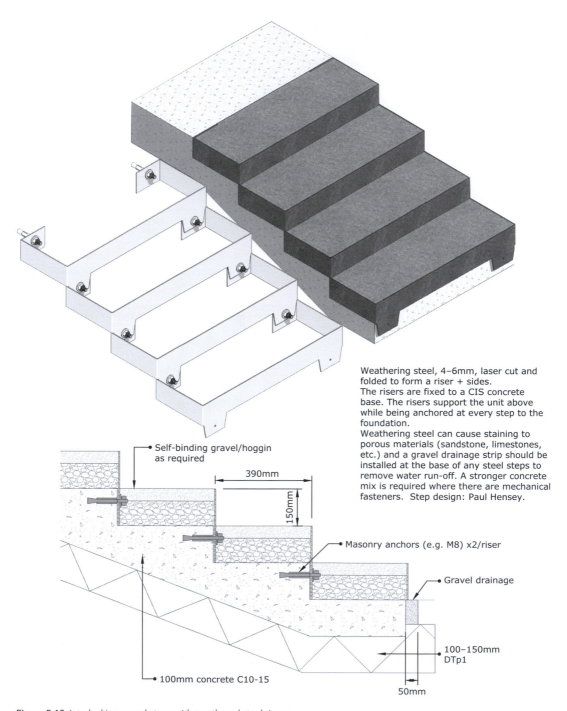

Weathering steel, 4–6mm, laser cut and folded to form a riser + sides.
The risers are fixed to a CIS concrete base. The risers support the unit above while being anchored at every step to the foundation.
Weathering steel can cause staining to porous materials (sandstone, limestones, etc.) and a gravel drainage strip should be installed at the base of any steel steps to remove water run-off. A stronger concrete mix is required where there are mechanical fasteners. Step design: Paul Hensey.

Self-binding gravel/hoggin as required

390mm

150mm

Masonry anchors (e.g. M8) x2/riser

Gravel drainage

100–150mm DTp1

100mm concrete C10-15

50mm

Figure 5.13 Interlocking gravel steps with weathered steel risers

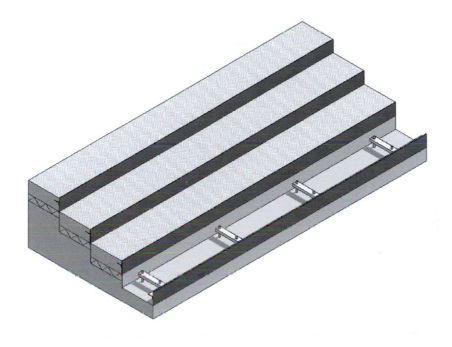

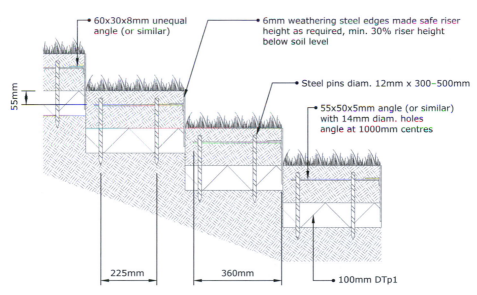

60x30x8mm unequal angle (or similar)

6mm weathering steel edges made safe riser height as required, min. 30% riser height below soil level

Steel pins diam. 12mm x 300–500mm

55x50x5mm angle (or similar) with 14mm diam. holes angle at 1000mm centres

55mm

225mm

360mm

100mm DTp1

Construction is indicative only, alternative arrangements of rear support can be used.
The unequal angle (60x30x5mm) acts to stiffen the weathering steel edge. Step design: Paul Hensey.

Figure 5.14 Grass steps with weathered steel risers

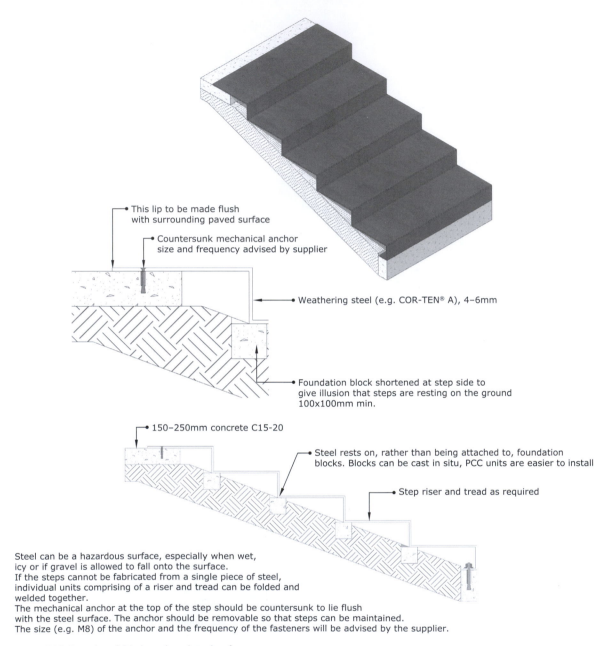

This lip to be made flush
with surrounding paved surface

Countersunk mechanical anchor
size and frequency advised by supplier

Weathering steel (e.g. COR-TEN® A), 4–6mm

Foundation block shortened at step side to
give illusion that steps are resting on the ground
100x100mm min.

150–250mm concrete C15-20

Steel rests on, rather than being attached to, foundation
blocks. Blocks can be cast in situ, PCC units are easier to install

Step riser and tread as required

Steel can be a hazardous surface, especially when wet,
icy or if gravel is allowed to fall onto the surface.
If the steps cannot be fabricated from a single piece of steel,
individual units comprising of a riser and tread can be folded and
welded together.
The mechanical anchor at the top of the step should be countersunk to lie flush
with the steel surface. The anchor should be removable so that steps can be maintained.
The size (e.g. M8) of the anchor and the frequency of the fasteners will be advised by the supplier.

Figure 5.15 Steps from folded weathered steel surface.

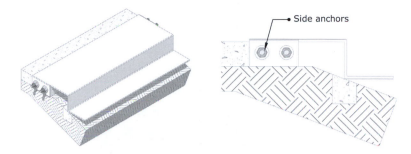

This detail is easy to access but leaves the fixings visible at the side of the top tread.

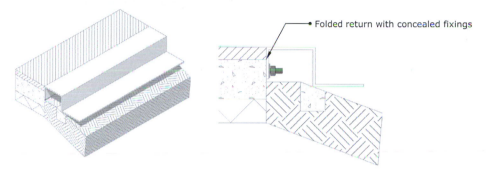

This detail allows the top tread to be flush with the final paved surface, while having the fixings concealed. Short vertical slots in the steel are better than holes, allowing the steps to be adjusted to suit the final paved level.

Figure 5.15 (Continued)

although the specification and installation guidelines should be consulted, not all such fasteners work with hardwoods, such as oak or in damp conditions.

Steps constructed entirely out of timber should be located above ground level and ideally on a cast concrete or strip foundation with a damp-proofing membrane (dpm) to reduce migration and absorption of water by timbers closest to or in contact with the ground.

Steps that are cut into the ground can be formed of standard construction techniques. The excavated surface will require retaining. This may be formed from **blockwork**, bricks or specialist retaining components. An inexpensive method is to use large format paving slabs (PCC, for example), on end and laid parallel to the angle of the steps. A suitable foundation and haunching will be required, along with a land drain at the rear of the retaining wall at the base of the flight.

A single step can be a hazard as its presence might be unnoticed; it is recommended practice to have steps in groups of three or more. The 'nosing' on a step refers to the small overhang at the lip. Building Regulations suggest that too large a chamfer or nosing can create a trip or slip hazard. Nosings can help create a shadow line on a step and thereby help identify the step better during ascent; 15–25mm is the recommended overhang. The size and orientation of materials used at the edge of a step are critical. For instance, bricks should never be used longitudinally, but at right angles (soldier course), the bricks are less likely to damage or become loose in this orientation. Nosings should be integral to the step and distinguished by colour and tone. Textured edges to the tread are frequently used where steps are exposed and likely to be wet or suffer from winter freezing. A range of materials are available to retrospectively attach to treads. These range from

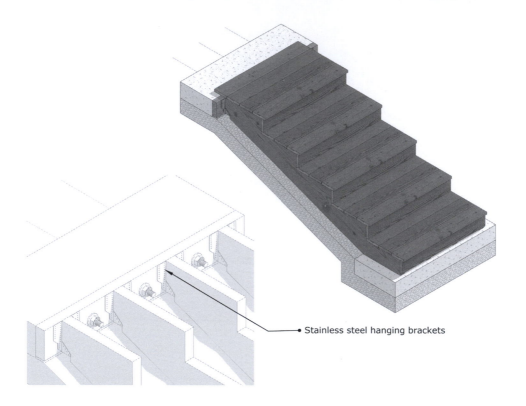

Stainless steel hanging brackets

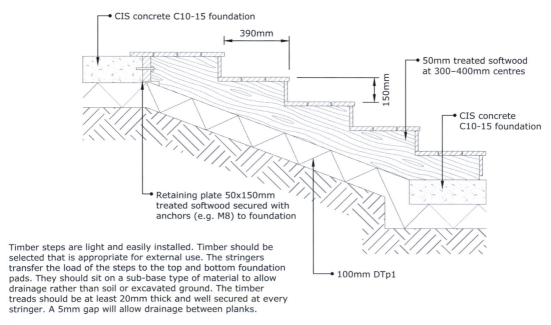

CIS concrete C10-15 foundation

390mm

50mm treated softwood
at 300–400mm centres

150mm

CIS concrete
C10-15 foundation

Retaining plate 50x150mm
treated softwood secured with
anchors (e.g. M8) to foundation

100mm DTp1

Timber steps are light and easily installed. Timber should be
selected that is appropriate for external use. The stringers
transfer the load of the steps to the top and bottom foundation
pads. They should sit on a sub-base type of material to allow
drainage rather than soil or excavated ground. The timber
treads should be at least 20mm thick and well secured at every
stringer. A 5mm gap will allow drainage between planks.

Figure 5.16 Timber steps with stringer

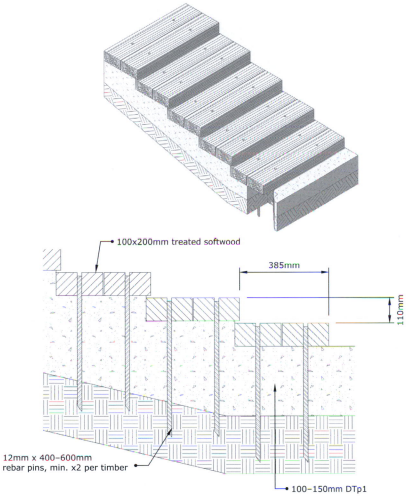

100x200mm treated softwood

385mm

110mm

12mm x 400–600mm
rebar pins, min. x2 per timber

100–150mm DTp1

Using a double tread brings the flight within the recommended step ratio. The timber is likely to move, so pinning is required. As a minimum, this should be to the risers but it is recommended that all timbers are secured with pins. Where the steps are built above ground level, side boards (50x150mm treated softwood) are required.

Figure 5.17 Timber 'sleeper' steps with double tread

temporary adhesive strips to aggressive inset textured strips. Some manufacturers supply treads with recessed channels along the tread edge to support bespoke anti-slip material inserts.

Aligned parallel to the direction of the steps, joints encourage water to be shed off the steps. A 5mm fall is recommended for regulation steps. Over a long flight this fall can make an adjustment to the number of steps necessary. e.g.

12 steps (risers) at 160mm rise each = 1920mm
total height rise of steps

a 5mm fall to each step = 12 × 5 = 60mm
overall reduction in the height the risers can attain

1920 − 60 = 1860mm the new total rise height when 5mm of fall applied to each step

1860 ÷ 160 = 11.6 the number of steps now required

the fraction of a step needs to be divided by the remaining steps

1860 ÷ 12 = 155mm the new riser height for 12 steps, or 169mm for 11 steps.

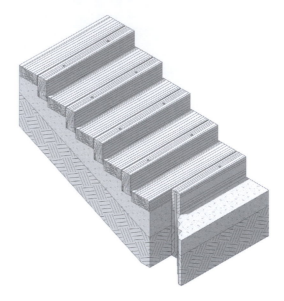

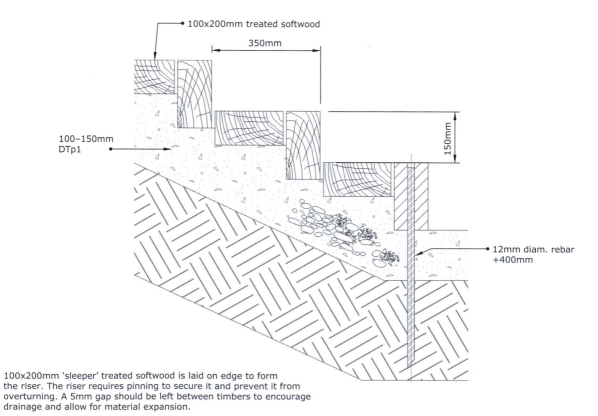

100x200mm treated softwood

350mm

100–150mm
DTp1

150mm

12mm diam. rebar
+400mm

100x200mm 'sleeper' treated softwood is laid on edge to form
the riser. The riser requires pinning to secure it and prevent it from
overturning. A 5mm gap should be left between timbers to encourage
drainage and allow for material expansion.

Figure 5.18 Timber 'sleeper' steps with on-edge riser

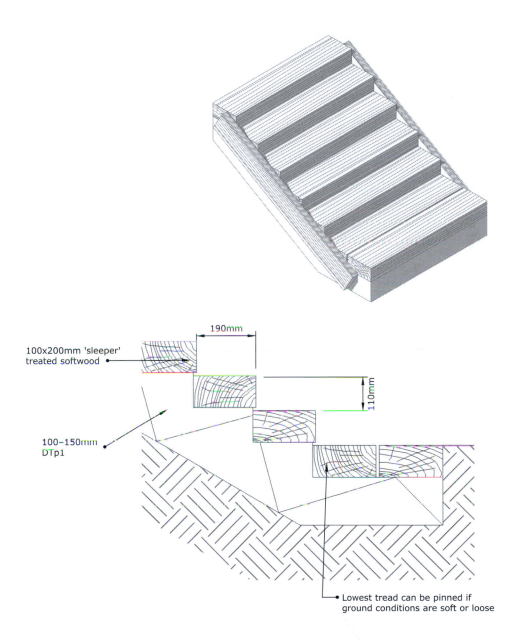

100x200mm 'sleeper'
treated softwood

190mm

110mm

100–150mm
DTp1

Lowest tread can be pinned if
ground conditions are soft or loose

Timber steps can be a quick and economical method of creating steps. They are easily laid over a consolidated bed but they must be retained by a side board (50x150mm treated softwood) to ensure that there is no movement. Sleepers can be pinned with 12mm diam. rebar (to +400mm) if the ground conditions are soft or loose or there is any risk of movement. The riser height and tread length will determine the step ratio, which can be outside of that recommended by Building Regulations.

Figure 5.19 Timber 'sleeper' steps

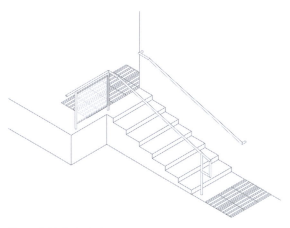

Figure 5.20 Protected steps.

Steps should always be made available as an alternative to ramps that are steeper than 1:20. Steps in public spaces, for use by groups or disabled people, must have a corduroy hazard warning surface at top and bottom of the stairs extending 400mm min. beyond flight width.

Curved steps are measured along the centreline of the tread width. The minimum going is measured 270mm from the internal curved wall and the maximum going is 270mm from the external curved wall.

BALUSTRADES

Balustrades are required in and around dwellings where there is an immediate change of level of 600mm or more. A balustrade is also required in buildings other than dwellings, where there is a difference between levels of two or more regulation risers (or 300mm if not part of a stair). This is intended to safeguard areas where people may infrequently gather and be less familiar with the space, making any change in level in a potentially crowded area a hazard.

Any balustrade, whether along a stair or to defend a drop (used where a drop is in excess of 600mm), must not be climbable (i.e. horizontal balustrade elements are not acceptable if a child can use them to climb the rail or balustrade). There are creative solutions to these regulations and advice on compliance to the

UK Building Regulations should be sought directly from the system manufacturer. No opening in any balustrade should allow the passage of a 100mm sphere (simulating a small child's head). Part M (UK Building Regulations) also gives guidance on the size of the handrail, ideally circular in section and 60–75mm from the supporting wall.

The height of balustrades should be min. 900mm from the finished paved surface, ideally 1000mm to 1100mm.

Corduroy surfaces should also be used at intermediate landings where there is access other than by the stairs, or on large landings where the handrail is not continuous.

Document K of the Building Regulations 1992, Stairs, Ramps and Guards, gives provision in the design and building of stairways which form part of the structure of a building and offers guidance on the aspects of geometry and the guarding of stairs.

RAMPS

The relationship between the gradient of a ramp and its going (horizontal length) is given in the UK Building Regulations, Part K. The longer the ramp, the shallower the pitch.

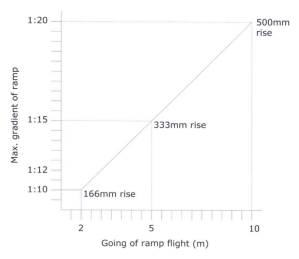

Figure 5.21 Gradients of ramps by overall length

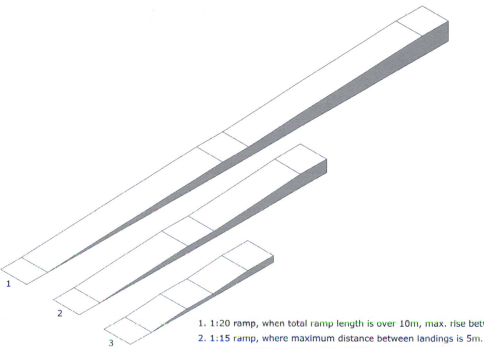

1. 1:20 ramp, when total ramp length is over 10m, max. rise between landings 500mm.

2. 1:15 ramp, where maximum distance between landings is 5m.

3. 1:12 ramp, where maximum distance between landings is 2m.

The start and end landing to be min 1.2m long, with intermediate landing 1.5m long. Ramps to be min. 1.5m wide to allow for disabled access.

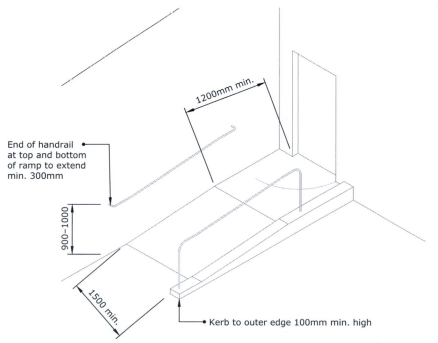

Ramps should be provided as an alternative, not as a replacement for steps. Gradients, dimensions, handrails should meet the requirements of Building Regulations, Part M. Where the rise is less than 300mm, steps are not required.

Figure 5.22 Comparison of ramp gradients

Source: Charnwood Borough Council, Loughborough Building Control (2011)

(Continued)

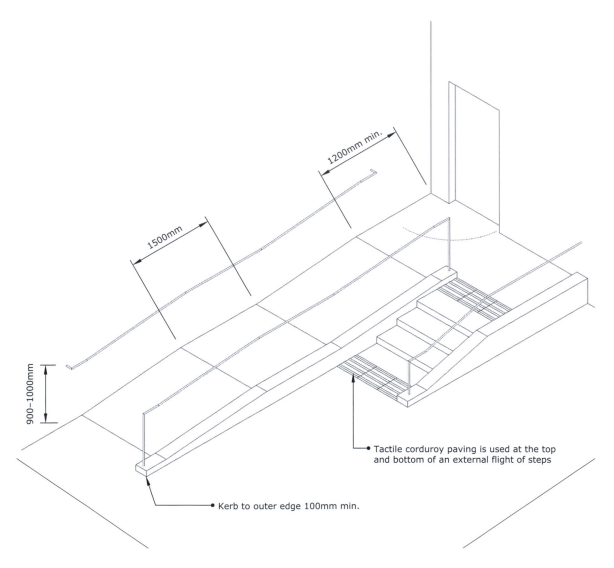

1200mm min.

1500mm

900–1000mm

• Tactile corduroy paving is used at the top
and bottom of an external flight of steps

• Kerb to outer edge 100mm min.

Where there is a rise greater than 300mm, ramps should be accompanied by steps.
If the total rise exceeds 2m an alternative means of access (e.g. a lift) should be provided.

Figure 5.22 (Continued)

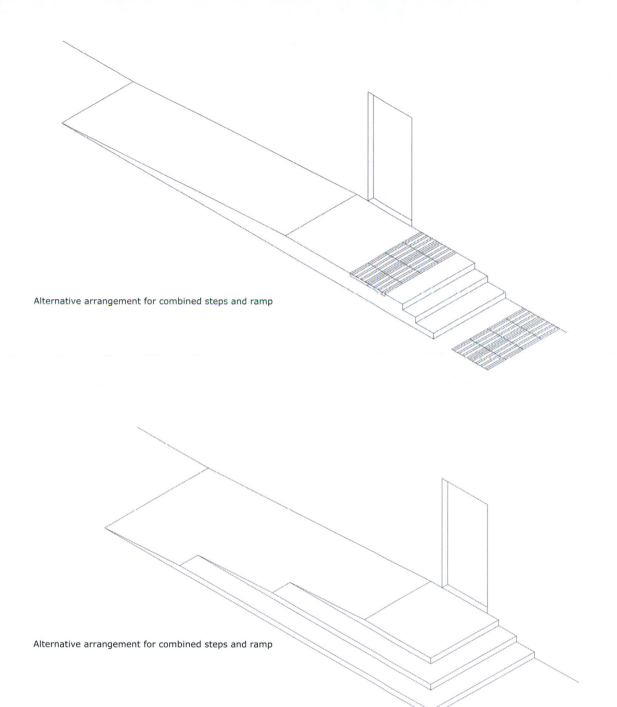

Alternative arrangement for combined steps and ramp

Alternative arrangement for combined steps and ramp

Figure 5.22 (Continued)

(Continued)

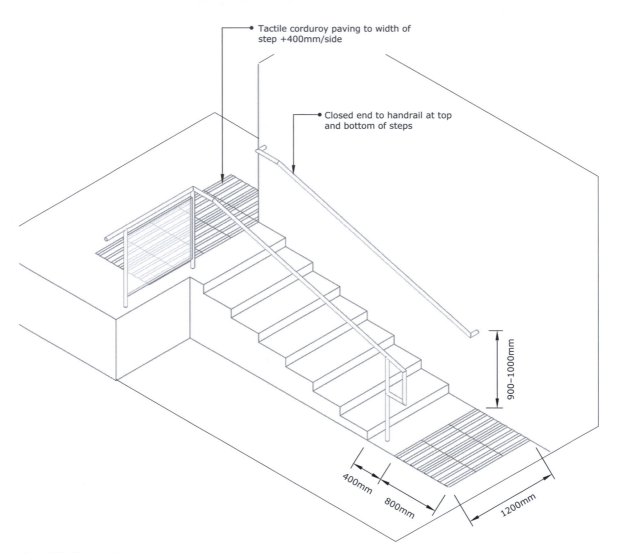

Tactile corduroy paving to width of step +400mm/side

Closed end to handrail at top and bottom of steps

900–1000mm

400mm

800mm

1200mm

Figure 5.22 (Continued)

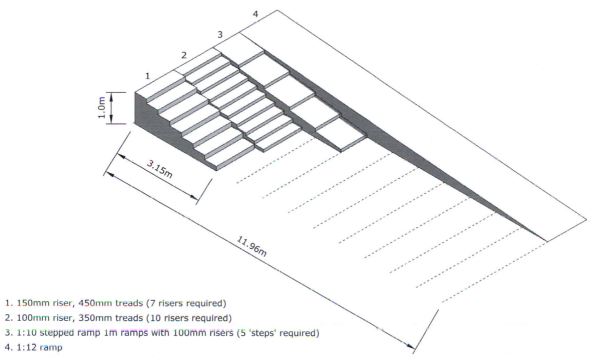

1. 150mm riser, 450mm treads (7 risers required)
2. 100mm riser, 350mm treads (10 risers required)
3. 1:10 stepped ramp 1m ramps with 100mm risers (5 'steps' required)
4. 1:12 ramp

Figure 5.23 Comparison of steps and ramps

Ramp surfaces must be slip-resistant, therefore the selection of suitable materials and applied textures is important. Ideally the incline surface should also be of a colour that contrasts with that of the landings. The slip-resistant characteristics of the ramps and the landings should be similar. As with steps, the tread course should be orientated to be parallel to the direction of the ramp to minimise the risk of a brick becoming displaced.

On the open side of any ramp, it is recommended to have a kerb or suitable upstand of 100mm min. Where the change of level is more than 300mm, provide two or more steps in addition and in the very near location to a ramp. Less than 300mm, a ramp can be used exclusively.

Handrails for ramps

For ramps that provide disabled access, a minimum width between handrails or kerbs of 1500mm is required, to allow two disabled users to pass at the same time.

Handrails or barriers are required where the total change in level from the top of the ramp (including landings) to the bottom is greater than 600mm. For ramps less than 600mm in height gained, no handrails are required. Ramps less than 1000mm wide require one handrail and for those over 1000mm wide, a rail is required on both sides.

Ramps can be successfully combined with steps, either along the side running parallel to a ramp, or as a faster means of gaining height as a ramp switches direction. **Prefabricated** concrete units or custom-cut stone will keep construction detailing relatively simple. The use of smaller format materials, such as brick, will take some manipulation and detailing, if courses are to be aligned on the ramp as well as along the steps. A wheelbarrow ramp, included as part of a flight of steps, is a common example. The gradient for a wheelbarrow should be treated as if it were a wheelchair and the same guidance followed for length and pitch of the slope. Steps alongside such a ramp will be long, the actual length being determined by the riser required for the steps and what will fit into the sectional silhouette of the ramp.

Figure 5.24 Stepped ramp traversing a slope

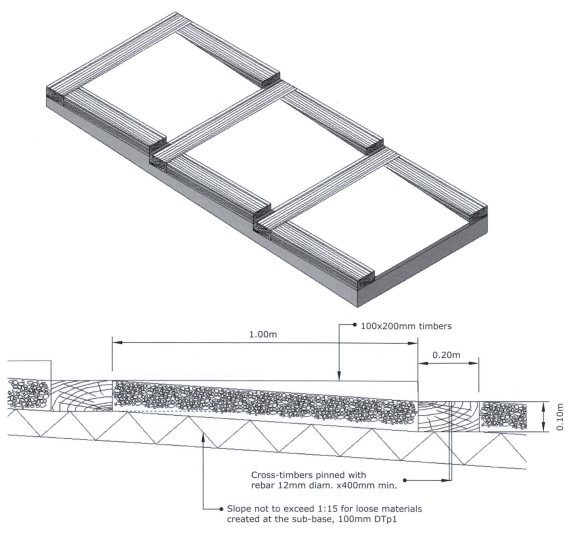

1.00m

100x200mm timbers

0.20m

0.10m

Cross-timbers pinned with
rebar 12mm diam. x400mm min.

Slope not to exceed 1:15 for loose materials
created at the sub-base, 100mm DTp1

The ramp treads can be formed from a variety of materials: brick on edge, self-binding gravel, even grass.
A cement and aggregate mix will set, to leave a highly tactile solid surface.

Figure 5.25 Timber ramp with 'sleeper' sides

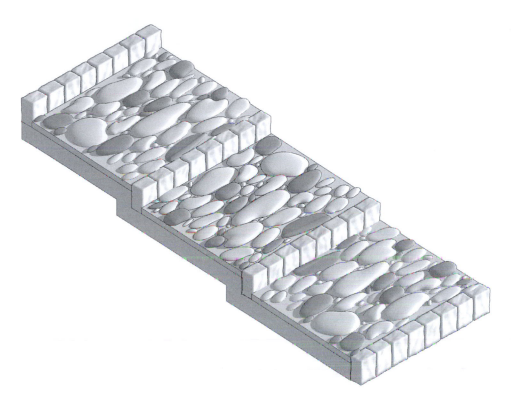

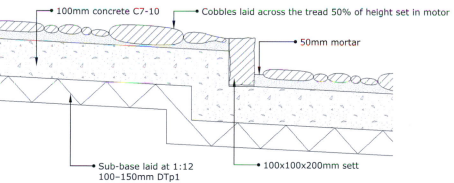

100mm concrete C7-10

Cobbles laid across the tread 50% of height set in motor

50mm mortar

Sub-base laid at 1:12
100–150mm DTp1

100x100x200mm sett

Cobbles used as a tread infill can created a hazardous surface, as accumulated water will make the surface slippery. Cobbles should be coursed across the tread for maximum traction. The tread should be laid to grade (1:12) at the sub-base level to encourage drainage. In addition, a cross-fall can be made to shed water to the sides of the steps.

Figure 5.26 Ramped steps with sett risers and cobble treads

Stone or PCC blocks to specific ramp gradients are available to create ramps with side steps.

Figure 5.27 Ramp with side steps

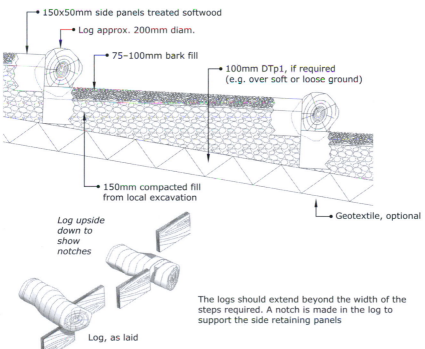

- 150x50mm side panels treated softwood
- Log approx. 200mm diam.
- 75–100mm bark fill
- 100mm DTp1, if required (e.g. over soft or loose ground)
- 150mm compacted fill from local excavation
- Geotextile, optional

Log upside down to show notches

Log, as laid

The logs should extend beyond the width of the steps required. A notch is made in the log to support the side retaining panels

Figure 5.28 Log steps with bark tread

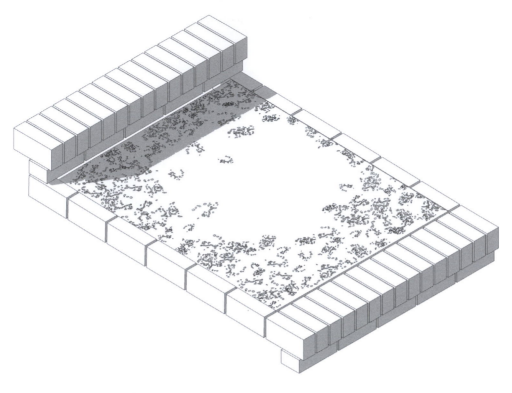

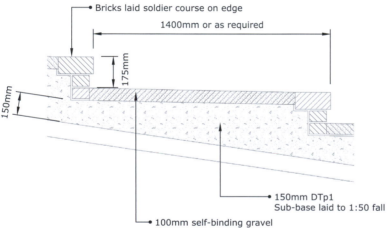

• Bricks laid soldier course on edge

1400mm or as required

175mm

150mm

• 150mm DTp1
Sub-base laid to 1:50 fall

100mm self-binding gravel

Width of steps to be full brick dimension. Self-binding gravel or hoggin can be a hazardous material used as a step tread. Not all locations are suitable (e.g. damp or shady) and it should be used with caution and installed as directed by the material supplier.

Figure 5.29 Long hoggin steps

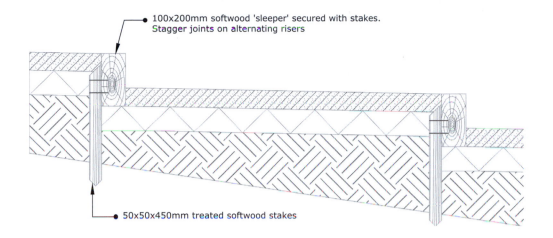

100x200mm softwood 'sleeper' secured with stakes. Stagger joints on alternating risers

50x50x450mm treated softwood stakes

Alternative riser construction using 'sleeper' sized timbers (100x200mm) on edge with rear support stakes

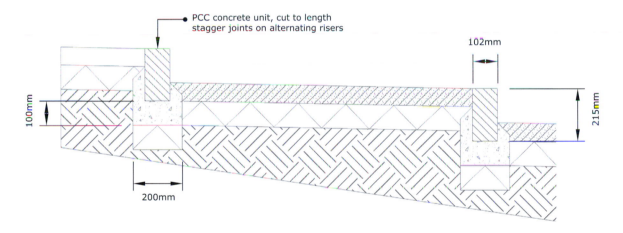

PCC concrete unit, cut to length stagger joints on alternating risers

102mm

100mm

215mm

200mm

Alternative riser construction using PCC concrete kerb units (e.g. 102x215mm), set in a concrete haunch (to +50% of the height of the kerb unit).

Figure 5.29 (Continued)

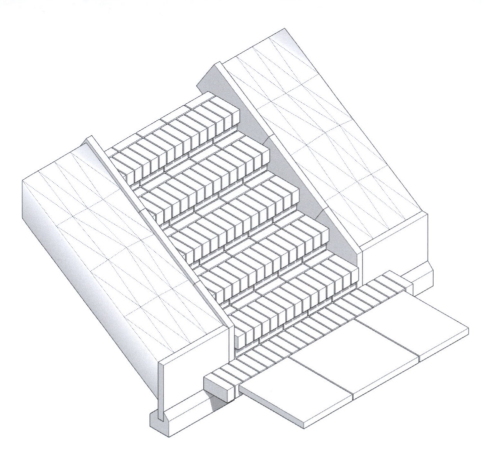

Steps (brick/concrete paving block) cut into a sloped bank. A retaining wall could be built but a successful solution is to support the earth sides with standard PCC paving units (25–50mm). The sides can be 600x300mm with the PCC units at the base of the slope 600x400/600mm to ensure that their footing is below the paved surface. The side walls experience little load as the soil and hygroscopic (water) pressures act down the slope and the brick steps ensure that at last 50% of the slab surface is supported. A drainage pipe may be required at the rear of the slabs at the bottom of the slope. The width of the steps is created to be a whole brick dimension, with no cuts. Tactile paving may be required where steps are located in public or high traffic areas.

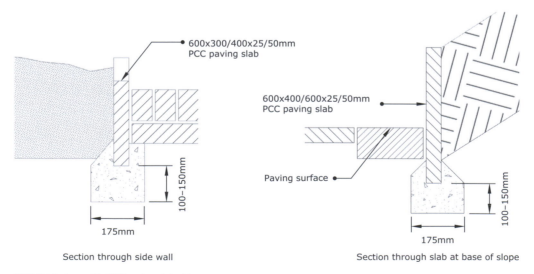

Figure 5.30 Brick steps with PCC paving slab sides

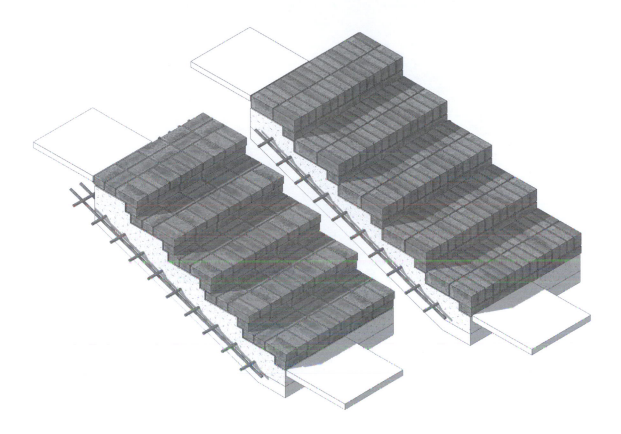

Weld mesh is shown for illustrative purposes only

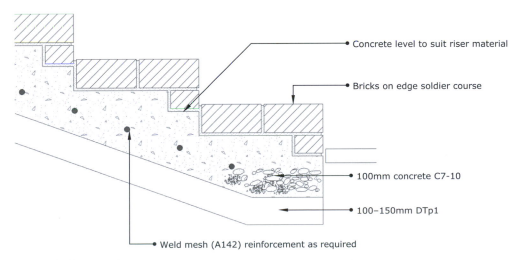

Concrete level to suit riser material

Bricks on edge soldier course

100mm concrete C7-10

100–150mm DTp1

Weld mesh (A142) reinforcement as required

Figure 5.31 Brick steps, double coursed

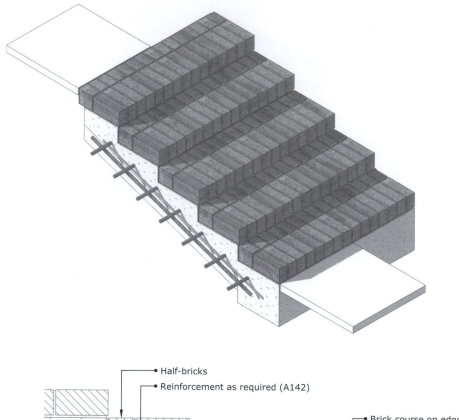

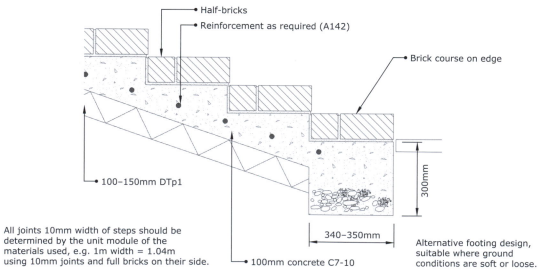

• Half-bricks

• Reinforcement as required (A142)

• Brick course on edge

100–150mm DTp1

300mm

All joints 10mm width of steps should be
determined by the unit module of the
materials used, e.g. 1m width = 1.04m
using 10mm joints and full bricks on their side.

340–350mm

• 100mm concrete C7-10

Alternative footing design,
suitable where ground
conditions are soft or loose.

Figure 5.32 Brick steps, header and half-course

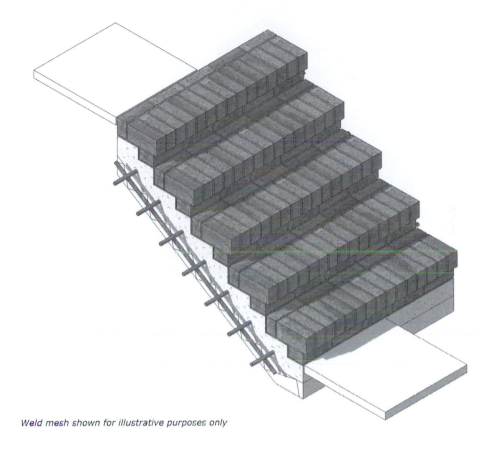

Weld mesh shown for illustrative purposes only

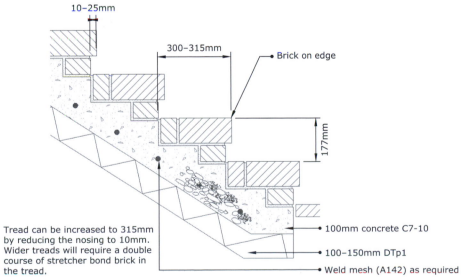

10–25mm

300–315mm

Brick on edge

177mm

Tread can be increased to 315mm by reducing the nosing to 10mm. Wider treads will require a double course of stretcher bond brick in the tread.

100mm concrete C7-10

100–150mm DTp1

Weld mesh (A142) as required

Figure 5.33 Brick steps, narrow tread

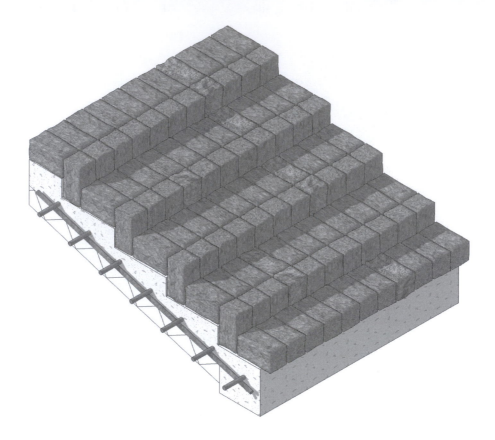

Weld mesh shown for illustrative purposes only

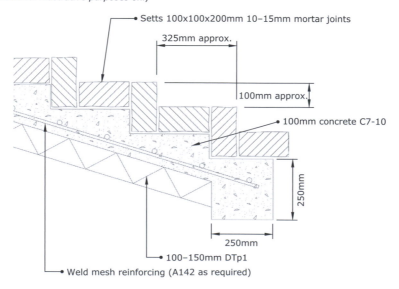

Figure 5.34 Steps with sett treads and risers

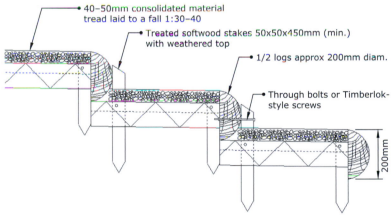

• 40–50mm consolidated material tread laid to a fall 1:30–40

• Treated softwood stakes 50x50x450mm (min.) with weathered top

• 1/2 logs approx 200mm diam.

• Through bolts or Timberlok-style screws

200mm

Loose fill treads can be hazardous, the material should be consolidated as per the suppliers' recommendations.
Logs should be supported by stakes at the front to retain the tread material, and the rear to provide support for the side retaining panels of 150x50mm treated softwood. Side retaining panels can either be shaped to fit the log or the log can be notched to accommodate the panel end.

Figure 5.35 Half-round log steps

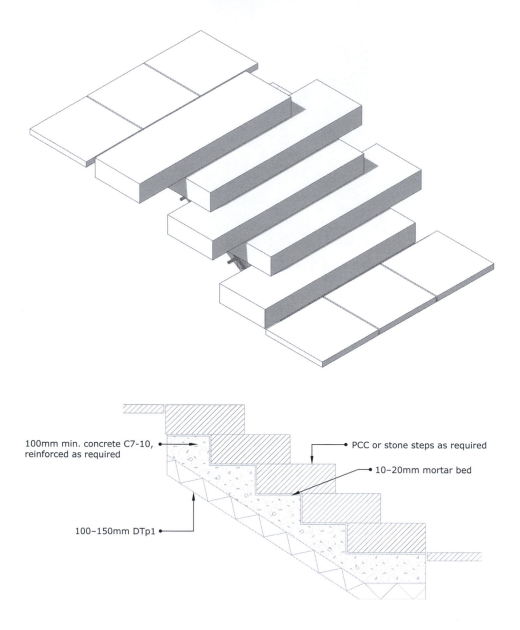

100mm min. concrete C7-10, reinforced as required

PCC or stone steps as required

10–20mm mortar bed

100–150mm DTp1

Steps that are laid with a stagger or offset give a contemporary feel. The steps can appear to float, with planting breaking up the outer edge of the flight. The steps are best installed as single stone pieces or PCC units over a concrete foundation. The step blocks should be set on a 10–20mm mortar bed. The foundation need not extend to the edges of the steps but there should be a core foundation section that is a minimum of 50% the overall width of the steps.

Figure 5.36 Staggered stone steps

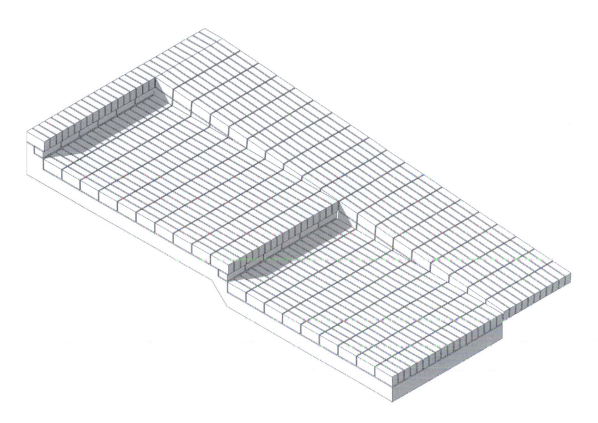

A combined step and ramp can be useful in gardens for wheelbarrow access. A maximum slope of 1:12 is recommended for laden barrows and the slope is designed as for wheelchair access. It is possible for the tread length to be designed such that the riser location and height match a course of material (e.g. bricks) in the ramp surface. The long steps should have a small fall (e.g. 1:40) to shed water. The fall is used to help align the riser edge to the ramp. The thickness of the mortar bed should be used to make fine adjustments to ensure the riser edge follows through into the corresponding course in the ramp.

Figure 5.37 Brick ramp and long step combination

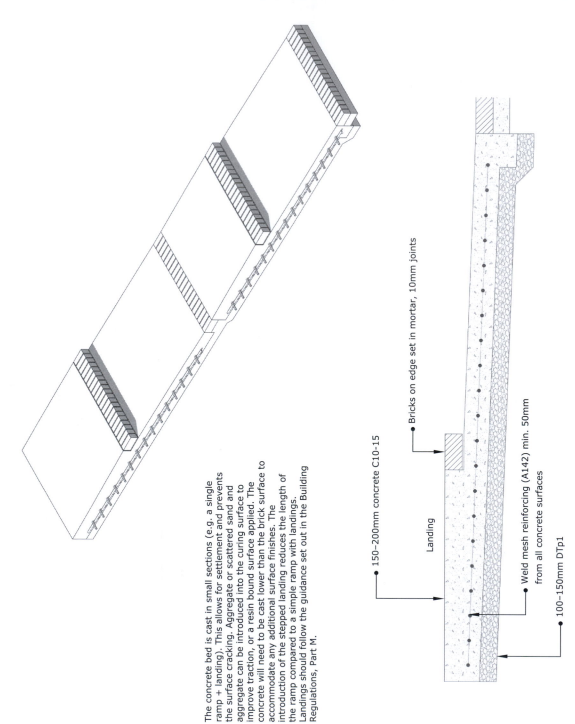

The concrete bed is cast in small sections (e.g. a single ramp + landing). This allows for settlement and prevents the surface cracking. Aggregate or scattered sand and aggregate can be introduced into the curing surface to improve traction, or a resin bound surface applied. The concrete will need to be cast lower than the brick surface to accommodate any additional surface finishes. The introduction of the stepped landing reduces the length of the ramp compared to a simple ramp with landings. Landings should follow the guidance set out in the Building Regulations, Part M.

150–200mm concrete C10-15

Bricks on edge set in mortar, 10mm joints

Landing

Weld mesh reinforcing (A142) min. 50mm from all concrete surfaces

100–150mm DTp1

Figure 5.38 Stepped ramp with landings

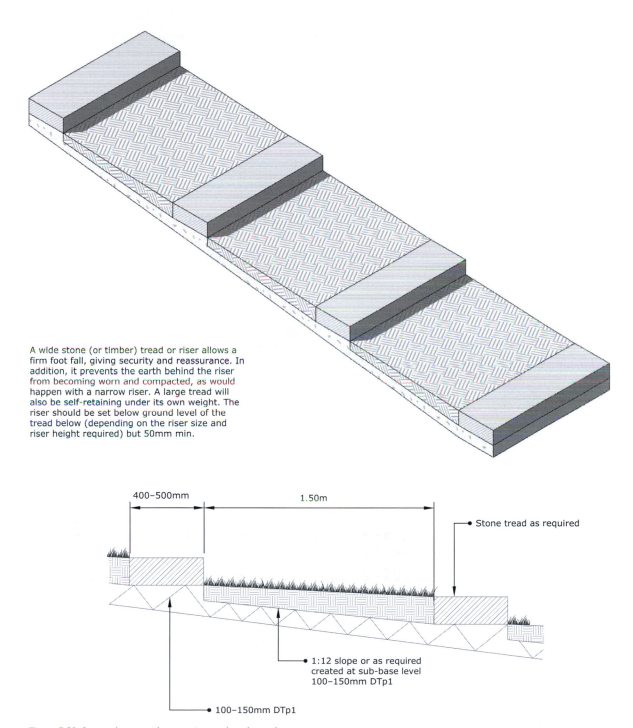

A wide stone (or timber) tread or riser allows a firm foot fall, giving security and reassurance. In addition, it prevents the earth behind the riser from becoming worn and compacted, as would happen with a narrow riser. A large tread will also be self-retaining under its own weight. The riser should be set below ground level of the tread below (depending on the riser size and riser height required) but 50mm min.

400–500mm

1.50m

Stone tread as required

1:12 slope or as required created at sub-base level 100–150mm DTp1

100–150mm DTp1

Figure 5.39 Stepped ramp with stone riser and earth tread

REFERENCES

Standards

BS 5395-1:1977 Stairs

BS 5395 Part 1 1977 Stairs, Ladders and Walkways, covers the design of straight stairs

BS 6180 1982: Code of Practice for Protective Barriers in and about Buildings

BS 8300: Lighting for Ramps

BS EN 1339:2003

BS EN 14081:2005 Visual Grading of Timber

BS EN 1995-1-1:2004+A1:2008 or Eurocode 5 Design of Timber Structures

Book

Holden, R. and Liversedge, J. (2011) *Construction for Landscape Architecture*. London: Laurence King.

Guidance

Building Regulations (2010) (Part K) Protection from Falling. Available at: www.planningportal.gov.uk/buildingregulations/approveddocuments/partk

Building Regulations (2010) (Part M) Access to and Use of Buildings. Available at: www.planningportal.gov.uk/buildingregulations/approveddocuments/partm

Department for Transport Practical Guide to Streets Works, available at: www.gov.uk/government/uploads/system/uploads/attachment_data/file/4382practicalguidetostreetsworks.pdf

Department of Transport and Regions (2007) Guidance on the Use of Tactile Paving Surfaces. Available at: www.gov.uk/government/uploads/system/uploads/attachment_data/file/289245tactile-paving-surfaces.pdf

DDA 2004 (Disability Discrimination Act)

Disabled Persons Act 1981

Planning Policy Guidance Note 25 (PPG25) SUDS

Suppliers

www.bison.co.uk   precast concrete stairs

www.breedon-special-aggregates.co.uk   self-binding aggregates

www.concretesteps.co.uk/mexboro   precast concrete tread with riser

www.haddonstone.com   standard reconstituted stone risers and treads

www.kinleysystems.com   metal edging systems

www.marshalls.co.uk   concrete paver step treads and risers

www.weland.co.uk   steel stair supplier, also laser cutting specialist

Online resources

www.cae.org.uk/   Centre for Accessible Environments stair guidance

www.forestry.gov.uk/   timber grading

www.legislation.gov.uk/ukpga/2000/37/pdfs/ukpga_20000037_en.pdf   Countryside and Rights of Way Act 2000

www.pavingexpert.com   practical advice on the construction of paths and paved surfaces

www.woodcampus.co.uk   timber selection and grading

Glossary

Approved documents: also known (in the UK) as Building Regulations.

Arris: the sharp edge created where two planes, usually at right angles, meet.

Attenuation: a system of water management for both rainfall and captured water.

Ballast: an unregulated mix of material that might be used as either a sub-base or laying course. Requires inspection to determine if it is suitable.

Baluster: the vertical element that supports the handrail of a balustrade.

Balustrade: the vertical barrier that protects a drop or change in level in steps.

Barface paving: a type of tactile paving, specifically used on ramps at subways and underpasses.

Batch: the total number of pieces produced in a continuous process. The batch is said to end when the production equipment is switched off or the process stopped to allow maintenance, replenishment of raw materials. The combination of new raw materials, different operators, changes in the atmosphere, can all contribute to a variation in the supplied product. Every batch will be identified on the order/delivery documentation. When materials are ordered, it is preferable that they are supplied/drawn from the same batch to reduce variation in both physical and aesthetic attributes.

Beany: Kerb drain systems, generically known as 'Beanys' after the civil engineer who developed the system. Kerb units are formed hollow with large holes on the roadside face that straddle the waterline.

Bed/Bedding: the layer, where used, immediately beneath the top course of paving. This can be either a wet or dry mixture; rigid or flexible.

Blister paving: a type of tactile paving. There are two types: offset blister, used at platform edges and blister, used at pedestrian crossings.

Blockwork: describes the constructed skin of a horizontal or vertical face that used concrete blocks, whether large or small format.

Bonds: the standardised patterns used in the laying of rectangular building materials, such as paving blocks and slabs.

Bound: surfaces with bound bedding are impermeable. Often cement-based, bitumen bound bedding is used but this is not typical in the UK, although common in the USA.

Breedon gravel: a trade name for a particular type of gravel (12mm to fines), described as 'self-binding'. It is particularly suited to very large paths and drives and is used extensively by the National Trust. It requires specific installation.

Butt joint: usually describes the junction between two materials/building components. They components may touch or have a gap to accommodate drainage or adhesives.

CBR (California Bearing Ratio): a standard method of measuring the ability of a soil to withstand imposed loads. The higher the number, the more suitable the soil.

CDM (Construction Design and Management): these Regulations define the legal duties for those involved in UK construction. The regulations apply duties of responsibility on the client, contractor and designer and they apply for the life of a construction project up to and including its removal or demolition.

Cement bound: a type of sub-base used in road construction where the aggregate is mixed with cement to form a solid, impermeable layer.

Chamfer: the angled bevel between two surfaces, added to create a neat appearance and to reduce the risk of spalling (see: Spalling).

Chat: see: Shot sawn.

CIS: Cast in situ, refers to concrete cast into its final form, on site.

Civils: a term used for public landscape work, and in particular the building components (kerbs, drains etc.).

Construction drawings: the drawings made by the designer or the manufacturer to communicate the intent of the detail to the contractor. Information relating to the location on site, extent of the work required, quality of the finish, specification of materials and finishes necessary to complete the work to the required quality. Drawings may extend over several sheets and be extensively notated with descriptions, references and dimensions.

Contract: The formal legal agreement between the designer and the client or the client and the contractor. The scope of work, agreed fees and timeframe for completion should be included.

Contractor: the company, team or individual who will execute the construction work. There should be a contract in place with the client which outlines the scope of works, fees and timeframe for completing the works. There may be more than one contractor appointed to a scheme (e.g. for specialist work) and there should be a clear line of authority, responsibility and liability in place.

Controlled crossing: pedestrian crossings at traffic signalled junctions with pedestrian phases (puffin, zebra, pelican and toucan types).

Corduroy paving: a type of tactile paving, specifically used at level crossings.

COR-TEN®: a trade name for a type of weathering steel. Desirable for the rust-like patina that develops over the first few years.

CPR (Construction Products Regulation): a European-wide standard that requires construction products to comply to a minimum safety and performance standard. Such products carry a CE mark.

Crusher run: a type of sub-base material that is formed of an uncontrolled mix of 'everything' from dust to a specified aggregate size (e.g. 60mm). Suitable for domestic applications only.

Deterrent paving: material that has been arranged so as to prevent or discourage incursion from vehicles or pedestrians (e.g. pebbles set in mortar).

DTp1: also known as MoT1 (UK), 804 Type A (Ireland), a premium and controlled specification of aggregate used to form sub-base layers. It is a granular material comprising particles of stone 40mm to dust, providing a high degree of interlock. This is the highest grade of sub-base. Ideally suited to roadways and areas subject to high loading, such as roads. Must comply with the Department of Transport for Highway Works, clause 803. It is unacceptable to simply specify DTp1. Clarity is required for the type of aggregate to be used, e.g. DTp1: crushed concrete. All sub-base materials should be compacted in layers not exceeding 100mm to ensure optimum performance. Once compacted, Type 1 and Type 2 are not permeable.

DTp2: contains a higher ratio of fines and therefore has reduced load-bearing properties. Suitable for some vehicular areas such as drives and mostly used for paved/pedestrian areas. Must comply with the Department of Transport for Highway Works, clause 804.

DTp3: permeable, due to lack of fines and dust particulates. It is usually specified for use as a sub-base below gravel paving, grass paving systems, resin bound and permeable paving. Must comply with the Department of Transport for Highway Works, clause 805.

DPC (damp-proof course): older properties may not have a DPC.

Flexible paving: materials that are granular in nature and usually tipped into position and compacted are described as being flexible; e.g. gravel, hoggin and asphalt.

Folded plane cuts (also known as envelope cuts): diagonal cuts made in flexible/slab paving to accommodate changes of level (such as drop kerbs).

Gauged: natural stone paving that is lightly machined so that it will lay flat without rocking, the thickness can vary between slabs.

Geotextiles: a term used to describe a large range of membranes and fabrics used in subsoil construction to separate two layers. They can be permeable to allow the infiltration of water.

Going: the term used for the horizontal surface of a step or landing. The 'total' going for a flight of steps or a ramp is the horizontal distance the steps or ramp extend. (see also: Total run).

Gradient: the term used to define or specify the angle of a slope. It can be expressed as a ratio (1 in 20), as a percentage (15%) or less commonly as an angle (12 degrees).

Gully: an open channel for removing water. Can refer to both a natural or man-made structure.

Hardcore: a generic term used for sub-base materials.

Hoggin: a loose laid material comprising dry clay mixed with sharp gravel of various sizes. Typically used for forming pedestrian and even vehicular paved areas. It is relatively cheap and easily repaired.

Honed: a smooth (not gloss) finish, created by polishing.

Hydraulically bound: material, usually sand that has had cement or lime added. This will draw moisture from the sand and cure or 'stabilise' into a continuous, solid mass.

Impermeable: material or accumulated materials that impede the passage of liquid, usually water.

Infiltration: a method by which water (rainfall or captured) is directed into the ground and allowed to percolate through to the water-table.

Kerb: an upstand at the edge of a road or path, greater than 25mm.

Landing: the horizontal platform between two flights of steps or two ramps or inclines.

Laying course: (see also bed/ bedding course), the layer of material onto which the uppermost paved/wearing layer is laid.

Light rapid transport (LRT): a public transport system that runs on dedicated rails or tracks, usually at street level.

Lime: a type of mortar common before it was mostly replaced by cement-based products. It is flexible and aids rather than prevents moisture transpiration through structures. Ideal for flint work and Code 5/6 construction where cement-free specification is important.

Linear drain: also called a slot drain. There are various styles of drains but most comprise two components: a drainage channel, the deeper, the more water volume can be accommodated, and a cover/grille. The grille is specified according to the type of traffic that it will support.

Macadam: see: Tarmac.

Monolithic: a constructed surface that is or appears to be constructed without seams or joints and of a single material or colour.

Nominal size: the dimensions at which a product/component is designed to be (e.g. a 400mm square slab is nominally 400mm square before applying any tolerances). This is the size usually quoted in product specifications.

Nosing: the projecting edge of a stair tread.

OPC: Ordinary Portland Cement.

Paving: a generic term used for the wearing surface of roads and paths. It is most commonly applied to materials that are laid in patterns (e.g. block paving, paving slabs).

Pavior: can be used to describe a person who paves or a type of block/brick that is designed specifically for paving applications.

PCC: precast concrete.

Pen: the term used to measure the softness of a bitumen surface.

Penetrating sealers (silicone/siloxane/fluoro polymers): these are applied as a liquid to the uppermost, wearing surface and are partially absorbed into the stone. They can repel oil (oleophobic) and water (hydrophobic).

Permeable: material or accumulated materials that allow the passage of liquid, usually water.

Planings: material derived from the resurfacing operations in highway maintenance, used as an economical sub-base material in road and carriageway construction.

Point: the load of a structure or building element can be concentrated at a single location, foundations will require additional depth to locally support such loads.

Polished: a buffed, glossy surface used particularly for cladding and decorative surfaces.

Porcelain: a man-made paving product created from natural materials fired to temperatures up to 1240°C. Porcelain paving is full-bodied, typically 20mm thick, the colour and texture are carried through the entire thickness of the tile, making them virtually impervious to wear. They are supplied in a wide range of textures from smooth to riven and a very wide range of styles, colours and finishes. They can be almost indistinguishable from high quality sawn stone.

Porous: material or accumulated material that allows the free passage of water, can also be referred to as permeable.

PPV: polished paver value, value applied to the surface as a whole. Paving for large/public spaces may require materials with a specific value/resistance to wear.

Precast: typically used for concrete building elements that have be manufactured off site in a controlled environment to meet specific design criteria. These may be unique or batch produced items (see: Batch).

Prefabricated: components which have been assembled or part-assembled off site. Installation may require finally assembly in situ. Prefabricated items usually carry specific warranties and improved life cycle characteristics as the manufacturing process has been controlled and undertaken by specialists.

PSV: polished stone value, how much an aggregate polishes after repeated wear. Paving for large or public spaces may require materials with a specific value or resistance to wear.

PVA: a liquid added to mortar that improves its strength and adhesion, similar to SBR (styrene butadiene copolymer).

Quarry scalpings: consist of crushed and recycled stone material, derived from the everyday operations of a quarry. The variety of material is considerable and only local knowledge will identify if the scalpings/waste are suitable as a load-bearing fill.

Reinforced grass/gravel: a cellular/interlocking system of panels that are laid over a permeable sub-base. The panels can be made from concrete or plastics and are backfilled with soil or gravel as required. There are different grades depending on the application and type of traffic anticipated.

Rigid paving: the wearing surface of a carriageway/path that has been formed from material laid in a continuous process (e.g. concrete).

Rise: the overall, vertical height gained by a single or series of flights of steps or ramps.

Riser: the vertical surface of a step.

Riven: the resulting surface after stone has been split by the application of a load to one or more edges.

Sawn: also known as calibrated; where all faces are smooth, the thickness is even across a slab and all slabs are identical. Calibrated paving is typical of public spaces and high traffic areas.

Scalpings: crushed stone recovered from mining operations and quarry work. Quality can vary considerably.

Sett: although also referred to as cobbles, cobbles are usually rounded/tumbled to give a softer appearance. Setts are made from mechanically split or sawn stone, usually sandstone or granite. They are available in a range of sizes but usually between 60×60mm and 100×100mm.

Shot sawn: also known as chat, where natural stone paving is given a coarse finish created by using a slurry of abrasive material while cutting.

Silane impregnator: a type of sealant for stone, makes a permanent molecular bond with the stone material. The pores are coated rather than blocked and the breathability of the material is maintained. The inherent surface qualities of the stone, whether natural or mechanically enhanced are not changed or compromised.

Slurry: a fine concrete, used as a wet grout for pavers and setts. Poured onto the finished surface, it fills all voids between units, excess slurry is brushed off.

Soak-away: a sub-surface chamber lined with a water-permeable membrane. Water, from run-off, overflows and drains are directed into it. An outflow allows excess water to proceed down the drainage system.

Spall/spalling: the flakes and chips of material that are broken off the edges of blocks, paving and concrete. This can be as a result of impact or vibration but also weathering and chemical attack.

Specification: the annotations and descriptions that a designer uses to identify specific materials, assembly techniques, finishes, suppliers and other detailed information. This is usually in addition to the construction drawings and may identify any applicable standards and regulations.

Spot bedding: the technique whereby four or five 'dabs' of mortar are placed to support a paving slab.

Sub-base: usually the first constructed layer of a load-bearing structure. Laid onto the excavated/prepared sub-grade, it is essential to support and dissipate the load of the overlaying surface or structure.

Sub-drain: drains are usually located at the periphery of a pavement and below the aggregate sub-base. This is an essential component in vehicular pavements built over heavy or colloidal (clay) soils, to prevent heave.

Sub-grade: the term used to describe bare earth, after it has been prepared (i.e. stripped of vegetation and excavated to the required level).

SUDS (sustainable drainage system): SUDS are a series of water management practices and structures designed to drain surface water in a sustainable manner. Legislation (UK) was introduced to ensure that construction now takes account of water management and there is a direct impact on the type of surfaces/sub-surfaces that can be laid, for instance, to driveways.

Swale: a low lying piece of land used to retain water run-off. The water is allowed to naturally infiltrate the soil.

Tactile paving: paving surfaces with a specific profile or texture to provide guidance or warning to the visually impaired.

Tarmac/Tarmacadam: macadam is an historic development from loose gravel, whereby graded gravels, in a determined ratio, were compacted to form an impermeable surface. Tarmacadam introduces a bitumen binder to the graded gravel.

Tolerance: the permitted range of dimensional variation for a product or assembled components. This is usually expressed as +/− mm (e.g. +/−5mm). All manufactured materials will have a tolerance; this is usually found in the small print of the product specification. A 400mm square paving slab with +/−5mm may be delivered at a maximum size of 405mm or minimum size of 395mm, and it would be within tolerance. Products from the same batch (see: Batch) are more likely to have the same dimensional characteristics and tolerance range.

Topical coating: (acrylics/polyurathanes). These are applied to the surface of paving stone, sealing the pores. These can be slippery when wet. They typically lend a glossy sheen to the surface, and moisture embedded or taken up from the stone surface in contact with the ground can be prevented from migrating to the uppermost surface of the paving.

Total run: (see also: Going) The total run for a flight of steps or a ramp is the horizontal distance the steps or ramp extend.

Tram lines: are created from narrow (300–600mm) lines of bricks, blocks, asphalt or concrete, laid over a suitable sub-base. The area between and around the tracks can be surfaced in gravel or planted. The actual paved areas are so small that standing water will not cause problems, although a slight camber can help reduce ice formation in winter.

Tread: the horizontal surface of a step, (also see: Going). In a flight of steps there is always one tread less than the number of risers.

Unbound: material that is loose and without any form of binding agent (such as cement), also called loose material.

Uncontrolled crossings: Pedestrian crossings where there is no difference between the level of the footway and the carriageway; usually found on side roads.

Visually impaired: people who are blind or partially sighted or suffer severe loss of vision.

Wearing course: the topmost surface of a road, highway or paved area.

Weld mesh: also called 'fabric'. Weld mesh is supplied in standard sheets (4.8m × 2.4m) and is used to reinforce large areas of concrete. It usually has a rusted appearance; this is not detrimental to its performance.

Wet cast: Concrete that is supplied/cast with water premixed (typically water: cement ratio of +0.4).

Yorkstone: a dense, hard-wearing sandstone, used as paving and cladding for centuries. Naturally textured and aging to a dark patina. Reclaimed Yorkstone is prized for the weathered look and characteristic blemishes.

Resources

PUBLICATIONS

Some publications that offer good information and advice

Baden-Powell, C., Hetreed, J. and Ross, A. (2011) *Architect's Pocket Book*. London: Routledge.

Bisharat, K. (2004) *Construction Graphics: A Practical Guide to Interpreting Working Drawings*, Chichester: Wiley.

Ching, Francis D. (2008) *Building Construction Illustrated*, 4th edn, Chichester: Wiley.

Ching, Francis D. (2010) *Visual Dictionary of Architecture*, Chichester: Wiley.

Pheasant, Stephen & Haslegrave, C. (2006) *Bodyspace: Anthropometry, Ergonomics and the Design of Work*, 3rd edn, London: Routledge.

Vernon, S., Tennant, R. and Garmory, N. (2013) *Landscape Architect's Pocket Book*. London: Routledge.

ONLINE RESOURCES

www.acronymfinder.com   acronyms and abbreviations
www.buildersengineer.info   general information on construction processes

Specifications

The inclusion of a written specification is a necessity for any built garden or landscape. At its most simplistic, the specification can be annotations on the relevant construction drawings. There are frequently aspects of a scheme where no drawings are required but guidance and details are still necessary. A written document is where such information is kept. A convention for specifications is that while a construction drawing illustrates how things are to be built, the actual references and detailed specification for individual components and materials are located within the written specification. It is therefore necessary to ensure that both the written specification and any associated drawing are cross-referenced. This typically takes the form of a label on a drawing, directing a contractor to the relevant clause for clarification on what the component, finish, supplier should be. Clauses within the written specification would include any drawing references so that construction details are clarified.

An advantage to keeping such detailed specifications in a separate document is that any changes made are independent of any associated drawings and the revision process is kept simple. It is essential that both the construction drawings and the written specification are kept up to date. If changes are made, then the document and any associated drawings must be reissued. The revision must be clearly identified (for instance, from version A to B) and dated. A drawing register is a useful document, recording which drawings are associated with a project as well as what their current revision status is and to whom they have been issued. The specification should be treated as if it is a drawing and its release controlled.

CONSTRUCTION DESIGN AND MANAGEMENT (CDM)

All those who work in the construction industry have a part to play in ensuring their own health and safety as well as those who implement the work. On all projects, designers will need to eliminate hazards and risks during design and provide information about design, assembly and maintenance.

Where projects are notifiable, under the Building Regulations, designers must also check that the client is aware of their duties and that a CDM co-ordinator has been appointed. The specification document provides the main point of reference and the starting point for such information.

CDM is constantly being reviewed. The scale of work and what constitutes a notifiable project as covered by the CDM regulations are subject to frequent debate and it is essential that a designer is informed when the regulations will apply.

CDM is maintained by the Health and Safety Executive and their website includes all of the information and advice required: www.hse.gov.uk/construction/cdm.htm

There are no prescriptive methods and formats for creating a specification. In the UK there are several systems that have been adopted by those designing exterior spaces, and the choice of which system to employ may be as much a matter of price as one of scale. Custom specification documents are perfectly acceptable so long as they are easy to navigate and capture the details.

NATIONAL BUILDING SPECIFICATION (NBS)

A wholly owned division of the Royal Institute of British Architects, NBS comprises a suite of products that capture and distribute the specification of the majority of commercially available building products.

NBS Landscape comprises hard and soft landscaping specifications. This is currently available for PC Windows only: www.thenbs.com

CONSTRUCTION SPECIFICATIONS INSTITUTE (CSI) MASTERFORMAT™

This is applicable in the USA. A numeric-based system that standardises information about construction components and activities so that they can be communicated between all parties concerned. It is the most widely adopted specification writing standard for commercial design and construction projects in the USA: www.csinet.org/masterformat

THE HEATHER MODEL SPECIFICATION FOR LANDSCAPE AND GARDEN CONSTRUCTION

This specification template has been developed and is distributed by the Society of Garden Designers (UK). Like many specification templates, it takes the form of a series of standardised clauses with accompanying notes. Those clauses that are not pertinent to the project being specified are simply removed. As with all specifications, custom features and constructions may require the creation of a unique clause. These should be saved into the master specification and removed if they do not apply to subsequent schemes. Available at: www.sgd.org.uk

Professional and Trade Associations and Bodies

American Society of Landscape Architects
www.asla.org

BALI
The British Association of Landscape Industries
t: 02476 690333
www.bali.co.uk

Building Research Establishment (BRE)
www.bre.co.uk

Concrete Society
t: 01344 466007
www.concrete.org.uk

Construction Industry Publications
t: 0121 722 8200
www.cip-books.com

Environmental Protection Agency
www.gov.uk/government/organisations/environment-agency

Interlay
The Association of Block Paving Contractors
t: 0116 22 9840
www.interlay.org.uk

Interpave
Concrete Paving Producers Associations
t: 0116 253 6161
www.paving.org.uk

Landscape Institute
Chartered Institute for British Landscape Architects
t: 0207 299 4500
www.l-i.org.uk

SGD
The Society of Garden Designers
www.sgd.org.uk

Graphical representation

Construction drawings require that different materials are shown next to one another. This can lead to some confusion and ambiguity. To ensure consistency, an international palette of graphical representations has been developed. These are usually available within CAD software. In practice, most landscape and garden structures are simple and have a limited number of materials. Artistic licence is acceptable and digital-based textures are easily rotated and scaled to permit greater differentiation. Figure A1 shows the graphical symbols used.

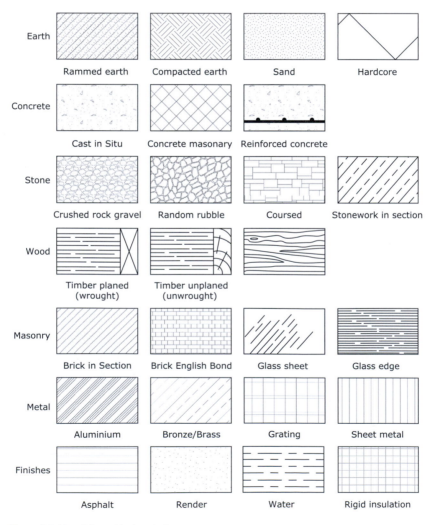

Figure A.1 Material graphical symbols

SketchUp CAD Modelling

All of the illustrations featured in this book and available for download from the companion website were created in SketchUp 2014/2015.

SketchUp is available in both a free (Make) and subscription (Pro) version. The principal difference is that Pro comes with an additional unit called Layout . This allows drawings and documents to be created and was used to scale and dimension all of the cross-sections. I do not add dimensions or text in SketchUp, but use layout.

Annotated models and elevations, when exported, lose some quality and text in particular starts to break up.

Plugins have been essential to my workflow and I have listed those that were particularly useful in Table A1.

Many of the plugins/extensions for SketchUp are made available, free of charge, through the generosity of their authors. If a plugin has helped solve a modelling problem or contributed to improving the workflow of a project, please consider making a donation to the author.

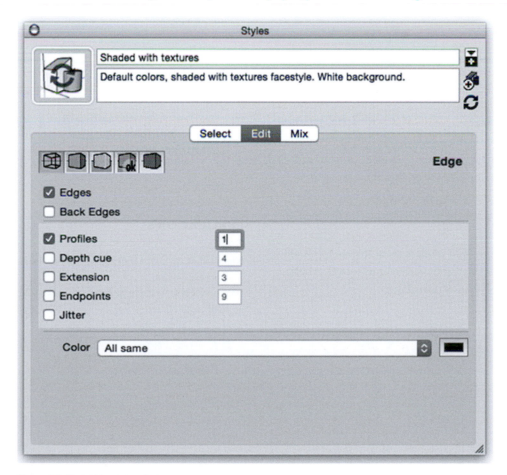

Figure A.2 SketchUp screen shot

Table A.1 Useful plugins

Plugins used (author)	Plugin source	Used for
1001bit	Extension Warehouse	Divide edges into segments
		Extrude along a path
		Fillet
		Staircase generator
Arc centre point finder (Chris Fullmer)	Extension Warehouse	Circles and arc centre points
Erode (Eneroth)	Extension Warehouse	Naturalistic stone faces
CleanUp3 (ThomThom)	Extension Warehouse	Removes stray geometry
Select Only (ThomThom)	Extension Warehouse	Edges or face selection
Curviloft (Fredo6)	Extension Warehouse	Creates surface between unlike profiles
Round Corner (Fredo6)	Extension Warehouse	Rounds corners
Convert to Construction Line (daiku)	Extension Warehouse	Converts any line to a construction line
Section cut face (TIG)	SketchUcation	Creates group from a section cut
Artisan (Whaat)	Extension Warehouse	Organic forms such as pebbles
Skalp	www.skalp4sketchup.com	Dynamic cross-sections, released after the illustrations in this book were completed.

STYLES

Organic, curved or cylindrical geometry does not usually have edges visible in certain viewing styles. In particular, the black and white style (i.e. texture and colour switched off) used for the majority of illustrations would have meant that many features would have been invisible. A simple adjustment to the Styles palette 'switched' on these edges.

In the Styles/edit window, set profiles to 1. This will ensure that curved and circular forms such as pebbles and cylinders display their edges.

SKETCHUP RESOURCES

www.SketchUcation.com hub/ forum for all things SketchUp
www.mastersketchup.com tutorials and advice on SketchUp, especially useful for Layout

PUBLICATIONS

Brightman, M. (2013) *The SketchUp Workflow for Architecture*, Chichester: Wiley.
Donley, M. (2014) SketchUp to Layout (e-book). available at: www.sketchuptolayout.com

Index